Greenhill Books

THE ROAD TO ISANDHLWANA

The Road to
ISANDHLWANA

**Colonel Anthony Durnford in Natal and Zululand
1873–1879**

R.W.F. Droogleever

**Greenhill Books, London
Presidio Press, California**

The Road to Isandhlwana
first published 1992 by
Greenhill Books, Lionel Leventhal Limited, Park House,
1 Russell Gardens, London NW11 9NN
and
Presidio Press
P.O. Box 1764, Novato, Ca. 94948, U.S.A.

British Library Cataloguing in Publication Data
Droogleever, R. W. F.
Road to Isandhlwana: Colonel Anthony Durnford in
Natal and Zululand
I. Title
968

ISBN 1-85367-118-5

Library of Congress Cataloging-in-Publication Data available

Quality printing and binding by
Butler & Tanner Ltd, Frome and London

CONTENTS

LIST OF ILLUSTRATIONS

LIST OF MAPS

ACKNOWLEDGEMENTS

THE thesis from which this book derives was accepted for a D. Litt. et Phil (History) at the University of South Africa in October 1982. I am grateful to the University for their approval to use this thesis for publication.

Thanks must go too to Mr Gary Fountain of Hoppers Crossing, Victoria, for the time, effort and patience he spent on improving my original mapwork.

Photographs are mostly my own handiwork but I acknowledge the copyright on photos obtained from the National Army Museum, London; the Bodleian Library, Oxford; the Royal Engineers' Library, Chatham; the Killie Campbell Africana Library, Durban and the State Archives, Pietermaritzburg. I have also to thank the following for granting me permission to use photographs from their collection: Mr. John Young; the Brenthurst Press, Johannesburg; The State Archives, Cape Town.

Mr. John Young and Lt. Colonel Ian Bennett have given generously of their time and have been most helpful in providing many small details that I believe have enhanced the quality of the text.

PREFACE

A NTHONY DURNFORD is best remembered for his controversial role during the annihilation of British troops in the
battle at Isandhlwana in January 1879. In the film *Zulu Dawn*, the
American actor Burt Lancaster played the part of the gallant
colonel, and who can forget his dramatic end as a spear was
plunged into his breast as he fought his way out of a donga? But
the true manner of Durnford's end was different to that in the
film, and indeed, there was much in the film which the script-
writer, Cy Endfield, committed to the licence of his imagination.
It made a ripping yarn, but the audience would have left the
film with merely a superficial impression of a very complex and
intriguing man, and would have been none the wiser as to
whether Durnford could have been held responsible for the
defeat. My account, I hope, does make this issue clearer and
also, I trust, exposes the personality of Durnford for the reader's
interest and evaluation.

Durnford, as a first captain in the Royal Engineers, arrived in
South Africa in 1872 aged forty-two, outwardly with the hope that
he would both further his career and enjoy the excitement of battle.
But inwardly he was desperate to know whether he had the qualities of leadership expected of an imperial officer. Natal and Zululand were to afford him the opportunity to achieve these aims, but
circumstances were to involve him in continual controversy.

In 1873 when a petty chief, Langalibalele, refused to cooperate
with the Natal colonial authorities in having guns registered, a
colonial detachment under Colonel Durnford was sent to appre-
hend him. It was chased away by the chief's tribespeople at the
Bushman's River Pass. The courage of the troopers was placed
under scrutiny by a court of inquiry. The men were 'relieved
of censure' for their behaviour but the local press focussed its
displeasure upon Durnford.

His period as acting colonial engineer in Natal (November 1873 to October 1875) was an unhappy one: he was unpopular with influential members of the Legislative Council, with colonists and their press. He involved himself in politics: under the influence of the bishop of Natal, John Colenso, he successfully struggled for the rehabilitation of the Phutile tribe, unjustly punished by the colonial authorities for allegedly aiding Langalibalele. He courageously stuck to his principles and this endeared him to the bishop's attractive young daughter Frances, with whom he established a close and lasting relationship.

In 1877 he participated in the military preparations leading up to and beyond the British annexation of the Transvaal. He sat on the Boundary Commission that resolved the Zulu-Transvaal dispute over the Blood River territory and then played a major role in Chelmsford's Zulu war preparations. He was given command of one of the army columns. The battle of Isandhlwana was to be the test of his ability to command, for the debacle of 1873 had placed some doubt on this ability. What evidence there was from survivors on those few hours of resistance in the camp on 22 January 1879 left this issue in a mist of controversy among his contemporaries.

This account, I hope, dispels some of the mist.

There is much fresh historical material here. Included is the only full narrative of the skirmish on the Bushman's River Pass. The creation of a Natal Field Force, prior to the British annexation of the Transvaal, is looked at in some detail. There is some fascinating information on the involvement of Durnford in Natal Colony's African policies, and when it was seen that the Zulu War seemed imminent, Durnford was asked by the commander-in-chief, Lord Chelmsford, to draw up a plan for the use of native contingents. Finally, there is a thorough analysis of that most infamous of all British defeats at Isandhlwana. The study of the latter is derived from primary source material – some forty-eight survivors' statements – and consequently there are a number of differences from the well-worn secondary versions that are perpetuated by armchair historians: the Zulu army was in considerable disorder due to the premature movement of the Umcityu regiment, and a number of strategic blunders were made; the Zulu regiments attacking the camp have been relocated; the

British line was penetrated by the Zulu at a number of points simultaneously at the vulnerable stage of retiring; the Natal Native Contingent cannot be held responsible for the collapse of the front; some success has been achieved in establishing the movements of the NNC companies; the construction of the ammunition boxes was not a major cause of the failure to maintain an adequate supply of ammunition to the troops, and a closer look has been taken at the question of command at the camp. Of course, Durnford holds centre stage during the unfolding of this drama.

I extracted much of the early period of Durnford's life from his brother's biography *A Soldier's Life and Times in South Africa*, but Edward had only limited early material, for the bulk of Anthony Durnford's private correspondence was, according to his brother, destroyed in a fire, and there was simply no other source available. Attempts to track the movements of his daughter got no further than her marriage to a Mr Rapp, a German who most likely returned to Germany with his bride. However, the Colenso Papers in Durban, Pietermaritzburg and Oxford, were an invaluable source on all aspects of Durnford's life in Natal and Zululand.

Verification of sources can be obtained from my D. Litt. thesis 'A Figure of Controversy: Colonel Anthony Durnford in Natal and Zululand 1873–1879', undertaken with the University of South Africa, over a six-year period from 1976 to 1982 and from which this book is written. Copies of the thesis are with the Royal Engineers Library at Chatham, the South Wales Borderers Museum at Brecon, the University of Natal Library in Pietermaritzburg, the Killie Campbell Africana Library in Durban, and the State Library in Pretoria. As my guide for Zulu spelling I have used Webb and Wright's *James Stuart Archives* editions, and where they could not help me I turned to George Chadwick and the late Harry Lugg, both noted local historians and linguists. Most of the topographical information on Isandhlwana was obtained through George Chadwick from elderly Zulu residents in the area, which is under the administration of the Zulu authorities. It would be both proper and sensible if historians used the Zulu names when referring to the landmarks around Isandhlwana.

R. W. F. Droogleever

INTRODUCTION

THE FIRST FORTY YEARS

'He is calculated to make a very good officer'–
(CO, Corps of Royal Engineers, Chatham
December 1849)

T HE central character in this story, Anthony William Durnford,
was born on 24 May 1830, at Manor Hamilton in the county
of Leitrim, Ireland. He was the eldest son of the marriage of
Edward William Durnford and Elizabeth Rebecca Langley. His
father, a lieutenant with the Royal Engineers, was serving with the
Ordnance Survey.

According to his mother, Anthony grew up to be all that a
mother could desire – 'a perfect infant, a lovely child and a noble
youth'. Young Anthony received only his primary education in
Ireland. When he turned twelve, he was sent to Düsseldorf in
Germany where he continued his education under the eye of his
uncle, J. T. Langley, who may well have provided most of the
finance.

Edward Durnford wanted his son to follow a military career in
the Royal Engineers – the Durnford family having had a member
in the corps since 1759. In September 1846 Anthony, aged 16
years, entered the military academy at Woolwich as a cadet. He
was commissioned as a second lieutenant in the Corps of Royal
Engineers on 27 June 1848, having obtained first class passes in
mathematics, fortification and French.

He then proceeded to the Corps of Royal Engineers headquarters at Chatham for specialised instruction. Eighteen
months later the young lieutenant had satisfactorily completed
this course and was posted to Scotland. He took with him a com-
mendation from the commanding officer at Chatham which
gave him praise for his 'intelligence, abilities, zeal and high

principles', and which also predicted that he would make a fine officer.

Durnford's next posting was in October 1851, when he was transferred to Trincomalee in Ceylon and attached to the command of Admiral Sir Fleetwood Pellew. Trincomalee had been captured by the British from the Dutch in 1795 for use as a naval base. Its value lay in its protected inner harbour, which was separated from an outer harbour by a peninsula dominated by Fort Frederick, a solid stone structure built in 1676 by the Portuguese on the ruins of a sacred Tamil temple.

Very little is known of Durnford's service in Trincomalee, but from the official correspondence between the Engineer's department in Ceylon and the War Office, one can deduce that he was an active and efficient officer who was rated most highly by his immediate superior, Lieutenant-Colonel J. I. Hope, commanding Royal Engineers in Ceylon.

On 17 February 1854 he received promotion to first lieutenant. By 1855 he was employed as Assistant Commissioner of Roads and Civil Engineer to the colony in addition to his military duties, it being fairly common practice in Britain's lesser developed colonies to appoint members of the military establishment to such positions when there was a shortage of suitable civilian applicants.

More is known of his social life in Trincomalee. He lived in one of the little bungalows which had been erected for officers' use around the outer edge of the grassy courtyard within the fort. A typical evening among the officers was described by him in one of his letters home:

> 'Twas our custom to dine with each other in turn, every man bringing his own dinner, there being no mess ... One of the most common dinners was mulligatawny soup, roast fowl and plaintain fritters ... On moonlight nights as the midnight hour drew near we often had our tables set outside in the grassy quadrangle and there with converse and cheroots, whiled away the time till nearly daylight when all retired, the lazy ones to lie in bed till 9 or 10, the active ones for an hour or so till dawn, when a brisk gallop on horseback round the inner harbour followed by a bath, braced one up a little to encounter the intense heat of the day.

Despite the apparent regularity of the evenings there were distractions. It is possible that it was at this time that he acquired his taste for gambling which, according to his younger brother Edward, who later became his biographer, developed into a compulsion which even marriage could not terminate. One of the less frequent distractions was the grand social occasion when a ball would be held and the young officers at the fort would be invited. Six foot tall and slim in build, the young Durnford was a handsome figure with pleasing, if sharp, features and a ready wit. He seems to have won the affection of one Frances Catherine Tranchell, for on 15 September 1854, Anthony and she, the youngest daughter of a retired lieutenant-colonel of the Ceylon Rifle Regiment, were married in St Stephen's Church in Trincomalee.

Historian Donald Morris has suggested that by marrying at such an early age, and at the lowest rung of the ladder for commissioned officers, Anthony Durnford committed a 'rash act', for the 'low pay, long hours in primitive posts and the lack of pension' would place considerable strain on the marriage. Durnford's father had married early and although there probably were financial difficulties, his marriage had been a most successful one. This success possibly encouraged his son to tie the knot early. Unfortunately his marriage was not to last.

In 1854 war against the Russians in the Crimea had broken out and many of Durnford's contemporaries were sent to the front. He too was eager to get into battle and applied for a transfer. At last, in November 1855, his transfer came through. He was ordered to Malta, but his departure was delayed by a bad dose of fever. It was only in March 1856 that he was able to join the reserves at Malta as adjutant to his father who was lieutenant-colonel commanding the Royal Engineers there. He was too late to be posted to the front, for the war was very nearly over. It is likely that his disappointment was aggravated by the fact that six of the twelve lieutenants who had received their commissions with him in 1848 saw service in the Crimea.

A further misfortune in 1856 was the death of an infant son whom he buried on Malta. The loss was a great blow to him, for apart from the normal paternal instincts, he was a deeply sensitive parent who wanted desperately to have a child. The next year was a happier year for the family for his wife gave birth to a girl,

Frances, who was to outlive both parents. He was devoted to her and in later years, when in South Africa, grieved at having to be away from her.

In February 1858 he returned to England and took up duties as an itinerant instructor in field work at various military academies. He was appointed in a permanent capacity at Chatham in September 1859 where in the sixteen months of his incumbency he numbered among his friends Captain Charles George Gordon (shortly to make a name for himself in China) who was for some five months seconded to Durnford as instructor in field works.

In 1860 a second child, whom the Durnfords had christened Julia Brabazon Durnford, was lost in infancy. Memories of the death of his infant son weighed heavily upon him. Yet his brother made no mention of the anguish this second death must have caused him.

Undoubtedly he found it difficult to come to terms with personal misfortune. There seemed to be no one, not even his wife, in whom he confided during times of suffering. His correspondence with his parents never dwelt upon his personal problems. His happy lively letters home are frequently mere narratives of events: the pain from the loss of his infants and from the setbacks in his career, is never mentioned.

This unwillingness to share his grief and disappointment was to find some form of comfort in physical activity. He is at his happiest on expeditions, sleeping in tents, riding on horseback over miles of difficult terrain – the punishment to his body distracting him from his emotional stress. Through failure to communicate intimately and openly it may well be that he blamed his wife for the death of little Julia and that this brought about their separation and his subsequent decision to leave for Gibraltar.

There seems little purpose in determining who was to blame for the separation, though one writer has confidently asserted (on somewhat flimsy evidence) that fault lay with Frances and that the Durnfords accordingly 'turned her picture to the wall' in the tradition of Victorian England. It is true that Durnford's parents put her out of their lives and that Edward, his biographer-brother, made no mention of her after the marriage, but not all the Durnfords treated her as a pariah; Anthony's youngest brother

Arthur, who followed him into the Engineers seems to have kept
contact with Frances after Anthony's death, for it was he, who, in
1886, secured for her a 'grace and favour' apartment at Hampton
Court.

The family tried their best to hush up the scandal – for scandal
it was in Victorian England in the 1860s. Historian John Roberts
declared that in Victorian times 'the sanctity of the family was the
keystone of social morality'. Divorce would have been out of the
question: Anthony's prospects for promotion in the Engineers
would have ended. Separation was the least painful exercise but
it was most difficult to keep it a secret. The best solution was for
the husband to take a posting abroad.

In December 1860 he left for a four-year stint in Gibraltar as
lieutenant in command of the 27th Company of the Royal
Engineers, a period in his life which appears to have been
uneventful but for his promotion to first captain in his final year
there. In August 1864 Durnford returned to England, but before
the end of the year had set sail for China, possibly in the hope of
joining his friend Charles Gordon, who four months previously,
in the service of the Chinese government, had concluded a brilli-
ant campaign against the Tai'ping rebels, and who was now busy
on an ordnance survey of Shanghai. He would have welcomed
an engineer of Durnford's calibre who could relieve him of his
engineering duties while he devoted his energies to training a
new Chinese army. But fate once again denied the young officer
his opportunity of going on campaign, for on his way there he
became dangerously ill from heat exhaustion and had to be disembarked in Ceylon, where he remained in hospital for three
months. His brother Edward claims that he was nursed by Gordon
during this time, but there is no evidence to support this.

When he recovered some of his strength, in January 1865, he
was invalided back to England where he was to be stationed at
Devonport for the next five years, before moving to Ireland for
a short spell of duty.

What sort of man had these first forty years produced? His
energy and intelligence seem to have been noted by many of his
superiors, and his undoubted competence in field work presumably led to his appointment as an instructor at the various military
academies. His humour, which added to his charm but never

distorted his impeccable manners, was at this stage frivolous, and only developed a cynical vein later in Natal. His personal appearance was always neat and his bearing upright. His significant feature, his famous drooping moustache, which hung practically to his collarbones, he had started to grow while he was stationed at Malta.

Despite his attributes and his promising potential as a leader he appears to have held a fear of failure as a soldier. His desire to be involved in battle was an ambition which circumstances seemed to deny him. While his contemporaries fought in the Crimea or went to India to help quell the mutiny or adventured in China, Anthony Durnford remained in the wings, exasperated and inactive.

His father was a highly distinguished soldier who had gained battle experience in China in 1847, and by 1870 had become a major-general in the Engineers. Although he may well have had an influence on Anthony's appointments and postings – family connections were valuable in facilitating promotion and transfer – his father's successes possibly heightened Anthony's sense of failure. The abortive trip to China, his father's old battleground, must have been a serious blow to his self-esteem.

There were also disturbing signs of instability in his character: his impetuosity in marrying too young and to a partner with whom he could not establish a permanent relationship; his gambling; his inability to share his emotions; his restlessness, and his failure to deal positively with his personal problems. These character traits lay at the root of the controversies which later surrounded him.

All these factors possibly had some bearing upon his decision to serve in Southern Africa – a land which had seen little peace in the last forty years and which seemed to offer him ample opportunity for escape, adventure and advancement.[1]

---

[1] An overseas appointment would generally mean a considerable increase in pay, as much as two-thirds, e.g. a captain would have received 11/- per day plus an extra 8/- for service overseas. (See *Royal Engineer Corps' History*, Vol 1, p. 534).

CHAPTER I

COLONIAL LIFE:
A COMMISSION AND A CORONATION

'They sang a war song, a song without words, ...
wonderfully impressive ... yet warlike in the
extreme.'

(Durnford at Cetshwayo's coronation)

S OUTHERN AFRICA at the beginning of 1872 was a complexity
of British colonies (the Cape, Natal and Griqualand West),
Boer republics (the Orange Free State and the Transvaal), and
African tribal units. Black–white relations were not stable and the
intermittent warfare between Boer and Sotho on the Orange Free
State–BaSotholand border in the 1860s had discharged its spark
of conflict into other areas of friction, notably the eastern frontier
of the Cape Colony where, since 1779, white and black had battled
through eight frontier wars and countless skirmishes. The most
recent disturbance there, in Thembuland, had been quelled by a
colonial unit, the Frontier Armed and Mounted Police (FAMP) in
1869, but the area simmered as the ripples of unrest spread to
Xhosa tribes across the Kei River.

Durnford reached the Cape on 23 January 1872 and a few
days later he boarded the *Syria* for Port Elizabeth. His ultimate
destination was King Williams Town on the eastern frontier,
where he was to relieve temporarily Colonel G. S. Tilly, RE.[1] He
arrived there on 3 February 1872 and had the good fortune to
meet Commandant James Henry Bowker of the FAMP, who was
eight years his senior. This hard-working son of one of the first
British settlers in this region, made a deep impression on the

---

[1] Durnford, pp. 1/2. It is not clear what the nature of his appointment was;
it appears that he was to be officer commanding the Royal Engineers in the
district until Tilly returned from leave.

newly-arrived captain of Engineers. Bowker had fought in three frontier wars against the Xhosa; had been decorated for bravery and had been employed by the Imperial government on a number of confidential missions to African chiefs. His knowledge of the frontier tribes was considerable, and Durnford became an eager student of African traditions and history. In November 1872 he took the opportunity to accompany a royal commission to 'Kafirland' – north of the Kei River, where there was widespread dissatisfaction among the tribes with the Imperial government's territorial settlements. Durnford's impressions of the 'kafirs' as 'honest, chivalrous and hospitable . . . Thoroughly good fellows', might have raised a few eyebrows among white settlers and officials on the frontier who had come to see every black as a potential cattle thief. But within four years 'Kafirland' was in the throes of another frontier war, and many of the 'fine men' that Durnford met on that expedition were to be struck down by the bullets of the Imperial troops sent to exact justice on Chief Gcaleka's Xhosa for attacking their Mfengu neighbours.

In January 1873, Durnford, by now a major,[1] returned to Cape Town, where for four months he was quartered at the castle. During this time he acquired Prince, a dog which his brother Edward described as a 'kangaroo breed' – a mongrel which appeared to bear a close resemblance to the Rhodesian ridgeback.

Early in May Durnford was instructed to join the Imperial garrison at Fort Napier in Pietermaritzburg in the colony of Natal. Pietermaritzburg was the administrative capital of the colony. Durnford described it as being no larger than an English village. Its dark-brown soil, its tile-covered houses, its rose-hedges, its trees and its gardens, did indeed give it the appearance of an English village. The town was founded by the Dutch Voortrekkers in 1838 as the capital of the Republic of Natalia; it had continued to be the capital after the British had annexed the territory in 1843, despite the fact that Durban was larger, busier and more heavily populated.

Many of the Dutch had left Natal, and English immigrants slowly

[1] He became a major on 5 July 1872 as a result of a change in the system of ranking introduced into the Royal Engineers in that year. Second captains became captains and captains became majors. See Durnford, p. 4; WO 25/3913, Service Record of the Royal Engineers: A. W. Durnford.

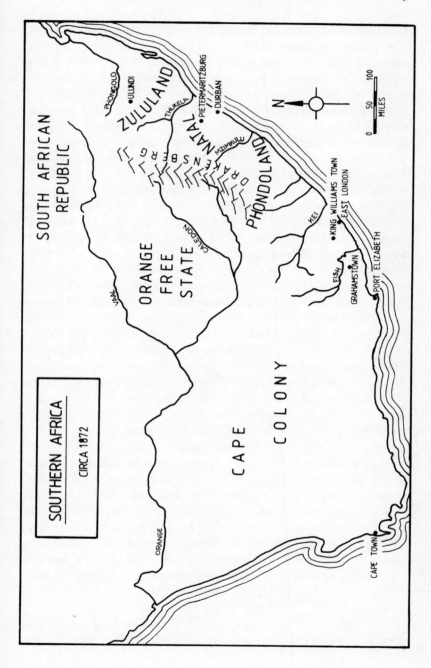

filled the void. The colony had a limited form of representative government in a legislative council made up of fifteen elected colonists and five officials. But the course of government was determined by the Queen's representative, the lieutenant-governor, and his Executive Council made up of the five officials.

In 1872 responsible government had been granted to the Cape Colony and naturally influential men in Natal began to press for the same privilege. But Natal's situation was vastly different from that of the Cape. For one thing it had a greater ratio of blacks to whites. It was estimated by the colonial authorities in Natal that in 1873 there were an African population of approximately 282,000 and a white population of 17,290. Furthermore, its borders were flanked by large African tribes: the Mphondo and Bhaca along the Mzimkulu river in the south, and the Zulu along the Thukela in the north. This situation gave rise to a strong feeling of insecurity among the white colonists who were grateful for the presence of an Imperial garrison at Fort Napier. It is hardly surprising that, under the circumstances, the Imperial authorities did not seriously consider pleas by Natal's colonists for responsible government.

Over the last twenty years the Africans in Natal Colony had been placed by Theophilus Shepstone, the Secretary for Native Affairs in Natal, into a number of reserves or locations. These were superseded as administrative units by magisterial districts but instead of streamlining African administration, little improvement was made, for the magistrate found that his control was hampered by the tribes splitting and spreading into other magistracies. Magistrates threatened and bullied the Africans, for law and order had to be maintained at minimum expense. The magistrates were answerable to Shepstone, who, according to historian Norman Etherington, 'stumbled along pragmatically from problem to problem with no very clear idea of where he was going'. The use of Native Law confused rather than clarified the system of justice among Africans. In theory Native Law was a collection of Nguni laws and customs, but the magistrates, largely ignorant of custom, relied on precedent, the chiefs and common sense. This resulted in great inconsistency and anomalies.

Although the lieutenant-governor of Natal was, as a means of securing the loyalty of all African chiefs, recognised as the

Supreme Chief of the Africans, it was Shepstone, known as *Somtseu* (which, according to historian Jeff Guy is Sotho for 'Father of Whiteness') who was the architect (and manager) of African administration in the colony.

The shortage of magistrates led to Shepstone depending upon the chiefs who had a great deal of power but the administrative system was viewed with considerable distrust by Natal's small white population. By 1873 the pressures upon the system were mounting: land-hungry white farmers were eyeing the reserves; funds were in short supply; white councillors begrudged Shepstone's inviolable position and citizens questioned whether Natal could remain stable and trouble-free.

Intimately concerned with the welfare of the Natal African was the Anglican bishop of Natal, John William Colenso, who with his mane of white hair and his stern features, reminds one of a prophet of biblical times. Colenso had arrived in Natal in 1853 to take up the bishopric there for the Church of England in South Africa. He had devoted his time to both white and black. Revered by the blacks, among whom he had established a strong bond of trust, he acquired the Zulu name *Sobantu* ('The Father of his People').

Durnford arrived at Fort Napier in Pietermaritzburg in mid-May 1873. He was to be introduced to Colenso by Warwick Brooks, the Superintendent of Education, and a close friend of the bishop. There was much that Durnford came to admire in the bishop, and they found that they had a lot in common. Both were to fight against injustice and the tyranny of officials. Both were humanitarian in outlook, although Durnford's humanitarianism only began to reveal itself after 1873, possibly as a result of his close association with the bishop. Neither was to allow an increasing unpopularity among the colonists to influence his firm adherence to policy or principle. A bond of mutual respect was to give rise to a firm friendship.

There were to be differences: Colenso was doubtful of the benefits of Imperialism, but Durnford was a product of it and believed that it could bring order and sanity to colonial mismanagement and misjudgement. He accepted his role as a servant of the Imperial government: 'Duty is duty. That is all that is clear to me'. Colenso would not be so passive – order and sanity were not exclusively the attributes of the Imperial authorities which could be as guilty as the colonial regime of mismanagement and misjudgement. Durnford was to accept the Anglo-Zulu War as a necessary phase of Imperial expansion, and when called to the front went unhesitatingly. War, *per se*, to Durnford, was after all the final examination in all that he had been trained. Colenso believed that every effort should be made to avoid war, but he was, in his own words, 'no milk and water philanthropist' who would rule out war entirely as an instrument of policy. But he was to see the Anglo-Zulu War, when it came, as 'unnecessary and iniquitous' and believed that the Imperial authorities had made little effort to avoid war.

Although Durnford had an independent mind, he could not fail to be influenced by Colenso whose intimate knowledge of the colony's inhabitants so often provided Durnford with the *raison d'être* for his own opinions on the colonial government's policies.

In the months that followed, Durnford was a frequent visitor to the bishop's residence at Bishopstowe. Prince his dog became equally acceptable to the Colensos and was granted the unusual privilege of being allowed to enter the bishop's sitting room. In this pleasant atmosphere Durnford struck up a particularly close relationship with Frances, at twenty-four years of age the bishop's second youngest daughter and by far the most attractive of the three Colenso girls. The dashing 42-year-old major of the Royal Engineers won the admiration and later the love of this girl, but by law he was still married – and Frances Colenso knew this. Nell, as Frances preferred to be known, was strongly influenced by her father, and she was no doubt pleased that her father and Durnford valued each other's company.

Nell's sentiments toward Durnford are amply illustrated in *My Chief and I*, published in 1880 under the pseudonym 'Atherton Wylde'. Although it is useful in so far as it is one of the few unofficial sources on a number of controversial issues and incidents in Natal in the 1870s, it is fundamentally a sentimental eulogy of Durnford. The content of the book, in which the fictitious Atherton Wylde (Nell's alter ego) plays the role of either observer or reporter, covers the Bushman's River Pass skirmish, the blocking of the Drakensberg passes and the rehabilitation of the Phutile tribe. Throughout, the focus is on Anthony Durnford, and inevitably Nell's deep affection for him is frequently exposed: In recalling the narrow escape Durnford had on the Bushman's Pass in November 1873 Atherton Wylde declared: 'I longed to have been at his side, fighting with and for him upon that day.' But Atherton Wylde's role is overplayed. The character emerges from the book as a sycophant.

Written as an answer to the adverse and distorted criticism of Durnford by colonists and officials, it was published at a time when Durnford was being held responsible for the destruction of the camp at Isandhlwana. Despite the controversy over this latter issue, the book did not sell well. The loss on it did not discourage Frances Colenso from preparing, in 1884, a revised edition in which it was indicated that the author was a woman. This made no difference to sales and the gallant Edward Durnford stepped in to cover the loss, much to Nell's distress.

Historian Brenda Nicholls has suggested that Anthony Durnford and Frances 'may each have found in the other a means of assuaging an emotional wound.' There is much to support such a suggestion: Durnford was separated from his wife and daughter and was many thousands of miles away from his parents with whom he had a very strong bond. His mother in particular had a special place in his affections. For Frances Colenso, the arrival of Durnford into her life came at a time when she had but a year previously parted from Louis Knollys, a man many years younger than Durnford. There was so much in Durnford she admired: his old-fashioned courtesy, his intelligence, his courage, his high principles, even his quick temper. In a confidential essay 'On Friendship' she rationalised her close affection for a married man – obviously Durnford:

> In cases of enforced separation very real and honest friendships may temporarily spring up, without any prejudice to the absent spouse, and especially in the man's case, are usually founded on a capability on the woman's part for interest in, and sympathy with, the man-friend's feelings about his absent wife. Such friendship may be sincere, loyal and useful on both sides.

But Durnford was unattainable. The realisation of this might account for the poignant touch of self-pity in her reflection that 'The true subjects for real friendship are the unhappy ones of the earth.'

On Durnford's side it should be said that the relationship seems to have remained correct and proper. Frances Colenso no doubt took this to be the epitome of good manners, but it might also be seen as a reluctance on Durnford's part to establish too close a relationship – not only because of Victorian mores, but because of the painful experience of separation from Frances Tranchell.

Frances Colenso never married, despite her good looks and her strong personality. Perhaps her idealisation of Anthony Durnford had left her with a yardstick against which no other man could measure. After his death in 1879 she became sentimental in her search for reminders of his presence; was greatly distressed that he was held responsible for the destruction of the camp at Isandhlwana, and fought to her dying day to redeem his reputation. Not surprisingly she drifted into a close relationship with his brother Edward, whose marriage too appeared shaky. She pleaded with her sister-in-law, Sophie, (Frank's wife) to give her first son a second Christian name 'Durnford'. Sophie promised that she would do so but she produced only a daughter while Nell was alive.

The bishop and his wife knew of their daughter's love for Durnford and although they too considered him 'our very dear friend', they understood, or appeared to understand, the reason why he never wished to respond to her in as indulgent a manner as she to him. It was a melancholy relationship which, for Durnford, ended on the battlefield of Isandhlwana in 1879, but for Nell, remained with her till her death from tuberculosis in 1887.

Durnford had not been long in Natal when he was called upon to join a commission specially appointed to crown Cetshwayo king of the Zulus. After his victory over his brother Mbuyazi in 1856 Cetshwayo had become a powerful factor in Zulu affairs, although until the death of his father in 1872, he was never certain of succeeding him. Nevertheless the extent of Cetshwayo's support in Zululand marked him out as the logical successor to Mpande, a fact recognised by the Natal government in 1861 when Shepstone formally proclaimed Cetshwayo as Mpande's successor. Both Mpande and Cetshwayo were careful to cultivate a special relationship with Natal Colony as a counterpoise to their relationship with the Boers. Shepstone could also foresee the possibility of a political advantage to Natal in the continual dispute between the Boers and Zulus over territory in the Blood River area.

The origins of this dispute, which was to become a significant factor in the worsening of Anglo-Zulu relations after 1877, stemmed from the Boers' attempt in 1861 to use one of Mpande's emigré sons, Mthonga, as a means of securing title from Cetshwayo over land in the Blood River area. Cetshwayo, keen to reduce the number of half-brothers that challenged his preeminence to the succession, purportedly signed away the land in exchange for Mthonga. But once his brother was in his hands (and it wasn't to be for long) he repudiated the document which held his mark. The Boers, not to be outdone, began moving cautiously into the disputed territory. For reasons that are not yet clear Cetshwayo simply confined his irritation of increasing Boer encroachments to mutterings of discontent and dire warnings of the day of reckoning.

Upon the death of his father Cetshwayo took the opportunity to clarify his relations with Natal. A number of things distressed him: firstly there was the presence of at least four half-brothers in the colony, one of whom, Mkhungo, had a large following and was known to covet the Zulu throne. Mthonga, who had escaped to Natal in 1865, had also been intriguing against Cetshwayo and when in August 1872 Shepstone moved to put a stop to this, Mthonga fled into the Transvaal. It would indeed be worthwhile for Cetshwayo to secure from Shepstone a re-affirmation of his undisputed right to the throne.

Another vexing issue to Cetshwayo was the disputed territory in the Blood River area, where each passing day brought closer the possibility of conflict with the Transvaal. Now that Mthonga was with them once again the Transvaalers might find justification in attacking the Zulu kingdom. Shepstone viewed with alarm increasing Boer encroachment in the disputed area.

A further problem was the unsettled nature of the kingdom itself. It is known that there were many clans whose loyalty to Cetshwayo was doubtful. Many Zulus *expected* Cetshwayo's succession to be disputed. In the face of this disquiet a number of indunas believed that a simple act such as the crowning of

Cetshwayo by Shepstone would strengthen the unity amongst Zulus that at present looked so fragile, and was so deeply desired. Cetshwayo's position was also undermined by the interference of missionaries in Zulu politics and it was common knowledge that he wished to be rid of them. Would this be a stumbling block to improving Natal–Zulu relations? As it turned out, Shepstone would not consider this an important issue.

When, on 26 February 1873, Zulu messengers arrived in Pieter-maritzburg to notify Shepstone officially of the death of Mpande and to request of Somtseu that 'he establish what is wanting among the Zulu people', it seemed a golden opportunity for the administrator to strengthen his influence over the Zulus.

From Shepstone's point of view the opportunity to counter Boer activity had at last presented itself, and the plans that he had for the disputed territory might now be pursued. He foresaw the area becoming a location for surplus Natal blacks, and might also be used as a home for Zulu refugees. This area, he reasoned, could become a counter-attraction to the despotic Zulu kingdom, leading to the latter's ultimate disintegration and consequent absorption by Natal Colony.

Yet he also weighed up the immediate practical advantages. By crowning Cetshwayo he would have created a special relationship with the Zulu king and, in his words, it was 'an opportunity of acquiring a good deal of additional influence and real power, not only over the Zulus, but over all other native powers of South Eastern Africa.

This then was the background to Shepstone's coronation expedition in 1873.

Departure of the expedition had to be delayed until the arrival of the new lieutenant-governor, Sir Benjamin Pine, in July 1873. Pine was no stranger to Natal; this was to be his second term of office as lieutenant-governor of Natal, his previous term having been from 1850 to 1855.

Pine's authorisation for the visit was obtained and on 8 August 1873, Shepstone, accompanied by his sons Henrique and George, and 110 officers and men of the colonial volunteer force, the Durban Volunteer Artillery with two field pieces, and 300 black followers, in sum a most impressive escort befitting a Great White Chief, crossed the Thukela River and entered Zululand.

Durnford was attached to Shepstone's staff. It seems that his job would be to make a rough map showing the progress of the expedition into Zululand. Judging from what appeared on the map, he had to take note of the topography and the environment, most probably with an eye to future military activity. Other members of Shepstone's staff gathered information which included descriptions of armies, military fortifications, river crossings, areas of defence and forage useful to an invasion force. This intelligence, including the information on Durnford's map, contributed to the War Office's military handbook on Zululand published in 1879.

Durnford revelled in the outdoor life and the opportunity to broaden his knowledge of the Africans:

Chiefs escort us through the country; heralds proclaim our approach; cattle are slain when we halt to feed, and I am not sure that we shall not each return with at least half a dozen wives – Princesses of the Blood, who set off their dusky charms with red ochre well rubbed in with mutton fat!

Even after he had crossed the Thukela Shepstone continued to assert his authority. He instructed Cetshwayo not to put anyone to death while he was in Zululand. It is not known whether this order was carried out but if Cetshwayo's welcome was an indication of his goodwill then Shepstone had little cause to believe otherwise. Whenever possible, fresh meat and corn were brought daily to the commission on the king's orders.

The expedition averaged seven to eight miles per day. Although he gave the impression in his correspondence home that he was having a pleasant and interesting vacation, Durnford was in fact kept quite busy mapping the route – a job which he did with a great deal of care and detail.

During the course of the next nine days Durnford recorded that they made steady progress, passing through three rivers and a countryside of 'thorns, euphorbia, palms and erythrinas'. On the banks of the Nyezane River the band had a practice session – their audience being wide-eyed Zulu women from a nearby kraal, most of the men having left to participate in the coronation. The absence of men and of their cattle was considered by Shepstone an ominous sign and he became less confident of the safety of the commission.

The expedition halted at the Norwegian Mission station at Eshowe where Bishop Hans Schreuder, who, it was reported, had an intimate knowledge of the Zulu people and their politics, welcomed them and prepared to accompany them to the coronation. Schreuder was exasperated with Cetshwayo for harassing the Lutherans. Etherington suggests that Schreuder played a major role in persuading Shepstone to add to his agenda the question of the future of the missionary in Zululand. Schreuder even joined the commission as Shepstone's unofficial adviser in this matter.

On 17 August 1873 the expedition reached the Imfule River near Entonjaneni ridge. Here Zulu messengers brought Shepstone the news that Masiphula, Mpande's prime minister, had died and that the commission had to wait at the ridge for the four days set aside as the period of mourning. Masiphula had been seen as the leader of the traditionalists who were opposed to the installation ceremony being placed in the hands of foreigners. Most probably on his insistence, Cetshwayo's crowning had already taken place in the traditional way at KwaMagwaza at the beginning of the month. The political coronation conceived by Shepstone and awaited by Cetshwayo would provide both with an opportunity to take advantage of what the other had to offer.

It is likely that the death of Masiphula was welcome news indeed to Shepstone, for he was the most influential counsellor and while he was alive Shepstone believed that there was an element of danger to the commission. Cetshwayo was certainly not immune to Masiphula's influence: he had a nagging suspicion that Shepstone was playing a devious game. The delay in the despatch of the commission; the close consultation with Bishop Schreuder and the rumour that Mbuyazi, the same he had defeated in bloody battle in 1856, was still alive and that he was secreted among Shepstone's retinue, all combined to convince Cetshwayo that he should keep the whites at arm's length for a little while longer.

Shepstone sent assurance that Mbuyazi was not with the expedition, nor indeed were any of Mpande's sons, but the four days were to lengthen into six while Shepstone and Schreuder on their part sought guarantees for the expedition's safety.

A message finally arrived that Cetshwayo would meet the commission near the Norwegian Mission at Mahlabatini. A spot was found near a small stream some three miles from Cetshwayo's military kraal at Mlambongwenya and a camp which Durnford optimistically referred to as 'Runnimede' was laid out. John Dunn, one of the English settlers who was acting as Cetshwayo's adviser, met the commission. A battle of wills developed between Cetshwayo and Shepstone over who should go to whom. Was this to presage the tone of the discussions yet to come? It was Cetshwayo who finally relented, complaining of a swollen leg which had prevented him from being able to walk properly. When he was 100 yards from the camp an agitated John Dunn urged Shepstone 'to give the king confidence' by walking the short distance to meet him. Shepstone agreed, and accompanied by his staff, among whom was Durnford, walked forward to the monarch.

While the staff were being introduced to the king a salute was fired by the guns and the band struck up immediately afterwards as the king was guided toward Shepstone's camp. According to Shepstone the meeting that followed was most cordial, and during the afternoon of that Friday, 29 August 1873, the young king 'poured out all his woes' to his 'father', Somtseu. It was decided that the installation ceremony should be held on Monday, 1 September 1873, for there was much to consider beforehand, and Sunday would be needed for *ukubuzana*, when the Zulus had a discussion among themselves, settling matters connected with the previous reign and preparing a solid foundation for the coming one, and no doubt, considering the items that had been raised with Shepstone.

On Saturday, Shepstone repaid Cetshwayo's visit by appearing at Mlambongwenya. In the five-hour meeting, Theophilus Shepstone, his son Henrique, Major Durnford and the Natal black indunas, sat down in a tent with Cetshwayo and his counsellors and reviewed Natal–Zululand relations. Cetshwayo's manner had changed since the day before. Buoyed up with confidence from the preliminary discussions, he frequently took the initiative, and it was clear that Shepstone was unable to dictate to the king. However, of great reassurance to the whites was Cetshwayo's commitment that relations would continue on the same friendly basis as during Mpande's reign.

Etherington claims that in the final analysis Cetshwayo out-manoeuvred Shepstone: Further missionary activity was to be halted and the British had to deny the claims to the Zulu throne of Mpande's younger sons. Certainly Shepstone had achieved very little. His request for a proclamation of new laws which would reduce what was deemed to be the oppressive qualities of the Zulu royal power, was agreed to by Cetshwayo's counsellors, but the proclamation was couched in such ambiguous terms that interpretation was difficult. Furthermore, there was no time limit placed upon the introduction of these laws (the violation of which would later be used by the British as an excuse for war in 1879).

No satisfactory agreement was reached over Cetshwayo's treatment of Christian converts, so the matter was not pursued. In what was his only comment on the proceedings, Durnford wrote that, on what he had seen, there seemed to be no converts anyway, despite the existence of half a dozen missionary stations along the route taken by the commission into Zululand. Etherington confirms this, ascribing it to 'a determined resistance to Christian evangelism'. Durnford had discovered that the only reason that many Zulus had such a high regard for Bishop Schreuder was not because he was such a good Christian, but because it was believed that 'he had killed fifty lions and slain a leopard' with his bare hands!

There were a number of light moments to relieve the strain of the pre-ceremony discussions. While the serious talking was going on inside the tent Durnford could not have failed to have heard the sounds of what was considered to be a piece of grand comedy taking place outside, and which in its lighter vein contrasted with the cut and thrust of the debate taking place. Two *isibongi* (praisers) were yelling out the praises of their respective chiefs (Somtseu and Cetshwayo) and were trying their hardest to outdo each other. They worked themselves into such a pitch of excitement urged on by the crowd of both black and white that had formed a circle around them, that they were about to come to blows (and must have been most distracting to the occupants of the tent) when John Dunn stepped in and led Cetshwayo's man away.

Sunday was a busy day as everyone prepared for the crowning ceremony. Cetshwayo held the *ukubazana*. Warriors were still arriving at Mlambongwenya. Shepstone later paid a further visit to the king. Durnford accompanied him to the kraal but he was not required at the meeting so he used the time to explore his surroundings and pursue his interest in African tribal life. He and Bishop Schreuder, who acted as his interpreter, were given permission by Cetshwayo to wander around the kraal. They met some members of the royal family; Durnford was convinced that Cetshwayo's three sisters were the fattest women he had ever seen. He crawled into one of the sister's huts. 'How *she* got in I can't say,' he later wrote, 'for I, not very stout, had difficulty'. When he and the bishop moved on to the king's private apartments which housed fifty of Cetshwayo's wives, an agitated induna urged them to go no further for fear of upsetting the king.

On Monday the white troops pitched a large marquee in the central space of the kraal. It was decorated inside with colourful shawls, blankets and other items brought as presents. On one side stood a cloth-covered table. On the table in front of a mirror stood a headdress, an elaborate replica of the headdress worn by the king when at war. In front of the table was the colonial-made 'Chair of State', as Shepstone called it, with a scarlet and gold mantle upon it. The stage show was ready, and Shepstone, as master of ceremonies, prepared for the first act.

At noon the commission left their camp and processed to the kraal with band playing and the troops marching behind. It was all immensely impressive. The artillery under Captain Harry Escombe (one day to be prime minister of Natal), mounted men and the band of the Pietermaritzburg Rifles, formed on the right of the marquee, the Natal blacks on the left and Cetshwayo and his counsellors together with Shepstone and his staff, formed a group in front. Shepstone recalled:

> The Zulu people described three-fourths of a circle about fifty yards off, and may be estimated at from 8,000 to 10,000, mostly young men. These latter were forced into their position not by word of command so much as by the free use of sticks by their officers; it seemed to be many blows first and then a word, and some of them appeared to be severely hurt. I could not help thinking as I sat and noticed this violence ... how different the condition of the natives in Natal was ...

Durnford enjoyed himself immensely. Clearly he did not see the 'violence' that Shepstone had noticed; if he had, he thought nothing

of it. His disregard of this behaviour possibly puts it in better per-
spective. Durnford, after all, had no lieutenant-governor or Secretary of State for the Colonies to convince that the condition of the
Zulu people compared unfavourably with the Natal Nguni, for
whose well-being the Secretary for Native Affairs was responsible.

The delight shown by Durnford in simply being able to witness
the ceremony is infectious: 'They sang a war song, a song without
words, wonderfully impressive as the waves of sound rose, fell
and died away, then rose again in a mournful strain, yet warlike
in the extreme . . .' In his address to the assembly Shepstone
confirmed what he and Cetshwayo had agreed upon in previous
discussions. Cetshwayo then followed Shepstone and his staff into
the tent for the second act where the crown was placed upon his
head. He was then brought outside and a proclamation announc-
ing him as king was read to his people. A salute of seventeen
guns was fired and the band struck up. This was followed by
thousands of warriors lifting their shields and striking them in
unison with sticks. The volunteers had dismounted and their
horses were standing in line linked in sections of fours, one man
to a section. At the sound of the sticks striking the shields, the
horses became terrified and unmanageable. For a while there
was confusion. Fortunately they were eventually brought under
control but Cetshwayo had noted the inexperience of both horse
and rider. Durnford also saw the panic and reflected that he
would not like to rely upon volunteers in a crisis.

The show was now over. The marquee was left behind as a gift
to Cetshwayo. He in turn gave Shepstone four tusks of ivory and
a herd of fine oxen. Zulu councillors expressed the hope that the
good relations between the Zulus and the government of Natal
would prosper. On 3 September 1873, the expedition began its
return journey, arriving in Pietermaritzburg on 19 September
1873. Durnford found temporary lodgings kept by a Scots woman
but he had been there for only a month when he was recalled to
Fort Napier to help Lieutenant-Colonel T. Milles, of the 75th Foot,
and Officer Commanding Imperial Forces in Natal Colony, prepare an expedition against a rebellious African subject – one
Langalibalele, chief of the Hlubi people who lived in a location
situated adjacent to the Upper Bloukrans and Little Bushman's
Rivers, in the foothills of the Drakensberg Mountains.

CHAPTER II

LANGALIBALELE'S REBELLION:
THE REVERSE AT THE BUSHMAN'S RIVER PASS,
4 NOVEMBER 1873

'Would to God I could let you fire!'
(Durnford)

LANGALIBALELE had moved into Natal Colony in 1848 to escape the wrath of Mpande. For eighteen months, he and his people, the Hlubi, stayed in the Klip River District, but in 1849 Theophilus Shepstone, Secretary for Native Affairs, forced them to move into a location in the foothills of the Drakensberg to act as a buffer between white farmers and Bushmen raiders. Here the Hlubi prospered, and Langalibalele, whose influence as a 'rainmaker' spread far and wide among the clans in Natal and Zululand, was recognised as one of the most powerful chiefs in the colony.

Langalibalele's relationship with the Natal government had been no better nor worse than that of any other major tribe. By 1873 there was no indication that there was any likelihood of a conflict. However the situation in 1873 certainly had the ingredients for confrontation. Langalibalele's inclination toward the counsel of his younger, aggressive advisers; white fears of African rebellion; white envy of Hlubi wealth and land, and official concern for the maintenance of the Shepstone policy threatened by Langalibalele's 'impatience of control' and by reports of the Hlubi chief's association with Cetshwayo. But each of these factors need not necessarily have led to conflict if there had been restraint, patience and understanding from all parties. Unfortunately this was not to be the case.

During the course of 1873 Langalibalele evaded efforts by the magistrate of Weenen County, John MacFarlane, to get him to register guns paid to his people in lieu of cash for work on the diamond fields. This defiance may have been intended as a means of enhancing his popularity among his young men. If this were so then it was a foolish gamble. When finally Langalibalele disregarded the order of the lieutenant-governor to come to Pietermaritzburg to answer the charges against him, it seemed clear to the authorities that, if they wished to maintain respect for the white man's prestige, they would have to make an example of him, despite the fact that other tribes were equally lax in coming forward to register their firearms.

This then was the substance of the colonial case against Langalibalele.

In the last week of October 1873 the Lieutenant-Governor of Natal, Sir Benjamin Pine, officially announced the mobilisation of colonial volunteers, consisting of 6,000 African levies, 300 white volunteers, 200 British regulars and two field pieces. The shortage of Imperial troops in Natal – there was only the 1st Battalion of the 75th Foot – most likely dictated Pine's decision to mount a colonial campaign. Of course if the 'rebellion' could be quelled by the colonists it would be a feather in the cap of those who desired responsible government.

Most of the storekeepers, farmers, traders, labourers and gentlemen that assembled at their respective depots had had no military experience and the training appears to have been limited to parade ground drill. The military camp held in June 1873 had had little practical value contrary to the claims of the *Natal Witness* and it was likely that many of those assembling in October/November 1873 had not even attended. The lack of experienced fighters among the colonials could hardly have given the Imperial officers much confidence in them.

The now Colonel T. Milles, 75th Foot, was placed in control of the military operations. He asked Durnford, as next in rank among the Imperial officers, to act as his chief-of-staff and also gave him the responsibility of preparing a plan of campaign against Langalibalele.

A sketch of the location and surrounding countryside, together with the distances, was drawn by Durnford from the available maps – in particular from Major James Grantham's map made in 1863. Unfortunately Grantham's map was not contoured and gave little indication of the ruggedness of the terrain in the Hlubi location. Grantham was living in Pietermaritzburg at this time (he had retired on half-pay in January 1873) but surprisingly Durnford, who had a reputation for thoroughness, made no effort to interview him.

Additional information was gleaned from local sources but this turned out to be sparse and unreliable. The most useful of local sources was that of Hlubi, a young Sotho chief, son of Mbunda, who lived next to Langalibalele's location and whose people had so often hunted eland buck near the Bushman's River.

As the volunteers assembled to march against him, Langalibalele decided that to fight would be folly. He thereupon left a part of his livestock with his neighbours, the Ngwe (commonly known by the colonists as Phutile or Putini), and took the majority of his people and cattle up towards the Bushman's River Pass which was the only pass in his location that gave easy access into the mountain fastnesses of BaSotholand. The very young, the women and old men (all those who might slow down his escape) Langalibalele left hidden in the numerous caves and kloofs along the way, in the hope that they would be able to follow him at a later stage.

On 29 October 1873 Milles submitted Durnford's plan to Pine who gave his approval. Langalibalele and his people were to be prevented from leaving the colony. The head of the Bushman's River Pass would be seized by a forced march. The Hlubi tribe would be given until 6 November to place themselves and their property under the protection of the officer commanding the nearest detachment. Pine insisted that hostilities should not be provoked by the government forces firing the first shot. It was hoped that Langalibalele would be taken into custody, transported to Pietermaritzburg and there charged with treason. Interestingly Shepstone opposed the plan, not because he felt that it had any defects but because he expected Langalibalele to be betrayed by the Sotho, and so a military expedition seemed pointless.

Headquarters of the expedition was to be at the farm 'Meshlynn' on the southern border of the Hlubi tribe location, and between 40 and 50 miles from Pietermaritzburg. The Richmond Mounted Rifles and 500 African levies under Captain A. C. Hawkins were sent south of the Giant's Castle mountain. A similar force, 500 Africans and the Frontier Guards under Captain G. A. Lucas, was

to operate from the farm 'Cathkin' and watch the area around the
foot of Champagne Castle mountain, close by the Ngwe location.
Captain J. MacFarlane, the magistrate who had been defied by
Langalibalele, was, with 500 Africans and the Weenen Yeomanry
and Weenen burghers, to cover the area between the Little
Thukela and Bushman's rivers. Captain J. E. Boyes and his
detachment of 133 Imperial troops of the 75th Foot (Stir-
lingshires) were to act in a supporting role only.

Captain A. B. Allison, the border agent at Olivier's Hoek, in
command of 500 Africans, was to ascend the Champagne Castle
Pass (which turned out to be non-existent) and, acting as the
right hook, move along the top of the main range towards the
Bushman's River Pass. There he was to link up with the left hook,
a force under Major Durnford comprising 55 Natal Carbineers
from the Pietermaritzburg (Town) and Karkloof Troops, and 25
mounted Sotho, which was to hasten up Giant's Castle Pass.
Boyes's 75th Foot would follow in their wake.

If Langalibalele was to be captured before he escaped into
BaSotholand, then Durnford's and Allison's forces had to march
as soon as possible. It was most likely the urgency of the situation
that precluded Durnford from learning more about the land he
was about to ride over. On paper the plan looked effective
enough to stop the Hlubi tribe from leaving the colony, but in a
land of deep valleys and towering mountains it is simply not
possible to march along straight lines. The result of the failure to
take into consideration these difficulties – and it is not possible
that Durnford was unaware of them – was to lead to numerous
problems. Durnford does appear to have disregarded or under-
estimated the difficulties, although, in his defence, Pine or Milles
had imposed a time-limit upon him and under this limitation he
did the best he could.

Durnford was keen to get into action. When he left Pietermaritzburg with the troops on 30 October he had been given the
impression by his superiors that he would possibly be facing 'a
real army of bloodthirsty rebels'. Colonel Milles arrived at Fort
Nottingham, the temporary headquarters before the move to
Meshlynn farm, twenty-four hours after the troops on Sunday, 2
November. Captain Charles Barter of the Natal Carbineers was
the most senior officer of the volunteers, and had hoped to be

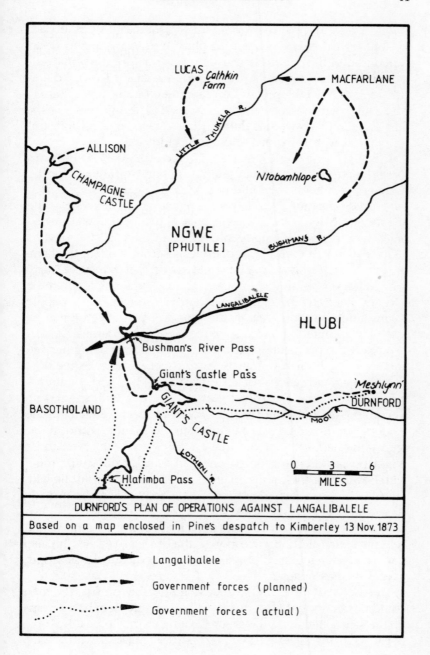

LUCAS · Cathkin Farm

MACFARLANE

ALLISON

'Ntabamhlope

CHAMPAGNE CASTLE

LITTLE THUKELA R.

NGWE [PHUTILE]

BUSHMANS R.

LANGALIBALELE

HLUBI

Bushman's River Pass

Giant's Castle Pass

'Meshlynn'
DURNFORD

BASOTHOLAND

GIANT'S CASTLE

MOOI R.

LOTHENI

0   3   6
MILES

Hlatimba Pass

DURNFORD'S PLAN OF OPERATIONS AGAINST LANGALIBALELE

Based on a map enclosed in Pine's despatch to Kimberley 13 Nov. 1873

Langalibalele

Government forces (planned)

Government forces (actual)

able to lead the force that would ascend the Giant's Castle Pass. But Milles had been reluctant to place him in command of an expedition of this nature because he was not a professional soldier and had had no soldiering experience. Major Durnford, the chief-of-staff, volunteered and was appointed in his place. Barter, who had been most energetic in preparing the Carbineers for this expedition, was no doubt piqued at this decision but cooperated with Durnford to the best of his ability.

At 8.30 p.m. on the evening of 2 November 1873, Durnford's force departed in the mist and rain from Fort Nottingham for the Giant's Castle Pass. He would not be stopping at Meshlynn farm but would be taking a direct route so that by the morning of the 3rd the force could be at the Bushman's River Pass. As it turned out, it was physically impossible for them to reach the pass so soon. This much could have been learnt from William Popham, the owner of Meshlynn, but he could not be found. Instead Durnford relied on his guide Hlubi, the young Sotho chief, whom he had appointed to the expedition on the strength of his people having hunted in the area. It was soon to be discovered that he had only a limited knowledge of the area of operations.

Already the preparations had the appearance of being hurried and superficial – hardly signals for the success of an expedition.

Each man had rations for three days and 40 rounds of ammunition. Few of the Sotho had guns. Those that had, sported an assortment of double and single smooth-bores and Dutch muzzle loaders. Ammunition was in short supply for the Sotho; those with guns had, on average, three rounds each but even these might be of little use, for no one had thought of issuing them with powder for their guns. Blame for this oversight must lie with Durnford, who seems to have made it his responsibility to provide them with food but overlooked their powder requirements. It is possible of course that Durnford assumed that the Sotho would rely on their traditional weaponry, the assegai. Perhaps he also saw them as being used only in a non-combative role, as scouts, guides or messengers.

The ascent of the Lotheni valley was a terrible ordeal. The men could not sit upon their mounts but had to pull them by the reins up the steep incline. As the going became more difficult the force began to string out as numbers of the less fit fell back with fatigue.

On the climb, at about 10 a.m. Durnford's horse Chieftain, a grey
BaSotho pony, lost its footing, fell down a steep decline dragging
Durnford with it. One of the Carbineers declared that Durnford
'rolled head over heels like a ball bounding down, for about fifty
yards'. Possibly the horse rolled over him, for his injuries were
many; a dislocated shoulder, two bruised ribs and a bad gash on
his head. His sword scabbard was bent double and the sword,
given to him by his father when he left for South Africa, could
not be made to fit in it, so he gave the sword to his guide Hlubi
to carry for him. The horse was uninjured. Durnford was then
helped to his feet, someone made his shoulder as comfortable as
possible, and he ordered the advance to continue. At noon he
called another halt to allow the stragglers to catch up. He also
sent a party of six Sotho to scout the top of the pass and to find
out whether Langalibalele's people were ascending the Bushman's Pass.

The worst of the ascent was still to come. Trooper Henry Bucknall of the Karkloof Troop (Natal Carbineers) recalled that

> everyone was too tired to give more than a passing glance at
> the stupendous masses of projecting rock above us like a
> rugged wall, half a mile high. We would scramble up 20 or 30
> yards then sit down, scramble another 20, and sit down again,
> leading our horses, which made it much more tiring than it
> would have been without them, for in keeping out their way
> we would slip down at almost every step.

Soon after 2 p.m. the small force, which had by now been
reduced to 36 white troopers[1] and 15 Sotho,[2] crossed the Bhodla
River, and followed the contour round a sharp spur. Captain
Barter, a farmer in his fifties and a member of the executive
council, was utterly exhausted. The climb before him appeared
insuperable:

[1] Barter claimed there were 32 left. The figure of 36 is merely an assessment based on evidence offered by Clarke, Barter, Varty, Durnford and
Parkinson. 13 or 14 seem to have been left behind.
[2] Three of the 25 had been sent by Parkinson to collect the pack horses
from Taylor; one had been sent to guide Taylor and his companions home
to Meshlynn and six had gone scouting.

The scene before us was savage in the extreme. Down the bare side of the mountain hung ribands of water, showing the spot to be the very birthplace and nursery of rivers; above, huge krantzes frowned while the masses of unburnt dry grass, hanging like a vast curtain, gave a sombre and malignant aspect to the scene.

During the course of the night ride Durnford had been brought to the foot of the wrong pass. Through no fault of the guide Hlubi, who in good faith had brought the troop to a pass believed to be the Giant's Castle Pass (even by some of the white troopers who had climbed this very pass before) Durnford was in fact, surveying the Hlatimba Pass six miles to the south of the Giant's Castle Pass. It was perhaps just as well that this error had been made for no horse would have been able to make a night ascent of the latter pass.

The day was to be an exhausting one. At sunset on 3 November 1873, some 100 yards from the top of the Hlatimba Pass, Durnford fainted from pain and fatigue. Trooper Robert Erskine, son of Natal's Colonial Secretary, hastened down to administer brandy to him and attend to his needs. Here Durnford's pain-racked body got some rest at last. For the next five hours, attended by Elijah Kambule, Shepstone's interpreter, and by Erskine (both of whom got very little respite themselves), the major slept fitfully. He no doubt hoped that, in the interim, Lieutenant E. Parkinson, whom he had left behind on the ascent to pick up the stragglers and the remaining pack horses, would soon be joining him. The rest of the men struggled on to the top of the pass. At 9 p.m. Durnford was wakened by one of the scouts who had returned to report that men and cattle were moving up towards the Bushman's River Pass. There could be no further delay. At 11 p.m. Major Durnford prepared himself for the arduous climb to the top. He was in intense pain notwithstanding the aid given by his guide Hlubi, Kambule, Erskine and Hlubi's brother who each held a corner of a blanket and pulled him up by placing it behind him. They had to halt every two or three steps and lay him down on the ground to let him rest. It took him three hours to get up an ascent which would have taken him fifteen minutes if he had been fit.

At the top of the Hlatimba Pass (9,323 feet above sea level)

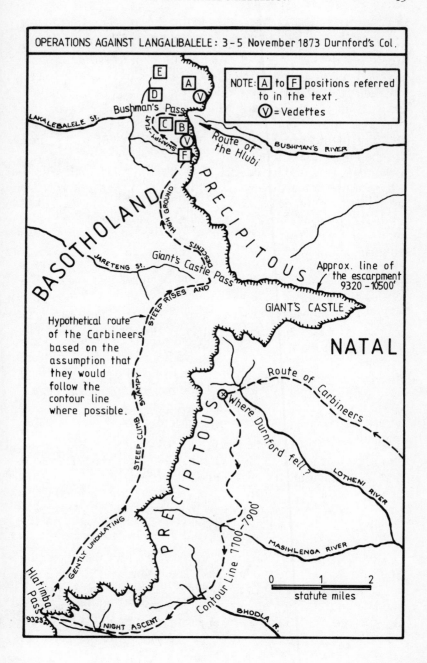

OPERATIONS AGAINST LANGALIBALELE : 3–5 November 1873 Durnford's Col.

NOTE: [A] to [F] positions referred to in the text.
(V) = Vedettes

Bushman's Pass
LAKALEBALELE ST.
SWAMPY FLAT
Route of the Hlubi
BUSHMAN'S RIVER

BASOTHOLAND

PRECIPITOUS

HIGH GROUND
DESCENTS
JARETENG ST.
Giant's Castle Pass

Approx. line of the escarpment 9320 – 10500'

GIANT'S CASTLE

STEEP RISES AND

Hypothetical route of the Carbineers based on the assumption that they would follow the contour line where possible.

NATAL

Route of Carbineers

Where Durnford fell?

SWAMPY
STEEP CLIMB

LOTHENI RIVER

PRECIPITOUS

MASIHLENGA RIVER

GENTLY UNDULATING

Contour Line 7700 – 7900'

Hlatimba Pass
9323

NIGHT ASCENT
BHODLA R.

0   1   2
statute miles

the men had tried to snatch a few hours' sleep in bitterly cold conditions. Soon after 2 a.m. Durnford reached the summit, weary but determined, and ordered the men to saddle up and proceed. A little after 2.30 a.m. the Carbineers and the Sotho were on their way, moving by moonlight slowly across the spongy grass, over the ridges and scattered rocks. Durnford took the Sotho on ahead until they were about two or three miles from the rest of the troop. After about three hours of riding they reached the crest of a hill overlooking the valleys leading to the Bushman's Pass, and in the early light of dawn watched the Hlubi tribe's cattle being driven toward the pass. It was not an easy ascent and a number of beasts lost their footing and were killed in the fall on to the rocks below. Jabez Molife, one of the Sotho, was sent back to hasten on the white troopers. An hour after sunrise, about 6.15 a.m. on 4 November 1873, the troopers reached the hill overlooking the pass. On the spur to the left of the pass (marked E on the map on p. 50) there were about 300 head of cattle and 30 herdboys.

Approximately 400–500 yards from the mouth of the pass next to a small stream the contingent halted. Here the force was split into two: half the force under Sergeants Button and Clarke, was instructed to follow as a reserve while Durnford and Barter took the rest of the men and the Sotho, and hurried ahead toward the pass. Close to the pass they rounded a corner where there was 'a large rocky projection'. Under this some herdsmen sat by a fire, cooking. A number were armed with guns, the rest had assegais. They were startled out of their wits; a few fled, but one stout heart snatched up his gun and pointed it at Major Durnford and Elijah Kambule. He was quickly disarmed, and the guns and assegais of the others gathered up. Durnford, who seemed to be under the impression that these men were Sotho, asked them whether they had met Langalibalele's people. 'We are they,' the herdsmen replied.

The advance troop continued at a fast canter for the remaining 300 yards to the mouth of the pass. The few tribesmen there fled in panic toward the left of the hill above the pass. The troop was then drawn up along the mouth. After about ten minutes of wait- ing the reserve troop was brought forward by the sight of the white-bearded Captain Barter waving his sword to get their attention. The time was about 6.30 a.m. The twelve miles from the Hlatimba Pass to Bushman's Pass had taken about four hours. Saddle-sore, exhausted both physically and mentally, the men found that Allison's force from Champagne Castle had not yet arrived. As it turned out Allison was unable to find a way to the top of the Drakensberg.

Already Hlubi tribe cattle that had come up through the pass were moving across into BaSotho territory, and several more large herds could be seen coming up. Durnford decided that he had to try and act without Allison and prevent more Hlubi people escaping into BaSotholand. He told the troopers of his decision but instructed them that under no circumstances were they to fire the first shot. Corporal J. W. Household was then sent to the top of the hill to the left of the pass (marked A on the map on p. 50) to watch through a telescope the Hlubi activity in the valley below. He hastened back to report large numbers of cattle and tribesmen but Durnford, with some impatience, sent him back to his post.

Of the bulk of the Hlubi people there was no sign. What Household had seen was probably the cattle-guard which possibly numbered no more than 500 men. In fact Langalibalele and the majority of his people had already crossed into BaSotholand.

On the summit all seemed quiet after the first flurry of activity. Some 300 yards away to the eastern rear of the pass a knot of tribesmen hovered next to a large herd of cattle grazing nearby. The men were ordered to dismount; the horses were linked and seven men ordered to hold them while the rest fell out and rested their exhausted bodies. In order to prevent tribesmen filtering up the pass along the sides, and to watch and report on developments below, two vedettes (Trooper M. Fannin and Corporal W. C. Shaw) were sent out to the right probably on to the hill known today as Mount Erskine (marked B on the map on p. 50) and two Sotho were sent on to the hill (A) to the left of the pass – thus relieving Corporal Household who rejoined his troop. Six Sotho were ordered to instruct those tribesmen on the pass to return to Natal with their cattle. The rest of the Sotho were placed on the right of the main force. Major Durnford then got down to writing a despatch to Colonel Milles (which was never sent) reporting his arrival at the pass, stating the absence of Captain

Allison and requesting reinforcements. He ordered the men to kill a cow – 'to stab it', not to shoot it, and this was done by the Sotho. But three or four had been stabbed before one was killed. The Hlubi people looked on disapprovingly. The cow was half-skinned when some fifty tribesmen joined the two Sotho on the hill (A) to the left of the pass. They had probably ascended by another pass nearby. The Carbineers thought they were Allison's levies. Some of the men, possibly anticipating being called in, breakfasted off the cow while it was still raw.

The six Sotho in the meantime were finding it impossible to get the tribespeople to take their cattle back down the pass. It seems that the Hlubi were emboldened by an indiscreet remark made by one of the Sotho, that the government forces had been instructed not to fire upon them.

Durnford sent off four Sotho to speak to the knot of tribesmen that had just arrived. They returned to announce that they were not Allison's men but were a group led by Mabuhle, Langaliba-lele's head man. Major Durnford thereupon went off with Elijah Kambule to speak to Mabuhle. He called for Mabuhle to step forward. He did so and listened respectfully to Durnford's assur-ance that all who surrendered to the government would not be harmed but that Langalibalele was required by the magistrate at Estcourt 'to answer certain charges'. Mabuhle, secure in the knowledge that Langalibalele was safe in BaSotholand, replied that the younger men might well decide to fight. He declared that it would be wise for the white men to leave first. This Durnford refused to do. The younger men who were grouped toward the rear of this party appeared to take this refusal with clamorous disapproval, and one hot-blood thrust his way to the front and gesticulated with his assegai in front of the major. He was struck down by one of the indunas but the action excited the rest of the young men who crowded round Mabuhle and the major, raising their voices and waving their guns and assegais. When Captain Barter saw the excited gestures of the warriors he passed word to the Carbineers to collect their horses and stand by them. The men were apprehensive. Bucknall recalled that they sat on their horses 'in close order watching [the tribesmen among the rocks on the right] sharpening their assegais and taking sights at us, and trying different positions behind the stones'. Sergeant Thomas

Varty declared that the men's confidence in Durnford began to evaporate when they saw him 'try to talk the kaffirs . . . into going down the pass'.

At last Durnford detached himself from Mabuhle and returned to his troops. Mabuhle, who had probably been notified by now of the order that the government troops would not fire unless fired at, sent messengers to command the cattle guard to hasten up to the summit and reinforce the numbers of tribesmen already there. Soon they were pushing past the troopers and the Sotho and moving among the rocks on the colonists' right flank, where they took up strategic positions with their fellows on the rising ground overlooking the government force (see C on the map on p. 50). Durnford wanted to return to Mabuhle, presumably with the object of putting a stop to this provocation, but the Sotho advised him against returning. He ordered the men to prevent the tribespeople pushing their way through but they were unable to stop them. Elijah Kambule urged the major to open fire but he refused. Trooper Robert Speirs, who was near Durnford, also suggested it but the reply was: 'Would to God I could let you fire', and he moved off.

In view of the increasing danger from the left rear (points A and E) and of the exposed position of his force Durnford re-deployed his men. Barter's troop was taken out in skirmishing order on to the rising ground 150 yards to the left (point D): four of the men were left near the Lakabalele spruit and four a little higher up. The remaining six were spread out below the spruit. The reserve troop was placed under Sergeant Clarke and was stretched across the mouth of the pass with about 15 paces between each man. But the Hlubi people were not discouraged by these acts and sat disdainfully among the rocks, hurling insults and sharpening their assegais or sighting their guns. Kambule approached Captain Barter and asked him to urge Durnford to retire the troops, presumably to higher ground, but Barter refused.

The reserve troop under Clarke, made up of the Pietermaritz-burg contingent and some of the Karkloof Troop, felt most unhappy with their exposed position and one or two of the 'oldest and steadiest' approached Barter and asked him to speak to Durnford and request of him that they retire. Barter sent

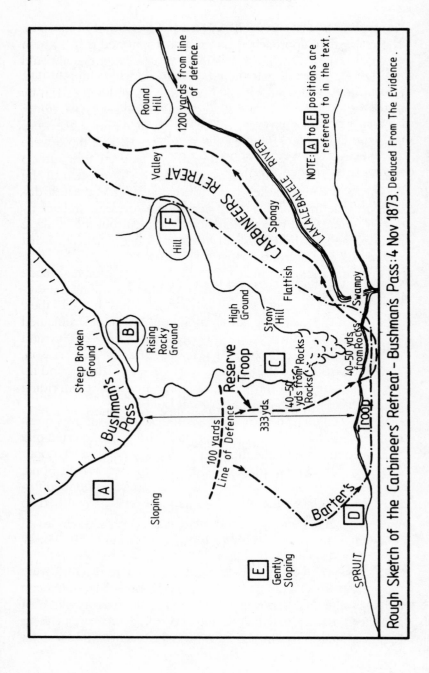

Rough Sketch of the Carbineers' Retreat – Bushman's Pass: 4 Nov 1873. Deduced From The Evidence.

Sergeant J. O. Jackson to tell Durnford of the mood of his men. The major then approached Barter who confirmed that his men were 'dispirited'. Durnford took this to mean that the men could not be relied upon, and their bearing convinced him of this. He thereupon gave orders for Barter's troop to be called in by Trumpeter George Ross and turned to address the reserve troop, presumably with the object of reassuring them, for there were possibly 300 Hlubi on the pass at this time. Most of these were on the left of the high ground opposite to where Barter's troop had been stationed, but the warriors among the rocks on the flank (point C) of Clarke's troop were causing the greatest discomfort. The men of this troop had tried to drive them back by threats, curses and riding their horses at them but the courage and boldness of the Hlubi had increased when it was seen that the whites would go no further than threats.

Durnford asked the men if the charge that Barter had made was correct. There was a great deal of muttering among the Carbineers and Sergeant Clarke, who considered himself their spokesman was heard by Barter crying out that if they remained they would be murdered. At this point Troopers G. Wray and F. Preller, who were apparently out scouting for some reason, joined the troop and the vedettes were called in. They found no easy passage through. 'My blood ran cold when I saw them riding through the rebels,' recalled Sergeant Button.

There seemed to be no positive response to Durnford's question, but the mood of the men alarmed Durnford who cried out: 'Will no one stand by me then?' From the reserve force Trooper Erskine stepped forward: 'I will, Major'. Troopers Edwin Bond, Charlie Potterill, Robert Speirs and Charlie Raw also stepped forward and declared their support. But the majority wished to retire.

Durnford now made up his mind. It was clear to him that the reserve troop could not be relied on 'in the slightest degree' and so, with a view to retiring the force to higher ground – they were about 100 yards from the mouth of the pass – he ordered Captain Barter to give the order 'to retire from the right, walk, march'. A great deal of time had been wasted and he was well aware of the risks involved in moving his men at this critical stage, but, as he wrote later, 'There was nothing else to be done; . . . there was no support'.

The major rode away to the right of his force with the object of calling Barter's troop to intercept the warriors who were seen to be working their way across the rear of the volunteers. The reserve troop would then be able to move unhindered into its new position. Most of the BaSotho had moved wide and behind the Lakabalele stream to the rear. There was no indication from the major of the seriousness of the situation and a few of them paused at the stream to have a drink. The majority were moving at a walk as the volunteers approached in column of fours. About four or five Sotho and Elijah Kambule remained close to Durnford, who by now was also at the stream and about 100 yards from the troopers.

The troop proceeded at a walk for about 200 yards along the same route that had brought them to the pass. Troopers Erskine, Bond, Potterill and Charlie Raw were in the rear. As the head of the column passed by the stony hill it was seen that a considerable number of warriors were moving among the rocks some 40 or 50 yards to the left. Sergeant Thomas Varty of Barter's troop in the front, gave the order: 'Form half sections', for the ground was difficult, 'boggy and stony, not suitable for riding four abreast'. In the middle of the movement a single shot was fired (by a tribesman identified as Jantje ka Silele, declared Hlubi later) and this was followed by a volley. Just before the shot was fired, a Sotho drinking at the stream saw the danger and cried out a warning to Durnford. This may have started the stampede.

The Carbineers lost all sense of discipline and dug their heels into their horses' flanks, driving the galloping steeds in the direction of the Hlatimba Pass. There were cries of 'Get out from under the hillside!' and 'Ride out of this!' Katana, one of the Sotho, was shot near the stream. Trooper Erskine was killed by Jantje, shot through the heart. Close by, Trooper Bond was shot in the head. Potterill's horse was shot from under him. Unable to find a spare mount and with no one to help him, he tried to run after the retreating column but was quickly overtaken by three Hlubi tribesmen. He turned to face his pursuers but was mortally wounded in the chest by a shot from the foremost of the three, who was identified as a warrior named Latyinga. As Latyinga threw himself upon Potterill, the Carbineer shot him dead. The two men fell in a heap together. The other two warriors arrived and administered the *coup-de-grâce* with their assegais.

Durnford had a miraculous escape. When the Sotho shouted out his warning Durnford was at the rear of the force with Kambule. They were soon cut off from the others as the tribesmen surrounded them. Kambule's horse was assegaied and fell. Durnford tried to assist Kambule to mount behind him on Chieftain, but at that moment the interpreter fell dead, shot through the head probably at close range by a tribesman believed to have been named Paluzamati. Two warriors grabbed Chieftain's bridle but they had great difficulty in steadying the horse, which had become most excitable. Durnford was assegaied in the left elbow and in the side – though this latter wound was later found to be superficial. He managed to shoot both these men with his revolver. Chieftain, frightened by the shooting and the clamour, plunged away toward the line of retreat, bowling over one man who had the temerity to stand in the horse's way and fire off his gun. The bullet grazed Durnford's cheek.

The major was in a bad way. His left arm hung limp by his side the nerve in the elbow severed. Undoubtedly he was very lucky to have escaped for it was found later that his patrol jacket was pierced and torn in many places.

After 40 to 50 yards some of the men slowed up and one or two turned as if to fire, but there was too much confusion, and Sergeant Clarke ordered the men not to fire for fear of hitting one of their own men, and to conserve ammunition in case they were cut off. They rode at a fast canter as best they could over broken and swampy ground for 400 to 1,000 yards. Varty's horse, shot in the flank, collapsed shortly after reaching the swampy ground, and seven or eight troopers halted to help him. Fortunately he was able to grab Erskine's riderless grey, but he had hardly travelled 200 yards further when a bullet cut down this mount as well. Sergeant Jackson and Troopers Bucknall, Fannin and Speirs quickly came to his assistance: the troopers kept off the enemy by firing one or two shots while Jackson procured another horse (Durnford's spare) and helped him saddle and mount.

Durnford had in the meantime joined the troopers around
Varty and called out to the rest to halt but it seems that they did
not hear him. Durnford's guide Hlubi was sent to call them back
but they paid no attention to him, so Fannin went after them, but,
according to Fannin, Sergeant Clarke refused to return, took his
men across a stream toward a hill and there declared he would
wait for the rest. Durnford had hoped to make a stand near where
Varty had halted (point F on the map on p. 50) – it was about
350 yards from the enemy – but when it was seen that the rest
would not return, one of the troopers remarked: 'It is no use us
staying here, look at those men,' pointing to the foremost of the
retreating Carbineers about a mile away. Clarke's party was about
60 yards away. Jabez Molife remembered that it was at this time
he borrowed Shaw's gun and fired a shot at the enemy. Another
Sotho borrowed Trooper H. Church's gun and fired two shots.
But Clarke was still not happy with his new position and declared:
'Don't halt here, take up a position to the right.' They then crossed
a second stream and travelled along its right bank.

Durnford claimed that the Sotho rallied at his command and
poured a volley into the enemy, with the result that they were
discouraged and momentarily halted. But there seems to be
no evidence to support this. The Carbineers denied that such
a stand was made and as most of the Sotho were not armed
with guns and no one had any powder, such a claim is unlikely.
It is possible that Durnford, in his weakened state, saw Molife
and the other Sotho fire at the enemy; there being other
BaSotho with these two perhaps this is the 'rally' to which the
major referred?

While the men on the right of the stream moved up a hill and
paused for two or three minutes under the ledge of a rock,
Durnford was moving on the left of the stream accompanied by
a solitary Sotho. The force seems to have been split roughly into
four: BaSotho, who were well ahead, and who were in fact the
first to arrive at the Hlatimba Pass; Clarke's unit of about twelve
whites and a few Sotho; the cluster with Varty, and also about a
dozen Carbineers, who were not far behind Clarke; and finally
the eight to ten men who could not be halted and were about a
mile ahead.

Sergeant Clarke who, contrary to some of the reports seems to have kept some discipline among those under him, seems guilty of poor judgement rather than cowardice. Being the drill instructor for the Carbineers, many of them looked to him for guidance and he in turn appeared only too willing to try and command when he should have deferred to Durnford.

He saw little point in stopping at the ledge, and his party continued their retreat over a hill which was estimated by Trooper J.J. Hodson to be about 2,000 yards from the Bushman's River Pass. When Durnford reached the top of this hill he dismounted; he may well have fainted as some claimed. Varty's group was with him, and both Varty and Trooper Dicks fully expected the major to make a stand here. He sent J.J. Raw to call the rest back but it seems that no one would return. The force was still being pursued by Hlubi warriors but their numbers were not large. The bulk of them gave up the chase after about two miles, but a few doughty ones persevered – two or three following the colonials the whole way to the Hlatimba Pass, where Durnford was able to get his men to halt at last.

Now that Durnford had his command together again, he contemplated returning to the fray. But no one would support him while he was in this frame of mind. Jabez Molife recalled that he and some of the Sotho had to chase after Durnford, for he had already turned his horse's head in the direction of the Bushman's River Pass again. When Molife drew up alongside he grabbed Chieftain's bridle and turned him round: 'I could not let him fling away his life by riding back alone amongst 300 fighting men who had tasted blood.' Even his loyal BaSotho saw little point in further aggression.

Lieutenant Parkinson, who had been waiting at the Hlatimba Pass with one of the pack horses and a few stragglers, asked the major whether they should not make a stand at the Hlatimba Pass (though Durnford later denied this). The colonel wanted to retire. Some of the men wanted to stay and eat now that they had met up with the pack horses and provisions, but Durnford was adamant that they get off 'this cursed mountain'. The ammunition was split up among the men and a number of BaSotho were detailed off as the rearguard.

Halfway down the Hlatimba Pass Durnford was met by a Sotho who gave him a packet of letters. One was from Theophilus Shepstone dated 2 November 1873, informing Durnford that he had instructed Chief Teteleku from the Swartkops location to follow Durnford's force up the Giant's Castle Pass with his African levies. Upon reading this he exclaimed: 'Would I had received that before.' There was also a letter from Captain Boyes of the 75th Foot asking for directions to the Giant's Castle Pass and for an indication of Durnford's whereabouts.

Trooper Fannin led the Carbineers down a shorter and easier route along the valley of the Mkomaas River (probably the Hlatimba River). But the going was still tough and the men inevitably began to string out.

Durnford remembered very little of the trip back to Meshlynn farm. On one occasion he fainted and was sustained by a mixture of gin and water administered by Sergeant Button. The Carbineers gave their wounded and weak commander every assistance in his passage down the Hlatimba Pass. Parkinson in the meantime had made his way to the front of the column. He passed Durnford and Barter resting near the Mkomaas. When he reached the head of the column some distance ahead he found the men and horses so tired that he ordered an off-saddle.

Soon afterwards Durnford rode up and demanded to know who had given the order to off-saddle. Parkinson stepped forward: 'I have given the order' and he explained why. Durnford rebuked him sternly and, according to Barter, said: 'In the present temper which your men are in, I shall not rest or let you rest until I get you out of the mountain.' The decision was wise for the area was too well commanded by the heights about for them to stop. The party up-saddled and continued the retirement.

It was an exhausting march. One of the pack horses carrying spare ammunition fell down a steep krantz and some of the ammunition was lost. Clarke's horse would go no further on one occasion and a number of men stopped with him. Durnford, possibly still bristling over Parkinson's misjudgement, rode up to ask him why he was halting. Clarke told him that his horse needed a rest, whereupon Durnford shouted at him that he should be ashamed of himself – 'an old soldier, setting such an example to other men'.[1] This so enraged Clarke that an altercation followed. The drill instructor, in recalling the incident a week later, vowed that he would never serve under Durnford again 'unless compelled by law'. They reached the Game Pass about 8 p.m. that evening, where they rested for an hour. They reached Meshlynn between 1 and 2 a.m. on 5 November 1873.

How does Durnford emerge from this conflict? Firstly, it could hardly be equated with his vision of war, and his disappointment was clear when he discovered that the enemy was not a 'real army of bloodthirsty rebels' after all. His task at the Bushman's Pass came to be that of the civil officer rather than that of the soldier. He tried to avoid conflict rather than seek it. When he failed to persuade the Hlubi tribesmen to return to Natal, and matters got out of hand, his force disintegrated and he was still left with the burning question whether he had the ability to command.

His rudeness to Parkinson and Clarke; his failure to have a roll taken at the Hlatimba Pass on the retreat; his inability to make up his mind during the flight of the force; his incredible physical strength and durability, exemplify the very deep frustration that had temporarily unbalanced him. At Isandhlwana, Lieutenant Alfred Henderson of the Natal Native Horse, was to record a similar assessment of him during the height of the battle.

When on his return to Meshlynn farm, he learnt of Captain Boyes's plight, he was still unpredictable, but his impulsive search for Boyes fortunately had a happy ending, and in some measure was to restore his mental equilibrium.

---

[1] Clarke had been a regular with the 43rd Foot and had served six years with them. He had seen service in the Kafir War of 1851–52. He had then served seventeen years with the Cape Mounted Rifles, ten of these as Troop Sergeant Major. At the time of his appointment as drill instructor of the Carbineers, he was on army pension.

CHAPTER III

RETURN TO PIETERMARITZBURG

'There have been sad sights – women and children
butchered . . .'

(Durnford)

As soon as he arrived at Meshlynn farm, Durnford, regardless
of his own injuries, hastened to discover the whereabouts
of the Imperial force under Captain Boyes, who, it will be
remembered, was making for the Giant's Castle Pass. He estimated
that Boyes would be at the foot of the mountain by now, but
nothing could be done to help him until morning. Colonel Milles
had moved his headquarters to Holmes farm, fifteen miles north-
east of Meshlynn, so Durnford scribbled an abbreviated account
of the debacle on the pass and sent a messenger off with it to
Milles. He then allowed Staff-Surgeon Major W. Bindon to look
at his wounds. By now he had lost all feeling in his left arm.
Bindon's inspection revealed that, apart from minor abrasions
and cuts, his left shoulder had been dislocated and that paralysis
in the left arm was due to the stab wound severing the nerve in the
elbow. After some medical attention Durnford retired to snatch a
few hours' sleep until first light.

In the morning a small volunteer detachment of four artillerymen, 46 infantrymen of the 75th Foot, six or seven Carbineers,
three of whom had been on the pass and still felt fit enough, and
30 of Hlubi's BaSotho, were mustered for the purpose of searching for Boyes. The day, 5 November, was one of mist, rain and
thunderstorms, and only by 11 p.m. that night had it cleared
sufficiently for the men to set out on the search. Ignoring the
entreaties of the surgeon that he should be resting, Durnford
insisted on leading the detachment. He was so weak that he had
to be lifted on to his horse. The men cheered him out of the
camp.

The weather remained inclement and after an exhausting three-hour march Durnford called a halt. By now the rain was falling in torrents and visibility was reduced to zero. It was only at 4 a.m. that the search could continue. For the next eight hours it was painful progress as each rise was topped and the blurred horizon scanned for a sight of Boyes or of the enemy. At last the red coats of the missing troop were seen and at midday on the 6th the two forces met. Boyes had indeed been lost and was still searching for the way to the foot of the mountain when Durnford arrived.

Colonel Milles, who had returned to Meshlynn on receipt of Durnford's note, sent a messenger after him to order his return to camp. But Durnford had found Boyes by the time the messenger caught up with him and was already on the way back. Milles, although he had good cause to rebuke Durnford for taking out a large portion of the Meshlynn garrison – a few scouts would have been sufficient – nevertheless generously commended him for his 'courage and coolness'.

Durnford was later recommended for a CMG by G. Gathorne-Hardy, the Secretary of State for War, but Lord Carnarvon, his counterpart in the Colonial Office, although sympathetic, turned the recommendation down:

> The expedition in which he had principal command was a disastrous, and in some respects, a discreditable failure and nearly involved us in very serious trouble ... It was only that being a soldier and a gentleman he did not disgrace himself like some of the runaway volunteers.

There were others that thought he deserved the VC. But all he was to receive was thanks from Milles on behalf of the military establishment, thanks from the Natal Colonial government and from the Colonial Office. His bitterness at official non-recognition of what Gathorne-Hardy was to call 'his exceptional merits', was demonstrated in his refusal to apply for a pension for the wounds he had received. According to his brother Edward, he declared that no amount of money could buy 'honour'. It was only as a result of strong pressure from his father that he registered for a pension, but on his death it was found 'that he had never drawn a penny of it.'

Had it really been necessary for Durnford, in his weakened state, to go looking for Boyes? It seems so. It may be unfair to ignore entirely his humanitarianism but the real purpose behind Durnford's action appears to be one of self-reproach. This apparent masochism was, in effect, a laxative for an aching conscience – blaming himself for the death of the men on the pass. It was not unexpected that he was to welcome Pine's fresh orders to return to Pietermaritzburg to pick up reinforcements and supplies for a second expedition against Langalibalele, the first plan having by now been abandoned and the forces recalled to their respective field headquarters.

By 9 November 1873 he was ready to move and at 2 p.m. he left Fort Napier with a detachment of the 75th Foot under Lieutenant E. O. Trower, artillery pieces, his loyal Sotho and 300 black levies under George Shepstone, one of Theophilus's sons.

In the early hours of 11 November, Durnford arrived at the field headquarters near Ntabamhlope. There was considerable bustle: parties had been sent out to search for Hlubi tribespeople and were returning with small numbers of captive women, children and old men flushed out of the caves and holes. Durnford wasted no time in getting together with Milles and other officers to plan the next stage of the operations against Langalibalele, who was now known to be in BaSotholand.

He was very keen to return to the Bushman's Pass to bury the dead and seems to have convinced everyone that in the process he could reconnoitre the route which would be taken by Allison and his 1,500 levies on their march into BaSotholand. Hawkins would be taking his force to the sources of the St John's River to cut off Langalibalele's line of retreat.

On 12 November he issued a 'Pass Order' calling for twenty mounted volunteers to be ready to leave for the Bushman's Pass either on the 13th or 14th for a period of four days. Although seventeen volunteers from the Karkloof Troop of the Carbineers put their names down, only one (George Shepstone) of the Pietermaritzburg Troop offered to go, despite the fact that the object of the expedition was to bury the dead of the latter troop. One vindictive member of the Town Troop triumphantly claimed that the lack of volunteers showed 'the opinion of the men with respect to [Major Durnford's] conduct'. The writer had undoubtedly read the *Natal Witness* of the day before in which it was 'confidently asserted' that Durnford had 'cast aspersions on the courage of the volunteers'.

In the place of the volunteers, Durnford decided to take Lieutenant William Beaumont with fifty men of the 75th Foot; Hlubi's Sotho and the 300 black levies under the command of George Shepstone, whom he appointed his orderly officer. But once again the weather delayed their departure and it was not until 17 November 1873 that they were able to leave.

In the interim the area around Holmes's farm and Ntabamhlope was being cleared of Hlubi tribesmen by MacFarlane's black levies. To those volunteers engaged in this work as well, it was mere sport hunting for refugees in the caves and holes. Every now and then they would meet a pocket of resistance from younger men; this would be ruthlessly overcome. Durnford, to whom reports of these operations were made, was contemptuous of the courage of the levies who were so loud in self-praise but who were, in fact, having to be forced by their white officers to enter the caves. They had joined the whites in the expectation of easy pickings from a helpless and cowed enemy. It only required one or two of their number to be killed for them to lose their appetite for the conflict and to desert in large numbers. It is not certain in what manner Durnford showed his displeasure of the brutality of the colonial forces, but he did assure the bishop that he had protested against it.

Durnford's forced inactivity made him impatient. The recent memory of Erskine's sacrifices on his behalf weighed heavily upon his conscience, and left him with a desire to avenge the young man's death. In a letter to the bishop dated 15 November 1873, it is clear that he was searching for indemnification – but it was to be in the form of action not self-analysis. He concluded: 'Tis useless now to talk; all that remains is to bury the dead and avenge him.'

These words are highly significant. Not only do they contrast with the bishop's philosophy that these deaths, though regrettable, were but a small measure in the wider context of colonial injustice towards black colonists, but they indicate the narrow focus of Durnford's nature when his emotions were tied up in an issue. He would have liked the bishop's concurrence for his decision but this was not forthcoming. Durnford's words disturbed the bishop, who needed Durnford as an ally to fight colonial injustice, not as a knight-courageous who wished to avenge the honour of a dead comrade in order to purge a guilt-laden conscience. Colenso wrote back on 17 November:

> I confess it jarred upon my mind to find you, a brave soldier and an accomplished gentleman, talking [in those terms] ... I, and *we all*, look to you to *check* when it can be reasonably checked, the effusion of blood. God help us, if men such as you will not interfere to stop the brutal acts of men such as ____ who wanted to kill nine prisoners in cold blood. Don't be angry with me because I have written as above. If I did not care for and value your friendship you may be sure I would not have done so.

The bishop would be making a similar statement to Durnford shortly before the latter departed to join the Zululand invasion force in January 1879.

Durnford was indeed pained to receive a rebuke which he felt was unjustified. He wrote back immediately:

> Your lordship has done me an injustice in thinking that I could wreak vengeance upon hunted men, women and children. My voice has ever been raised against such proceedings ... When I wrote to you I was on the eve of starting for the Bushman's pass and I hoped and prayed that I might find the enemy posted with arms in his hands, when, on a fair field, they should have received such mercy as they have shown to others ... The death of those three boys lies heavy on my heart and I shall never be content till I have avenged them – on a fair field, remember, for I am not an assassin, and would never countenance the slaughter of hunted creatures who know not which way to turn ...

It seems that the bishop had struck a raw nerve when he questioned Durnford's object in wanting vengeance against the Hlubi tribe. If he was to have his way then there was the likelihood that innocent Hlubi blood would be spilt as well.

Early on 17 November 1873 field headquarters was moved from Holmes's to a point on the left bank of the Bushman's River eight miles away. At 11 a.m. Durnford departed with his force for the pass. By the early evening everybody was on the pass. The major then took all senior members of the party over the area, describing in detail the circumstances surrounding the debacle two weeks previously. As they proceeded they came across the bodies of the slain. All but Potterill's were found in the stream where they had been stripped and laid by the Hlubi tribesmen. His body lay on the grass 50 yards away from the others. It had been mutilated by the Hlubi witchdoctor, who had cut off the right hand to make 'medicine'. The light was beginning to fail and the party hastened back to the others. The two small patrol tents were erected and Durnford and his officers squeezed themselves into these, while the men searched for cover among the rocks.

That evening was a sombre occasion. The men had great difficulty in making a fire in the damp conditions, but by 9 p.m. some goat's meat had been boiled and was passed round. Many of the whites had been too impatient to wait and had begged charred meat off the Sotho. Despite a generous tot of rum before bed few men got any sleep that night.

Durnford got the men up early on 19 November to prepare the graves. He personally supervised the digging while Lieutenant Beaumont and George Shepstone collected the bodies. Four Sotho brought the bodies of their comrade and of Elijah Kambule and laid them next to the whites.

Before the whites were interred Durnford cut a lock of hair from each of their heads and ordered Shepstone to ensure that, together with some everlastings, flowers that grew in profusion on the summit, it was later handed to relatives of the slain.

And so 'in the grey of the morning, with a cold sleet and rain falling' and to the accompaniment of three volleys fired by a platoon of the 75th, the Reverend George Smith, who had ridden with the troop, and who was later to win fame as 'Ammunition' Smith at the epic defence of Rorke's Drift, laid the men to rest. The three whites were placed in one grave and the two blacks in another by their side. The graves were filled in and, on Durnford's orders, covered by the levies with cairns of stones.

One last act had to be completed before the party returned to headquarters. According to Edward Durnford, the body of the tribesman Durnford had killed with his revolver was found wedged in a cleft of a rock. It had been covered with a shield, and weapons were in its hands. The major insisted that a cairn be built over him as well. This action was, in some respects enigmatic and yet explicable. The task of burying the dead colonials was over and with it came a large measure of peace of mind. The bishop would certainly have applauded the noble act that Durnford allowed to the dead tribesman.

While Durnford had been occupied on the expedition to the pass to bury the dead, the 'rebellion' had taken an unfortunate turn. Cattle were required for Allison's column, and the Phutile, the neighbours of the Hlubi, were ordered to supply 500 head. Only 130 were sent and seventy of these were of such inferior quality that they were returned. The energetic MacFarlane now felt that he had good cause to act against the Phutile whom he had long suspected of aiding Langalibalele. He therefore went with a large force to the borders of the Phutile location, made a personal visit to the chief, Mbalo, and demanded the cattle for Allison, plus 200 more as a fine. Meanwhile Allison's and Captain Lucas's forces joined MacFarlane's and encircled the location.

Mbalo admitted harbouring Langalibalele's cattle, so MacFarlane, who had been given carte blanche by Pine to act in this matter, laid a further fine of 2,000 head on the tribe and ordered the surrender of all firearms. Mbalo baulked at MacFarlane's excessive demands so the latter, 'with commendable promptness' declared the editor of the *Natal Witness*, disarmed the tribe and took the chief and his indunas into custody. By 21 November over 9,000 head of cattle and more than 200 guns were seized. The colony was committing itself to a course which was both unethical and regrettable.

The provocation of this tribe to violence was considerable, yet there was no reaction – indeed the tribe's response seemed to be one of passive disbelief that events were taking such an unpleasant turn. Before this incident MacFarlane had had no complaint against the Phutile and although the latter had watched

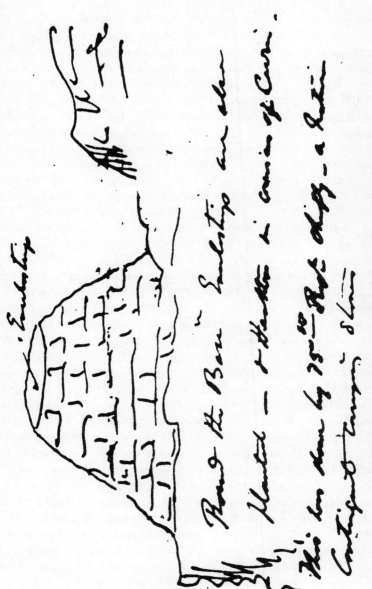

Extract from a letter dated 2 December 1873 written by Major Anthony Durnford to D. Erskine, Natal Colonial Secretary, informing him of the cairn built as a memorial to his son.

with some alarm the steps taken against Langalibalele, they had not sent any of their warriors to aid him. The act of harbouring Langalibalele's cattle could hardly be construed as complicity. The acts taken raise the possibility that MacFarlane was activated by other motives. The farmers in the Klip River and Weenen districts were known to have cast covetous eyes in the direction of the fertile land of the Phutile. On 26 February 1874, Pine notified the Secretary of State for the Colonies, the Earl of Kimberley, that he intended to settle whites in the Hlubi and Phutile locations, and during the next six months over 160 white settlers applied for the 2,000 acre grants of land offered by the government.

One man however, could have halted proceedings before it was too late: Sir Benjamin Pine. Yet Pine felt justified in acting against the Phutile. In a letter he wrote later in December 1874 to Lord Carnarvon, who was to succeed the Earl of Kimberley as Secretary of State for the Colonies when Disraeli's government came to power in February 1874, he spoke of the Phutile as having been in 'treasonable communication with Langalibalele ... in the winter of 1872', and marked the innocent acts of storing grain, looking after cattle and harbouring refugees as examples of treason and conspiracy against the colonial government. These were the reasons he gave for his proclamation of 17 December 1873 which declared his intention to break up the Phutile and banish its people from the colony. Carnarvon acknowledged Pine's letter enclosing the proclamation and asked what steps would be taken to fulfil the banishment. By the time this despatch arrived in May 1874, Pine was having second thoughts about the charges against Langalibalele's neighbours; he left it to Milles to inform the Secretary of State that a commission had been appointed to inquire into the complicity of the Phutile.

While MacFarlane was punishing the Phutile, Durnford was about to leave for the Bushman's Pass for the third time. He had hardly been in camp for two days when, as part of the general plan of operations, he moved off with seventy-six rank and file of the 75th Foot, the Sotho and a number of black levies under George Shepstone, to hold the pass, while the two 'flying columns' under Allison and Hawkins moved into BaSotholand, to catch the Hlubi warriors.

Pine's orders to all men in the field were to take all Hlubi tribesmen prisoner and confiscate all livestock. As an incentive he offered £1 for every able-bodied male captured and 100 head of cattle for the capture of Langalibalele. Any resistance from the tribesmen was to be ruthlessly put down.

Durnford's return to the pass was quite uneventful. The only thing of note was that on the night of 24 November, the rain and hail came down and it snowed along the top of the 'Berg – most unusual for that time of year. In the morning Lieutenant B. H. Woodward was ordered by Durnford to take twenty-five men to the summit and pitch the tents there. Throughout the 25th the men stayed at a camp on the spur 700 feet below the pass while the Sotho were sent to scout. There seemed to be no sight of the enemy.

The forced inactivity was trying to Durnford's patience. He was very keen to move on and pursue Langalibalele whom he estimated (probably on the evidence of the captured tribesmen) to be four days' march from the pass but he withstood the urge to go.

On 27 November Durnford, to save the men from boredom, and to occupy and to assuage his own restless conscience, ordered a pyramidal monument of stones with a base of approximately 80 feet by 80 feet to be built over the cairns of the dead colonials. This task took the men two days. The monument, which can be seen to this day, was topped with everlastings which formed 'a beautiful white covering', like a shroud.

On 30 November Durnford and his unit were relieved by Mr Lloyd and his command of 100 black levies.

Once again there was little time for rest at headquarters. He was ordered by Pine to write an account of the skirmish at the Bushman's Pass. This was done and sent off to Pietermaritzburg. It was a surprisingly terse account when one considers that the behaviour of the Carbineers at the pass had become a public issue. Although he still accused them of panic ('Two or three shots were sufficient to send them into headlong flight') he tempered his earlier version of the skirmish (made to Milles on 5 November), by admitting that the move he took to retire the men at the stage when the enemy were preparing to fire was 'a fatal line of policy', but that he had had no alternative if he wanted to save their lives. The panic that ensued, he had been told (most likely by Barter), was caused by Sergeant Clarke, the drill instructor. He indirectly pointed a finger at Pine too in his non-committal conclusion to the memorandum: 'The orders I received were "not to fire the first shot". I obeyed.' And yet both Durnford and Allison had been instructed by Pine to prevent Langalibabele's escape. Constraining the forces in the use of their firearms in what was expected to be an aggressive action, was an absurd decision.

Pine made a lame attempt to sidestep his responsibility for issuing such confusing instructions by hinting to the Earl of Kimberley that Durnford should have exercised his initiative: 'How far Major Durnford might, under the circumstances, have considered himself justified in disregarding the letter of the order, I cannot say . . .'

In the light of the furore over Durnford allegedly disobeying orders on arrival at Isandhlwana six years later, the above reflection is significant.

Although Kimberley wrote back giving his support to Pine for the action taken against Langalibalele, and exculpating Durnford entirely for the defeat at the pass, the matter was far from closed. For the moment it was out of Durnford's hands, and although the issue was kept alive by the *Natal Witness*, he had more immediate problems to deal with: the extension of the war to the Phutile location and the capture of Langalibalele.

On 1 December 1873 the men were mustered and marched out to operate in the Phutile location in support of MacFarlane, who was busy beyond the Little Thukela, and Captain G. A. Lucas, who was close to Champagne Castle.

By 5 December 1873, Durnford was back in headquarters camp. The forces were closing in on Langalibalele. The white volunteers and their black levies had, according to colonial sources, killed 150–200 tribesmen since the commencement of the first punitive expedition. The Hlubi and Phutile tribesmen had been dispersed and their cattle, horses and sheep plundered by the government troops, and later auctioned to local white farmers. Durnford was appalled at the excessive retribution taken upon these people. He wrote to his mother on 5 December:

All is over now and we return to Pietermaritzburg in a few days
... The results of the campaign are the destruction of two
tribes ... There have been sad sights – women and children
butchered by our black allies, old men too ... Thank God no
woman or child was killed by my command, no old men either,
but others have committed these atrocities for which there is
no defence to my mind ...

Durnford's good friend Bishop Colenso thought so too. It should
be mentioned that the press exercised no censorship when pub-
lishing letters from volunteers on the expedition, letters that
unashamedly exposed the cruelties the tribespeople were subjected to.

On 7 December 1873, Langalibalele and eighty-four of his followers were betrayed (as Theophilus Shepstone had predicted)
by their host, the Sotho chief Molapo, to the Cape Frontier Police.
Four days later Allison arrived to arrest him. Seven thousand head
of cattle, 260 horses and a great number of sheep and goats were
confiscated. Molapo received a gift of 2,000 head. Allison then
began the weary trip to Pietermaritzburg where he arrived
together with Langalibalele on 31 December 1873.

Langalibalele's humiliation was absolute. Forced to walk
through Pietermaritzburg encumbered with chains, he was spat
at, jeered and cursed. Old Potterill, who had, since the death of
his son on the Bushman's Pass, taken to drinking excessively,
rushed out of the crowd and struck the chief.

The trial of Langalibalele, which commenced on 16 January
1874, was a tragic farce. He was tried according to Native Law
before the Supreme Chief, Sir Benjamin Pine, who was assisted
by Theophilus Shepstone and other members of the Executive
Council, including Barter, who had been on the Bushman's Pass,
Erskine, the colonial secretary and Gallwey, the attorney general,
who were father and brother-in-law respectively to the dead Carbineer. Accused of treason, rebellion and murder, Langalibalele
was denied the services of a lawyer to defend him and was
pronounced guilty before the evidence was presented. Finally
on 9 February 1874 he was sentenced to banishment from Natal
for life.

Durnford had, together with the 75th Regiment, returned to

Pietermaritzburg on 10 December 1873. The next day he received news of his appointment to lieutenant-colonel. Since the news of the debacle on the Bushman's Pass and the rumours that Durnford had questioned the courage of the white volunteers, there had been an intensive crusade by Ridley, the editor of the *Natal Witness,* to whip up colonial displeasure against him. Although Colonel Milles had given the newspapers an account of the skirmish and had indicated gallantry by all concerned, Ridley was not satisfied and it was largely through his campaigning that a court of inquiry was to be sanctioned by Lieutenant-General Sir Arthur Cunynghame, Commander-in-Chief, Imperial Forces in South Africa, at the end of September 1874. It assembled in Pietermaritzburg in late October 1874. Its terms of reference were to inquire into all aspects of the ill-fated expedition relative to the Carbineers, and to decide whether those on the pass 'merited censure'.

Unfortunately the evidence recorded by the court was to be destroyed 'by statute' (order of the Secretary of State for the Colonies?) in June 1875 so one is forced to depend on the day to day reports that appeared in the *Natal Witness.* Although these are detailed, they place an inevitable constraint on an evaluation of the inquiry because of the absence of memoranda by the commissioners and the clerks of court. Furthermore, the depth and reliability of the newspaper's record must be treated with caution because of the aggressive standpoint taken by its editor toward the inquiry.

As a possible explanation for the destruction of the records of the court, perhaps a great deal of the evidence and correspondence would have been harmful to succeeding generations of prominent Natal colonists.

The inquiry appeared to be a most thorough one. Twenty-four witnesses were called before the court, three of these being Sotho. No Hlubi tribespeople were called but it is likely that the members of the court had access to the evidence given by Hlubi prisoners at Langalibalele's trial in January–February 1874 and later printed in a parliamentary bluebook. Members even took the trouble to cover the exact route taken by the Carbineers to the Bushman's Pass.

'The courage of the volunteers' was the subject under scrutiny, not Durnford's competence. The court's handling of the former issue was certainly impartial; there was very little in the way of cross-examination, and contradictory evidence was rarely queried. It is hardly surprising that its final 'Opinion' seems to have been framed with a view to finding the easy way to satisfy the greatest number of people. 'Extenuating circumstances' justly excused those who fled from the pass; Durnford was fairly praised for his courage and devotion to duty; Barter's behaviour was diplomatically passed over; Milles and Pine escaped criticism. The only questionable decision was the selection of Clarke as the scapegoat.

It was in Barter's letter to the *Times of Natal*, on 8 November 1873, that mention was first made of Clarke by name as having been responsible for starting the panic. Barter claimed that Clarke had shouted out while Durnford was addressing the troop just prior to retiring, that everyone would be murdered if they stayed where they were. When examined by the court Barter stated that Clarke had said words which 'did *not* lessen the feelings of disquietude and indignation among the men.'

Yet no other person was able to identify Clarke as having been responsible for this – if indeed it was said at all. In fact practically every Carbineer testified that Sergeant Clarke took command of some of the men with a view to making a stand. The only other sources which suggest Clarke's guilt in precipitating the panic were Durnford and Bucknall, and neither could produce conclusive evidence. The evidence they did produce was based on hearsay.

Whereas Barter and Bucknall had their knives out for Clarke, Clarke's target was Durnford. At no stage did he waver from his opinion that Durnford was a poor leader. He called the expedition 'one of the worse-commanded patrols that it ever fell to my lot to be in.'

Durnford was questioned by the court on 8 December, the last day of the inquiry. At no stage did its members question his decisions. They appear to have had a number of prepared questions which, it was hoped, would sort out some of the anomalies that had emerged from the questioning of the Carbineers. Durnford's replies were firm and convincing. It is unlikely that he was kept by the court for much longer than half-an-hour. The questions were led with a view to establishing the 'general bearing of the volunteers' and in this respect Durnford's replies vary little from what he had written in his memoranda to Milles and Pine in November 1873.

How did this inquiry affect Durnford? Sir Arthur Cunynghame, to whom the court's 'Opinion' was sent for judgement, alluded to many grave errors for which Durnford could be held wholly or partly responsible. An example 'not alluded to by the court' was the confusion among the volunteers over who commanded them: 'They did not clearly understand whether they were to act directly under their own officers or under the chief-of-staff (i.e. Durnford) . . .'

Cunynghame criticised the poor organisation and supervision of the transport of rations and ammunition – a situation for which the officers, Durnford included, could be held responsible. He also condemned the 'disadvantageous and unmilitary' instruction that the troop was 'not to fire the first shot' which gravely affected the morale of the troop and undermined the discipline. But all this would not have come before an inquiry if Allison's force had arrived at the pass, for Durnford's mounted troops were to be there in a supporting role only. Does he deserve castigation for remaining at the pass? Should he have ignored the escaping rebels? It was not in his character to do so, and under the circumstances it is doubtful whether any other Imperial officer worth his rank would have sat back and done nothing. However, the action he took does deserve censure. Greatly outnumbered, his advantage lay in the fact that his force was mounted yet, as Cunynghame stated, he advanced his troops 'to a position of the utmost peril' where there was no advantage to the mounted troopers.

One might add that the breech-loading Calisher-Terry carbine with which the troops were issued, gave them little cause for confidence. Although its hitting power was heavy (it fired a .45 bullet) loading was a laborious business, for before every shot a percussion cap had to be fitted. This made it slower to load than the Imperial issue Snider rifles which, according to information available at that time, could only manage an average of 18 rounds per minute in competent hands. In close combat conditions such as existed on the pass, the party would have been overwhelmed after the first shot. It is likely that the Terry would be more effective from a protected or fortified position, or in the Carbineers' situation, some distance from the enemy. Loading from a bucking, rearing horse must have been well-nigh impossible, for the Carbineers' horses were certainly in the main unschooled for and unused to battle. The shortcomings of the volunteers' mounts may not only have undermined their self-confidence but also might explain Durnford's lack of confidence in them.

Cunynghame adjudged that the circumstances in which the volunteers were placed would have been 'trying to the utmost of the most disciplined of troops' and in his final paragraph he urged Pine 'to relieve them of censure from the most serious imputations under which a soldier can labour.'

Although Cunynghame's criticisms covered the major factors that led to the retreat of the Carbineers, there were other issues not mentioned in the 'Opinion' and for which Durnford could be held responsible. He must accept some blame for the application of a plan based upon a map which provided woefully inadequate physical information. He can be blamed for neglecting the powder needs of his Sotho force. His lack of experience as a commander was, in some measure, offset by his personal bravery, and it was this latter quality which received the attention of the court. In fact the inquiry simply became an appraisal of courage. No matter how much Ridley might fume that Durnford should have been 'subjected to a searching cross-examination', there was little that could be done to place either Durnford, Milles or Pine in the dock.

What effects did this have upon Durnford's values? Ostensibly he was shown as a hero, but he must have realised that there was some controversy over his performance as a commander. One tenet he had always been firm on was his adherence to orders, a principle he had never questioned, but which now appeared to be on very shaky ground. Not only had Pine suggested that he should have used his discretion but an ex-Imperial officer, Captain A. N. Montgomery (late of the 7th Royal Fusiliers), had also publicly criticised his stubbornness.

It is reasonable to assume that when Durnford put his own interpretation to orders in January 1879, he recalled the occasion

on the Bushman's Pass when his inflexibility had brought about
the needless death of five men, and had laid open to doubt his
ability to lead men on the field.

CHAPTER IV

THE PHUTILE

'On every gentle slope and every rounded knoll
were to be seen the charred and blackened remains
of ruined kraals...'

(Atherton Wylde)

O N his return to Pietermaritzburg in December 1873, Durnford was able to attend to his duties as acting colonial
engineer. Since his appointment on 1 November 1873, the work
to be done was herculean. There was a great number of public
works that required maintaining, completing or commencing.
The labour force of the department was continually plagued by
shortages of both skilled and unskilled men. Overseers for road
parties could be found, but many of these men were lazy and
unreliable and had to be supervised themselves.

In order to improve matters Durnford had proposed to 'militarise' the department. In a minute dated 24 September 1873, laid
before the Legislative Council, he had recommended the employ-
ment of Royal Engineers' non-commissioned officers and men to
do the skilled work and that 500 blacks be trained as a pioneer
corps to do the unskilled work. The department would be run by
the commander of the Royal Engineers in Natal who would also
be colonial engineer. He would have two subalterns of the Royal
Engineers, one for the northern areas and the other based in Pietermaritzburg. The commander would take charge of the central district. 'There would be three officers of the Royal Engineers in Natal
knowing thoroughly the whole country, its means of communication, rivers, fords, military positions, as well as its value for food
supplies.'

The idea was a sound one, for it had been successfully applied
in India, Ceylon and Abyssinia. The advantage to the colony would
be the securing of an organised force for employment on public

works under the superintendence of well-trained and efficient men at very small cost. The pioneers would learn a trade and could also be used as a military force by the colony. However, the memorandum was introduced at the time when Langalibalele was causing trouble, and, with the editor of the *Natal Witness* at the van of opposition the council rejected the idea, for they feared establishing the nucleus of a trained corps which could simply substitute rifles for shovels. The council did, however, accept Durnford's offer to act as colonial engineer until a suitable civilian applicant could be found.

Military commitments kept Durnford in the field till the end of 1873. He was not a man to shirk his responsibilities, whether civil or military, and it seems that during the first quarter of 1874 he made an extensive tour of the colony to record what tasks the department was faced with. He found, that in the absence of his authority, little work had been done, and many were the reports of idle labourers, half-completed contracts and wasteful practices. He took steps to end corruption and tried to activate his subordinates, but his slender resources made things very difficult.

Despite his limited resources and the unrest in the north-western districts of the colony, he managed to get work to continue on most of the projects, and a number were finished within the time specified, but frequently through lack of available labour, construction jobs had to be temporarily suspended while repairs and maintenance were carried out on roads and bridges.

In 1872 the Natal Legislative Council, despite strong public opposition, had re-introduced Asians from India to work on the cotton and sugar plantations. The Engineer's Department could not persuade the council to attend to the department's labour shortage. It had difficulty attracting non-skilled workers to do the back-breaking labour on the roads and bridges. The Zulu showed little inclination toward this form of work. Other African tribesmen who entered the colony were quickly employed by the farmers. The shortage of labour for public works might have been reduced after 1874 as Tsonga labourers began to arrive in Natal in increasing numbers through Shepstone's agent, John Dunn, but those that were enticed away from the sugar plantations by the government were to be channelled into railway construction.

There was another avenue of labour: there were some 300–

400 men of the Phutile tribe who had been brought into Pieter-maritzburg the same day as Langalibalele, and were languishing in jail waiting for someone to decide their fate. The women and children of these men, left in many instances to fend for themselves (some had been attached to chiefs of other tribes as 'bonds-women') and now expelled from their land and deprived of their worldly wealth, wandered around searching for a home.

Durnford tentatively took up the cause of these unfortunate people. Initially Durnford's interest was with a view to alleviating the labour shortage in the Engineer's department, but he could not ignore the adverse social circumstances of the Phutile. It was not altogether unexpected. Although it must have been a difficult decision (being a servant of the colonial government, his position was a delicate one) he had to have some 'cause' to occupy his restless spirit. Denied the opportunity of honour *per bellum* it seems that he now continued the fight for honour against another enemy – that of injustice and tyranny. The bishop most likely had some influence over Durnford's decision.

Durnford's association with the bishop's philosophy now made him doubly unpopular with the colonists since Ridley's scurrilous campaign to discredit him for the actions of the volunteers on the Bushman's Pass. Forced to leave his abode in town and return to Fort Napier to escape the abuse, he had to live in a marquee close to the barracks. His dog Prince was poisoned, possibly by one of the colonists. But he remained firmly committed to his new undertaking.

He had, without realising it, reached a watershed in his life. In this new undertaking he was to reveal a strong sense of purpose, a tenacious concern for the well-being of the disadvantaged and down-trodden, and most important of all, he was able to achieve *real* results which gave him immense self-satisfaction. Yet, instead of seeing that his future lay in social work, he was bound to a military career by family tradition and expectation and by his own burning desire to succeed in this field. Social commitment had to be an activity subordinated to the call of military 'duty'.

He found work on the roads for the Phutile prisoners. He could watch over their welfare and reduce the backlog of maintenance work in the department. His brother Edward declared that Durnford 'had long been convinced that the government had committed a great mistake in "eating up" this tribe and [he] was determined to do what he could to get the error rectified.' His request to the Secretary for Native Affairs that the young Phutile men in the jail be employed on the roads was granted and they were immediately put to use on the Town Hill roadway (a steep winding road that gave Pietermaritzburg its only access to the north) which had been labelled by travellers as badly needing attention.

One particularly distressing problem for the department was the practice of wagon drivers of overloading their wagons, and consequently, when going down a hill it became necessary to lock the wheel with chains, the wheels acted like ploughs and created deep furrows. When the rain came the furrow became a watercourse and the road was destroyed.

It was about this time that Durnford got, what appeared to be, the strange notion that the passes over the Drakensberg between Olivier's Hoek and Giant's Castle should be destroyed by demolition. He proposed to use the Phutile prisoners for the work. He apparently gave two reasons why the passes should be blocked: it would give the inhabitants of the up-country districts some confidence, and secondly, horsemen and cattle would be prevented from escaping from the colony. However, it seems likely that one of the real reasons was that Durnford, tired of the hostility against both him and the Phutile, wanted to get away from Pietermaritzburg for a while. Not only would the absence of the Phutile perhaps calm those who had been calling for harsher treatment, but Durnford may also have seen in this move the opportunity for the Phutile to demonstrate to the colonists that they were not the ogres they were made out to be. He appeared to be determined to implement this plan; most likely he was well aware of the futility of blocking the passes, but this would be effort well expended if it could result in restoring the good name of the Phutile.

It will be remembered that the Legislative Council had rejected an earlier scheme of Durnford to drill a pioneer corps, so in expectation of difficulty from the council, he now went over their heads, much to the wrath of Ridley, who was also a councillor. While Sir Benjamin Pine was absent in the Cape, Durnford approached Colonel Milles, who was acting governor, and without any difficulty, obtained his permission to use the Phutile to block the passes.

From the government's point of view it seemed a sensible suggestion, for it would remove Durnford from Pietermaritzburg where he had become their conscience in the matter of the treatment of the Phutile. Theophilus Shepstone, in a letter to A. B. Allison on 25 May 1874, seemed to confirm this view:

> Too much zeal and too much severity also [was exhibited in government action against the Phutile] and I was glad to seize upon any opportunity that seemed to promise a means of escape, so when the cry for the destruction of the passes [over the Drakensberg] went forth and Colonel Durnford suggested that his 'Town Hill Gang' [Phutile men], who are highly efficient and in splendid order, should do the work, I readily consented.

It appears from the content of this letter that Shepstone was alarmed at and embarrassed by the punitive measures taken against the Phutile. Since the trial of Langalibalele in January 1874 he (according to historian Bill Guest) 'had had serious misgivings as to the manner in which the proceedings were conducted . . .' but he did not have the courage to speak out publicly, confining his concern to private correspondence. The suspicion that he was supporting a lost cause became more obvious during the months ahead (despite the approval of the vast majority of the colonists) for it was clear that the British government was unhappy with Natal's handling of the Langalibalele affair. Influenced by increasing public support in England for Bishop Colenso's stand against the Natal authorities, Lord Carnarvon, Kimberley's successor as Secretary of State for the Colonies, was not satisfied that the so-called rebellion of the tribes had been handled circumspectly. How uncomfortable Shepstone must have felt when called upon by Pine in July 1874 to defend the colony's acts against Langalibalele.

Before Durnford left for the Drakensberg he induced Shepstone to promise his ninety pioneers that if they behaved well and performed creditably they would be granted their freedom.

On 20 May 1874 Durnford left Pietermaritzburg for the passes. He had with him a company of the 75th Foot under Captain J.

Boyes and Lieutenant E. Trower, as well as his ninety pioneers. Even in his absence the *Natal Witness* still persecuted him: 'It was not sufficient for this recalcitrant Colonel that . . . members of the rebel tribe should have been chosen for this purpose [i.e. destroying the passes] which gives them abundant opportunity to escape . . . but they may be the more formidable when they do escape [for] the Colonel has been taking the trouble to drill them.'

At David Gray's farm, Cathkin, Durnford picked up Gray's son William to act as his guide. The wagons were left behind at the farm and everything was transferred to pack oxen. They then crossed the Little Berg into the Mhlwazini valley and camped at the foot of the mountain known as Ntunja, which is perhaps the Gatberg of today.

The first pass to be blocked was that known as Gray's Pass which gave access to the rear of Champagne Castle and lay close to the source of the Mhlawazini River. The rock had to be quarried from the faces of the cliffs on either side of the pass; they had no dynamite. Then followed the blocking of the Mlambonjwa and the Old Bushman's Passes between the Ndumeni Dome and Cleft Peak. The destruction of these three passes was completed by the first week in June. Everybody returned to base at Cathkin farm and on 18 June 1874, after replenishing the larder, moved toward the Mnweni where they commenced the blocking of the Amaponjwana Pass nearby. The weather was appalling. Heavy snow-falls slowed down the work and it was not unusual for Durnford to sport icicles from the ends of his long drooping moustache. Once he had blocked the Amaponjwana he returned to Cathkin to prepare for the long trek to the Bushman's River Pass. Two days later he was on his way. The bitter cold and snowy conditions followed him.

Accompanied by a patrol of Natal Mounted Police under Inspector George Mansel, the party passed through the lands of the Phutile. It was a depressing sight: 'On every gentle slope and every rounded knoll were to be seen the charred and blackened remains of ruined kraals . . .' Pine's orders had been faithfully discharged.

The party arrived at the foot of the Bushman's River Pass on 1 July 1874 and set up a tented camp. A wall of turf was built around the tents to keep out the cold biting wind. To keep themselves warm at night he and Mansel heated stones in the fires and took them to bed.

No work could be done in these terrible conditions and the Police returned to Estcourt. On 3 July the snow started falling heavily. When Durnford woke on the 4th the snow was two feet deep. He decided that all should retire seven miles to the valley below where the horses and cattle had been left.

On the 6th a comfortable camp was laid out in the valley, with the Bushman's River barely 55 yards away. On a sizeable rock, the cook of the 75th engraved a large '75' which can be seen to this day. Against this rock a substantial shelter, 'a cowshed', declared Durnford, was built of threaded branches and grass to act as a company mess, which Durnford shared with the men. The kitchen was outside and, according to Durnford, the cook of the 75th was a most ingenious fellow who produced the most nourishing 'roasts, stews and soups'. This was to be their home for the next twenty-two days.

It appears from his correspondence that the odd visitor to the camp reported that there was a changing attitude to him among the farmers in the Weenen district. There was without doubt a greater sense of security among them than there had been before his arrival in the district. Durnford felt that this was a victory indeed over his arch-enemy, the colonial press:

> The papers are now silent. They see their fears are moonshine, yet have not the manliness to say so and give credit where it is due.

It seems that Durnford's aim at restoring the good name of the Phutile was well on the way to succeeding. With this measure of success one can also identify a softening in the attitude of the government toward him. On 13 July 1874 Durnford was made a justice of the peace.

One day in early July his pioneers came into camp marching and singing, and drew up before his tent, in front of which he was enjoying a cup of coffee before a blazing fire. One of them stepped forward and presented a woman and child before him. The woman was Mkozana, the wife of the late Chief Phutile, and the child was Phutile junior, heir to the chieftainship. Durnford was asked to protect the two. In effect he was being made the guardian of the tribe's future. There was little he could do at this particular time but feed them well and send them on their way to her brother, who was with Zikhali's people to the south, with the hope that better days might come and that the Phutile one day be returned to their land.

It is possible that this visit had considerable impact upon Durnford for if he had any influence on the course of history in Natal then it was in the heroic manner in which he championed the cause of this tribe, the Phutile. As early as 2 July 1874 he had written to his mother, that once the work of blocking the passes was over he would return to Pietermaritzburg to secure their 'freedom'.

By the end of July 1874 the last of the passes had been blocked. When the party returned to Pietermaritzburg on 30 July 1874 Durnford busied himself with his self-appointed task. On 11 August 1874 Pine officially announced in front of his private secretary, the Colonial Secretary, the acting Secretary for Native Affairs and Durnford, that the whole tribe would be freed, but he made no offer to sustain them till the next harvest, although he permitted them to return to their old homes.

On 25 July 1874 Pine had sent Theophilus Shepstone, his Secretary for Native Affairs, to England to inform Lord Carnarvon of the affair of the 'rebellious' tribes. Carnarvon had a number of meetings with Shepstone during September 1874 and was most impressed with his breadth of knowledge of South African affairs. At about this time Carnarvon contemplated the possibility of a closer union of South African states and it was with considerable interest that he listened to what Shepstone had to say about Natal and Zululand.

Undoubtedly one of the greatest obstacles to a closer union was the absence of a workable policy towards, and on behalf of, blacks. Shepstone, well aware of the odium surrounding the Natal government's treatment of the Hlubi and Phutile people, abandoned his role as Pine's apologist and embarked on a role of political opportunism which had as its aim the ingratiation of himself with the Colonial Office, at the same time sacrificing Pine for the failure of the colony's policy towards its blacks. The Langalibalele affair, Shepstone claimed, had now got out of hand as a result of Pine's interference and because of irresponsible settler elements. The solution to this sorry state of affairs, Shepstone proffered, was a system of African administration which could cope with not only the Africans in Natal's locations, but with migrant workers and what was vaguely termed 'surplus' blacks. The latter two groups would, no doubt, be located in the disputed territory along the Blood River. As Etherington points out: 'By this simple expedient, uncongenial African groups in Natal would find a happier home, a vital labour supply route would be permanently secured, the Boer republics would be denied access to the sea and a road would be kept open to the north in an expanding dominion where Africans would be governed in accordance with Shepstonian precepts.'

Carnarvon ignored Shepstone's request for Natal to take control of the disputed territory and although Shepstone was to have little influence on the political matrix of confederation, he reinforced Carnarvon's intentions. In August 1874 the historian J. A. Froude was sent to South Africa to make a preliminary study on the prospects of confederation. His reports were to convince Carnarvon that confederation would solve the major problems of security and British paramountcy.

On 17 August 1874 Bishop Colenso had left Pietermaritzburg on his way to England, for the purpose of pressing the British government to reverse the colonial sentence imposed upon Langalibalele. His family and Durnford kept him up to date with events in South Africa. Shortly after he arrived in England he released a pamphlet detailing the colonial government's immoral acts. *The Times* published the contents in November 1874 and the matter was soon raised in Parliament. It hastened Shepstone's abandonment of Pine and strengthened his recommendation that changes had to be made to Natal's African policy.

Carnarvon's despatch to Pine of 26 October 1874 was the outcome of a number of meetings with the bishop. It was clear that Carnarvon was displeased with the lack of integrity shown by Pine in his treatment of the Phutile. The slightly mocking tone used by the Secretary of State would have suggested to Pine that his days as lieutenant-governor were coming to a close. He offered Pine an excuse that the 'injustice' perpetrated upon the Phutile was done 'in a moment of excitement' and he asked

Pine to give him a full account of all measures taken against the tribespeople.

While he remained in England the bishop continued to keep Carnarvon up to date with developments and in the process detailed the good work undertaken by Durnford. The Secretary of State's despatches to Pine became increasingly severe in tone. When in mid November 1874 Colenso complained on Durnford's behalf that young Phutile boys were still being farmed out to white colonists, Carnarvon requested an immediate explanation from Pine, adding, 'I sincerely trust that there is no ground for this apprehension . . .'

Carnarvon's support was a wonderful tonic to Durnford but the foot-dragging continued in the colony. By 21 December 1874 only 411 tribesmen had returned to their location or its environs. On 3 December 1874 Carnarvon wrote three further despatches to the lieutenant-governor: one of them outlined Shepstone's ideas for an overhaul of his present colonial African policy that Pine had so loyally upheld; one gave Pine notice of his recall to England, and a third constituted the Imperial government's final judgement in the matter of the rebellious tribes. Carnarvon, satisfied that he was fully acquainted with all the facts (even before he had received Pine's answer to earlier queries), signified his displeasure with the lieutenant-governor's handling of matters. Referring to Langalibalele, he denied that the evidence indicated conspiracy or rebellion, and reduced the charge to an illegal departure of the colony.

With regard to the treatment meted out to the Phutile, Carnarvon declared that he could find no evidence associating them with Langalibalele that could possibly justify 'the heavy losses and confiscations . . .' He ordered that the tribe be given fair compensation for these losses. Durnford was delighted with Carnarvon's response:

> Lord Carnarvon has at last made up his mind. It was just this –
> Mr Shepstone was sent home by the Governor to make things
> pleasant, and to explain away certain acts which he would
> probably have done, had not the Bishop of Natal gone home
> too to tell the truth . . .'

Durnford was not to know that Shepstone had side-stepped the blame by throwing responsibility on to Pine.

Carnarvon was particularly appreciative of the conduct of Durnford in ameliorating the situation of the Phutile, and praised his 'forbearance and humanity towards the natives'.

Pine was to be replaced by Sir Garnet Wolseley, the 'hero of Kumasi', who was to leave for South Africa in February 1875.

Shepstone escaped censure, much to the amazement and wrath of the Colensos, and returned to Natal entrusted with supervising the new African policy. He was at the waterfront to welcome Wolseley when he stepped off the *Raleigh* on 30 March 1875, and became a trusted adviser to the new Administrator.

Durnford's tenacity in ensuring that the Phutile were not discriminated against in any way paid dividends. He continued to find employment for the men on the roads and he was seen to be winkling out children that had been apprenticed to the white colonists at the slave wages of 2 shillings per month for five years. It was inevitable that he develop a paternal attitude toward these people, and they in turn responded by referring to themselves as his 'children'.

He was constantly visited by them in Pietermaritzburg. His success in enticing the menfolk to volunteer for duty on the roads where it had been necessary to obtain forced labour prompted him to write home: 'I am the only man in this land who has ever pulled such a following together from feelings of goodwill only, and I'm proud of it!'

Very few scholars give Durnford the large measure of credit that is his due for the part he played in bringing about the speedy rehabilitation of the Phutile. It was he and not the bishop who played the major role. He kept the bishop or the Colenso family informed of the colonial government's indolence, and in confronting officials he jeopardised his appointment as acting colonial engineer. Yet he never at any time made public his criticisms of the Natal government. His brother Edward explained that it was a matter of principle that caused him not to expose the evils of 'the government under which he had taken office', but it did not lessen his intent to influence that government to take 'the right and just course'. It does seem that the rehabilitation of the Phutile became a substitute for his desire to avenge the deaths of the young Carbineers. It had been as much a matter of honour to settle this question as it had been to fight on 'a fair field'.

CHAPTER V

THE DEPARTURE OF THE ACTING COLONIAL ENGINEER, 1875–76

'It is high time that he ceased to be at the head of
a spending department.'
(Wolseley on Durnford, 26 August 1875)

WHEN, on 2 April 1875, Natal's new administrator rode into Pietermaritzburg with his entourage, the *Natal Witness* declared: 'Sir Garnet Wolseley has arrived and the Colony is all agog!' Doubtless Natal Colony had not expected to be honoured with so distinguished a head of government.

Ostensibly he came to Natal 'to ease the tension between the Bantu and the colonists' but his real mission was to draw Natal away from its desired path of responsible government and set it on the Carnarvon road toward a confederation of South African states. Wolseley had to tread carefully in this realm of colonial politics, for the Natal colonists already possessed representative government, and if they were to be drawn into a wider political framework their constitution would have to be changed with their approval.

Durnford, who had been so frequently offended and frustrated by the Legislative Council, was strongly in favour of the re-establishment of Crown Colony rule in Natal. He believed that Imperial intervention would bring justice to all Natal's citizens, both black and white. At the end of 1874 he had had little hope for Natal. He wrote to his parents:

The natives have lost all trust in the truth and honesty of the white race. This loss of trust is the beginning of the end. Surely there will come a war of races – surely?

Wolseley hoped to be able to offer two things in exchange: security against Cetshwayo by an increase in the number of Imperial troops in Natal, and secondly an Imperial loan of £1 million for railway development. Carnarvon agreed to send the troops but baulked at the loan. Without this inducement Wolseley was left to think of other means. He had to get the colonists round to his way of thinking. So to do this he embarked upon a policy of wining and dining, and a self-exposure that resembled a present-day American presidential election campaign. He acted out the part most effectively. On the day after he had been proclaimed administrator in Pietermaritzburg, he wrote to his wife:

> I shall soon give a ball and intend feeding these people to gorging point. From the little I have already seen of them I think the men are about as ill-conditioned a lot of ruffians as I have ever met with. Low pettifogging politicians seeking their own aims regardless of the true and great interests of the colony and of the Empire to which they belong.

He was most annoyed to find Sir Benjamin Pine still in Natal. He believed Pine's presence would remind the colonists of the recent antagonism between them and the Imperial government, and make his task more difficult. According to historian W. A. Thompson he gave Pine 'a severe tongue lashing' and requested he leave the colony as soon as possible.

Wolseley made public his proposed constitutional amendments at a banquet given in his honour by the Durban Corporation on 16 April 1875. His Constitutional Amendment Bill, introduced on 5 May, had a rough passage before it finally became law.

To sweeten the pill, Wolseley now took steps to fulfil his promises of railway development and for a system of colonial defence. The Natal Government Railway Bill empowering the Governor to authorise the building of railways in the colony, arrived from England in the last month of Wolseley's period as administrator. In the Bill provision was made to extend the Durban railway inland. On 1 January 1876 Sir Henry Bulwer, who, as lieutenant-governor, was to succeed Wolseley, 'turned the first sod' of the inland line at Durban, and four years later the first train rolled into Pietermaritzburg station.

The question of colonial defence was tackled in a number of ways. The Natal Mounted Police, a permanent force of 50 white and 150 black troopers, formed in 1874 under Major John Dartnell (late of the 27th Foot) now had its establishment increased to 115 whites. The Defence Committee of the government, nervous of the large number of armed and disciplined blacks in the force, reduced its black troopers to 50. Wolseley was irritated. In a despatch to Carnarvon on 14 June 1875 he stressed the dangers to Natal of the military kingdom of Cetshwayo and recommended the garrisoning of a battalion (800 men) of Imperial infantry, a battery of mountain guns and a company of engineers. He further urged the enlargement of the establishment of the Natal Mounted Police to 250 white troopers. In 1876 Bulwer was to sanction an increase to 150, but by mid-1878 it was only 110 strong. It was claimed by a long-serving member of the force that the police had a settling effect on the black population and brought some measure of security to the whites. However, in reality numbers were too small to cover adequately the area that had to be patrolled and the volunteer system was still considered a necessary and vital part of colonial defence.

While Wolseley organised the reshaping of Natal's political future he found himself also committed to dealing with the effects of Pine's mishandling of the Langalibalele affair.

Wolseley had arrived shortly after Langalibalele had been released from Robben Island and sent to the Cape. He soon became irritated by the Colensos ('the Bishopstowe party') in their campaign for the full restitution of Hlubi and Phutile rights. This zeal, as far as Wolseley saw it, was like a disease – 'kaffir-on-the-brain', he called it. He had been briefed of the activities of the Colensos before he had set foot in South Africa, and, according to Thompson, had built up a strong dislike of the bishop. During his stay in Natal his dislike of the bishop did not lessen. However, he was not going to let himself get sidetracked by the Colensos.

He knew of Durnford's association with the Colensos before he met him, and on 3 April 1875, when he did have an occasion to speak to him in private, he warned him that his identification with the Colenso line of thinking made him so unpopular with the colonists that 'his usefulness as a public servant has been very seriously impaired'. Durnford was taken aback at this reprimand.

But Durnford was a minor figure and, as far as Wolseley could see, one of those who were of no value to him for as long as he toed the Colenso line. Despite Wolseley's pressure, the acting colonial engineer would not be shifted from his self-appointed task. This stubbornness led Wolseley to note in his diary: '[Durnford] is a man too much given to expressing in alarmingly strong terms his opinions upon men and their measures; he denounces everyone who does not agree with him, and thinks that because he is honest of purpose and devotes his time and purse freely to carrying out the line of policy towards the native tribes engaged in the late disturbances, that therefore his actions should command respect . . .'

Wolseley's relationship with Durnford remained an unhappy one from their very first meeting. Edward Durnford felt that the cause lay in Wolseley's prejudice against the Royal Engineers. But it seems that Wolseley did not know how to handle either Durnford or the Colensos. To court their friendship would alienate the colonists and this he could not afford to do. Mrs F. S. Colenso, the bishop's wife, believed Wolseley to be a negrophobe, and Wolseley on his part, believed that the Colensos were quite irrational over racial issues. His relationship with Durnford was also affected by Durnford's support for the bishop's desire 'to reopen the Langalibalele question' – a desire to which Wolseley simply turned a deaf ear.

Durnford was greatly disappointed in not having Sir Garnet as an ally. In a letter to his mother he stated bitterly: 'From the first [Sir Garnet] went in for conciliation [with the colonists], and therefore I suppose, did not desire to show countenance either to the Bishop or myself . . . So we two had "cold shoulder" . . .' It was a most perplexing situation for Durnford, who appears to have had the hope that Wolseley was the envoy of Imperial justice who had come to Natal to right all the wrongs committed by Pine and Shepstone. As late as 3 July 1875 Durnford was still wondering why Wolseley had come to Natal – 'He came out to carry some point, I imagine, not yet divulged . . .' The 'point' was, of course, confederation.

Wolseley was no humanitarian. He believed in the superiority of the white race over the black. In May 1875 he wrote to Carnarvon that 'one or the other must be the predominant power in the state, and if the very small minority of white men is to be that power, the great native majority must be taught, not only to confide in its justice but to realise and to acknowledge its superiority.' He later wrote in his Natal journal: 'I am convinced that for the management of a barbarous people the only punishments ever likely to be effective for keeping them in order are flogging and death.'

What support could Durnford and the bishop expect from a man who expressed these sentiments? Despite his disdain for the blacks they were to find Wolseley not altogether unsympathetic to the plight of the Phutile and Hlubi. By the end of April 1875 Wolseley had ordered the Legislative Council to pay the Phutile £12,000 compensation for the stock that had been confiscated by the government.

Durnford refused to heed warnings to cease 'meddling' in African affairs, so on 3 June 1875, Wolseley informed him that because he had disregarded his warnings, application had been made to England for 'an efficient Colonial Engineer'. Durnford later claimed that he there and then resigned from the post but that Wolseley would not accept it. Durnford was told that he should have resigned before trying to remedy the plight of the Phutile. He replied that what he had done was irreproachable 'as the Queen has endorsed that action'. He stressed: 'I led the government to the right path.' He later confided to his mother:

> I am very much disappointed in Sir Garnet Wolseley and I think he has treated me badly ... I am tied as regard future action in native matters and may soon expect to be relieved as Colonial Engineer.

In June 1875 Wolseley, accompanied by his staff and Theophilus Shepstone, toured the Phutile lands in response to Durnford's allegations that the people were starving. They began the tour at the Little Thukela where Phutile families had made some progress in reestablishing themselves. On the evidence in this area Wolseley triumphantly dismissed Durnford's report as 'grossly untrue', for the people, he claimed, 'looked fat and well-clothed and there were quantities of Indian corn and kaffir corn ready for use in the fields.' He did admit that there were very few cattle to be seen and that there was a severe shortage of hoes and ploughs.

As the tour moved along the foothills of the Drakensberg, a different picture began to emerge. Wolseley made no mention of the fact that from the Mooi River to the Little Bushman's the land was deserted and ruined kraals dotted the countryside. His hasty generalisation then was based on what he had seen near the Little Thukela. By the time he had passed by what one correspondent with the party called 'the remains of kraals' between the Little Bushman's and the Bushman's Rivers, he was at least prepared to admit that there was a need for blankets and that some of the women and children were 'badly off for clothes'.

It was clear to Wolseley that matters were far from satisfactory (though he would not admit this to Durnford) and on his return to Pietermaritzburg he provided relief for some of the immediate needs of the Phutile.

However, the Legislative Council continued to put obstacles in the way of payment of the compensation. Sir Henry Bulwer, who replaced Wolseley as Governor in September 1875, warned them of their 'morally untenable' position and had them set aside the money, some £7,000, in a separate fund. Carnarvon advised him to spend the money in a manner that would be of lasting benefit to the tribe.

On 10 October 1875 Durnford was officially relieved of his duties as colonial engineer. He was to leave the colony in May 1876. When he returned in February 1877 he found that nothing had been paid out of the fund and that once again it was necessary for him to prod an indolent government into fulfilling its responsibilities. Durnford's commitment to a line of action was unwavering, despite the risks involved – to his reputation; to his career prospects. Some might see this commitment as foolhardy; others as indicative of a principled and humane man. Although he could chalk up some success in his confrontation with officials over the treatment of the Phutile, Durnford's experiences as colonial engineer under Wolseley were less satisfying.

It was soon clear to Wolseley that the Engineer's Department was faced with a number of difficulties. He discussed with Durnford the shortcomings of the department and in May 1875 it seems he saw a possible solution in Durnford's earlier plan to 'militarise' the department's establishment. In proposing a similar scheme to the Colonial Office Wolseley gave no credit to Durnford. At this time Wolseley was at odds with Durnford over his involvement in African affairs.

It seems that Wolseley had no complaint against Durnford as an engineer, nor to begin with, against his capacity to head the department. In his scheme to 'militarise' the department he intended to retain Durnford as departmental head. However, he had not yet received the supplementary estimates for 1876 for the Engineer's Department. There is no doubt that fault for the financial chaos in his department lay with Durnford. For example, in 1875, the auditor, J. P. Symons, in his report for 1874, noted that the Engineer's Department had overspent its estimates on works and buildings by 400% and on roads by 70%. Furthermore, he had been waiting six weeks for the books to be balanced and was still waiting at the time he had made the report. Durnford had informed him that he did not know when the books would be ready, so rather than be delayed, Symons, who had already discovered 'irregularities', decided to bring these to the attention of the lieutenant-governor 'in order to secure a remedy and pre-vention for the future'. The most serious of these 'irregularities' was the unlimited overdraft facilities given to the Engineer's Department by the Natal Bank.

When a special advance of £3,300 had been advanced to Durn-ford to be used on the expedition for blocking the passes in the Drakensberg, no vouchers had been rendered to the Treasury to account for the expenditure. Durnford had merely submitted a statement of expenditure. When the Supplementary Estimates for 1876 were placed on Wolseley's desk in late 1875, his opinion of Durnford as departmental head altered:

[I] had a regular go in with Durnford about his extravagant estimate. He has no idea of spending only the money voted for the services over which he has charge. He is an active and hard-working man, but he is not a good man to be at the head of a spending department.

Two days later Wolseley was still working on the supplementary estimates. His greatest difficulty was to trim Durnford's 'reckless expenditure upon public works'. In fairness to Durnford it is likely that under his drive and energy and a real effort by all, he believed that great progress could be achieved by the department, and the results would justify the expense. Wolseley might have agreed, but expenditure *had* to be limited. Exasperated, he wrote in his diary:

> It is high time that he ceased to be at the head of a spending department. . . . Yet he is a fine fellow with many soldierlike qualities.

Wolseley's grudging respect for Durnford was confined to his private journals. He never explained why he admired Durnford; it might have been because Durnford was industrious or because he had displayed qualities of courage and fortitude on the Bushman's Pass in 1873. One might also add to the list the fact that Durnford had stood firm to his principles despite Wolseley's reprimands.

Although Wolseley had believed Durnford incapable of financial restraints as head of the Engineer's, he nevertheless admitted that there had been real progress in public works. He declared that the roads of the colony were better than they had ever been. Durnford's record in supervising the completion of public works within a reasonable time limit can best be gauged from these statistics: in 1875 there were fifty-two items of expenditure under public works, civil roads, canals and bridges. When one considers that over half the expenditure of the department was used on maintenance and repairs of roads and bridges, Durnford's achievements as colonial engineer were excellent considering his slender resources in manpower.

Wolseley left Durban on the *Florence* on 3 September 1875. Sir Henry Bulwer had arrived in Pietermaritzburg on 26 August 1875. The *Natal Witness*, in stark contrast to the speakers at the banquets held to bid Wolseley *bon voyage*, concluded upon his departure:

> Sir Garnet found Natal loyal; he leaves it servile. He found it hopeful; he leaves it downcast. He found it full of political life, he leaves it a political corpse.

Wolseley was elated with the success of his mission, ascribing it to the fact that he had hastened matters, 'never giving people here breathing time to think over what they were about until the deed was done.' Carnarvon was equally delighted with Wolseley's mission and wrote him a most flattering letter thanking him for preparing the colony as 'a very fair base of operations' for the advancement of confederation.

In the short span of five months Wolseley had changed the character of Natal. To the white colonists the economic horizon looked more promising than it had for decades with the prospect of railway development. A Native Administration Bill (passed on 5 December 1875) promised a more effective system of control over the black population, and the enlargement of the establishment of the Natal Mounted Police, gave added security. The overhaul of the public service, its establishment and financial policies, was imminent. The moribund harbour works were about to be revived, for it was recorded by the *Natal Mercury* that the new Colonial Engineer, Captain A. H. Hime, who had arrived in Natal on 27 September 1875, was an expert in marine engineering.

There were, of course, many difficulties unresolved: the shortage of labour; lack of white immigrants; Natal–Zulu relations and, as the *Natal Witness* had complained, the constitutional future of Natal. Although Wolseley had left Natal ready for absorption into a confederation, and Froude had tried to sweeten the pill, the refusal of the Cape to join such a union of South African states had left Natal's political future undecided (much to the wrath of those who had pressed for responsible government) and threatened to wreck Carnarvon's schemes for closer union.

Wolseley never publicised his displeasure with Carnarvon's insensitive appointment of Captain Hime as Durnford's replacement. Durnford, unfairly as it turns out, blamed Wolseley for having him relieved by a junior of his own corps. He wrote:

> Sir Garnet Wolseley will do nothing for me, of that I am sure ... One count against me, I find, is that I went to Durban to meet my friend the Bishop when he returned from England in January 1875, thereby plainly showing my sympathy. Some people threatened to tar and feather him, to prevent his landing! Well, as a government officer, I am told, *I should not have*

gone near him. Is that not a nice creed for a gentleman to hold? Desert your friends when trouble comes.

While waiting for a fresh posting Durnford was occasionally, as a justice of the peace, called upon to do a little magistrate's work. His arm and shoulder had been giving him a great deal of pain. In May 1876 he prepared to leave Natal on transfer to Mauritius. His relief as commander of the Engineers in Natal, Lieutenant-Colonel E. T. Brooke, had arrived and moved into Durnford's house at Fort Napier, buying his furniture and his horses (with the exception of Chieftain who was left with the Colensos) and re-engaging his servants.

Bulwer's letter of thanks to Durnford on behalf of the government 'for the zeal and ability' with which he had executed his duties as colonial engineer for the last two years, was sent by Broome on 5 February 1876. It enclosed too Carnarvon's acknowledgement of the value of his services to the colonial government.

Durnford's final official function was to attend a review of the Imperial garrison by Sir Arthur Cunynghame on 24 May 1876. Although his arm was giving considerable pain he nevertheless took part in the parade. One spectator later wrote to the *Natal Witness* that he was amazed at the colonel's 'complete horsemanship' for with his one arm he 'dexterously controlled an apparently restive animal'. Sir Arthur publicly paid him tribute on this occasion for his contributions to the colony. The kindest words came from a totally unexpected source. The *Natal Witness*, no longer in the hands of a vindictive editor, declared that Durnford had 'earned the gratitude of colonists in many ways', in particular for correcting 'many abuses' within the Engineer's Department and concluded by describing him as a perfect gentleman . . .

The Colonel was a brave, sensitive and high-principled man, and of blameless life. He was a thorough-going soldier and had a quick eye to what was wanted, but possessed in a remarkable degree the power of encouraging and seeing to all the wants of his subordinates. He was moreover, one with whom one could not converse with ten minutes without learning something, and that is a very special merit in a place like this.

Durnford left the colony on 27 May 1876 together with Cunyng-hame on the *Kafir*. He intended to seek medical advice for his arm in England first (and, as it turned out, would never get to Mauritius). He was also looking forward to the opportunity to meet his relatives, and in particular his daughter Frances, whom he had last seen four years ago.

Durnford's exit from Natal was, from his point of view, no doubt a sad one. Although he had very few friends, those whom he had gathered into his small circle deeply regretted his departure. While he would have been sorry to leave them, there was at least no longer a cause for him to espouse in Natal, and his departure was in consequence that much easier. The Langaliba-lele affair was now over and the Phutile about to be satisfactorily recompensed. As an officer of the Engineers he was at the beck and call of the military authorities. He would now have to take up the threads of his career once again and hopefully weave them into a pattern that would suit his temperament and ambition. Having experienced the excitement of conflict, the challenge of a cause and in some measure, the redemption of honour, it is unlikely that he would be satisfied with garrison duties in an isolated or peaceful area of the Empire.

1. Lieutenant-Colonel Anthony William Durnford, RE c.1878/79.
(*Institution of Royal Engineers Library, Chatham*)

2. *Left* Anthony's father, Lieutenant-General Edward William Durnford, Royal Engineers. (*Institution of Royal Engineers Library, Chatham*)

3. *Below* Captain Anthony William Durnford, RE and his youngest brother, Lieutenant Arthur Durnford, RE c.1864? (*Institution of Royal Engineers Library, Chatham*)

Two views of Brompton Barracks, Chatham, in the 1860s, showing: 4. general parade; 5. gun teams. (*Institution of Royal Engineers Library, Chatham*)

6. *Above* Group of officers (largely of the Corps of Royal Engineers at Gibraltar, 1863. Captain A.W. Durnford is seated next to the colonel. Lieutenant Arthur Durnford, Anthony's youngest brother sits on the colonel's left; young Lieutenant Moysey, whose daughter reminded Anthony of his own Frances, sits on the ground at Durnford's feet. (*Institution of Royal Engineers Library, Chatham*)

7. *Right* Anthony William Durnford, as a major in the Royal Engineers, from a carte de visite, c.1872/73? (*Institution of Royal Engineers Library, Chatham*)

8. *Left* Frances Ellen Colenso (*Bodleian Library, Oxford*)
9. *Right* John William Colenso, Bishop of Natal. (*Killie Campbell Africana Library, Durban*)

10. 'Bishopstowe', residence of the Colensos in Pietermaritzburg. (*The Graphic, 3rd May 1879*)

11. *Right* Sir Theophilus Shepstone (1817-93). (*State Archives, Cape Town*)

12. *Below* Langalibalele ka Mthimkhulu, chief of the Hlubi, (1818-1889) and his sons, 1873. (*Natal Government Archives, Pietermaritzburg*)

13. Cetshwayo's coronation 1873. Cetshwayo can be seen sitting on the chair in the centre of the assembly.
(Killie Campbell Africana Library, Durban)

14. View from the Bushman's River pass looking towards Natal, showing the broken nature of the land and the route taken by the Hlubi in their escape into BaSotholand.

15. *Above* Langalibalele's Rebellion 1873: Hlubi territory. The Giant's Castle pass can be seen on the skyline to the left.
16. *Below* The forbidding heights of the Drakensberg: Giant's Castle.

Langalibalele's Rebellion 1873:
17. *Above* On the Bushman's River pass showing the spruit (point D on the map) and on the right centre (point E) where the tribespeople were gathered.
18. *Below* At the mouth of the Bushman's River pass looking toward the rising rocky ground (point B on the map) and Mt Erskine.

Langalibalele's Rebellion 1873:
19. *Above* The Bushman's River – looking towards Giant's Castle.
20. *Below* On the Bushman's River pass showing the Lakabalele river which marked the line of retreat around the hill (marked F on the map) and back to the Hlatimba pass.

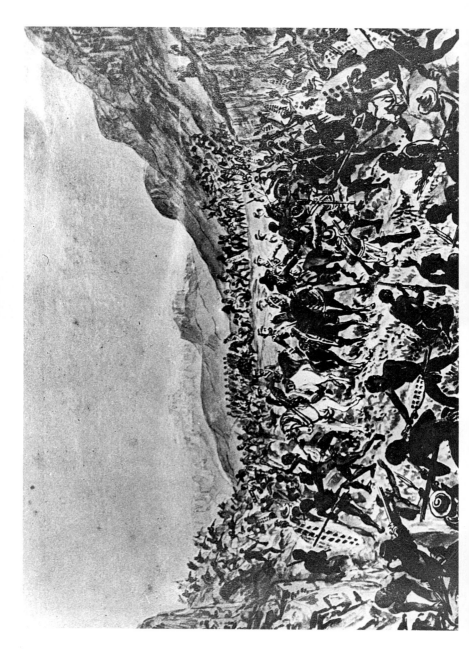

21. Photograph of a water-colour by Thomas Baines of an incident during the Lanagalibalele Rebellion of 1873. Durnford is shown expostulating with the amaHlubi at the summit of Bushman's River pass. The interpreter Kambule is at his side, and Captain Barter in the left foreground. Immediately behind Durnford are three of the young men who died in the subsequent skirmish. (*Killie Campbell Africana Library, Durban*)

The blocking of the passes 1874:
22. *Above* At the mouth of the Bushman's River pass.
23. *Below* Durnford's camp near the Bushman's River. The large rock (with the lean-to) is a short walk from the National Parks' camp at Giant's Castle. The large '74' chiselled into the rock is still visible. (*Killie Campbell Africana Library, Durban*)

The blocking of the passes
1874:
24. *Above* A parade of troops
in Colonel Durnford's camp.
25. *Left* At the Bushman's
River pass.
(*Killie Campbell Africana
Library, Durban*)

26. *Left* Sir Henry Bartle Frere, High Commissioner (1877-79).
27. *Right* Major-General Sir Garnet Wolseley, GCMG, KCB, Administrator of Natal, February-October 1875, in order to facilitate the federation schemes of Lord Carnarvon, the Colonial Secretary. Later replaced Lord Chelmsford as military commander in Zululand, July 1879.

28. Sir Garnet Wolseley and staff, Peitermaritzburg, 1875. Most of his staff had served with him in Ashanti and were known as the 'Wolseley Ring'.

29. Cetshwayo ka Mpande (1826-84), king of the Zulus.

30. The Ultimatum Tree, Thukela river, where, on 11th December 1878, the Zulus were given one month to disband their army, or face war. (*The Graphic, 8th February 1879*)

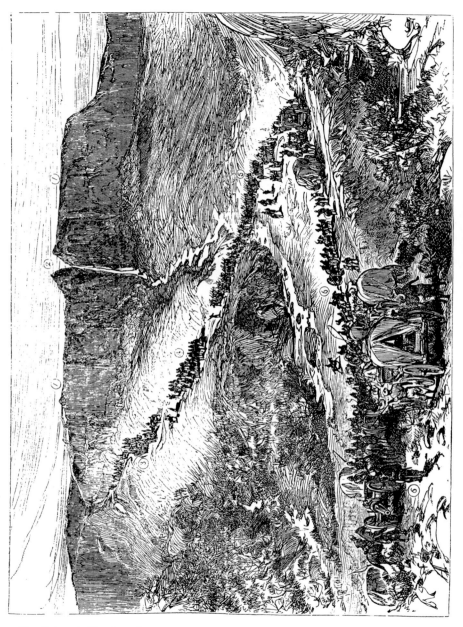

31. Colonel Glyn's column crossing the Buffalo River using Durnford's 'flying bridge' system similar to that used in India and Afghanistan. (*The Illustrated London News, 8th March 1879*)

32. *Right* Fort Pearson, overlooking the Thukela river, 1879. At the invasion point of the Lower Drift. (*Courtesy of the Director, National Army Museum, London*)

33. The 1st NNC on parade, January 1879. Colonel Durnford is on the white horse. (*Courtesy of the Director, National Army Museum, London*)

34. Rorke's Drift camp from the mission House. The drift where the invasion was carried out can be seen on the right. (*Courtesy of the Director, National Army Museum, London*)

35. *Left* George Shepstone (1849-79), Durnford's principal staff officer, KIA at Isandhlwana. (*Killie Campbell Africana Library, Durban*)

36. *Left* Lieutenant-Colonel H.B. Pulleine (1838-79), 24th Regiment of Foot. Killed when in command at the camp at Isandhlwana. (*Courtesy of the Director, National Army Museum, London*)

37. *Right* The view from iTusi of Isandhlwana. In the foreground are the dongas from the notch and the broken ground near where the rocket battery may have been trapped. To the left is the conical hill (Amatutshane) round which the Zulu left horn swept. The wooded area to the right is the location of St Vincent's Mission, built as a memorial to the battle.

38. The view of the Ngwebeni valley where the Zulu army was waiting on 22nd January 1879.

39. The donga of the Nyogane river defended by Durnford and his mounted troops on the British right at Isandhlwana. It is just over a mile from the nek.

40. Isandhlwana: The recovery of the wagons, May 1879. This shows the nek close to where Durnford's last stand was made. (*Killie Campbell Africana Library, Durban*)

42. *Right* Below iTusi. Is this where the rocket battery was overwhelmed? Lower down, the dongas peter out and the battery could have escaped with relative ease. The fact that it was on 'rocky ground' (Nourse's evidence) and attacked by Zulus from dongas on 'its left' (Johnson's evidence) suggests that the notch was out of sight. That can only be around the base of iTusi.

41. Was this the furthest point reached by Durnford on the plain? This is near the Nxibongo river looking back towards Isandhlwana, three miles away, and a mile from where the Rocket Battery was attacked.

43. Lieutenant Alfred Henderson, Natal Native Horse, with Durnford in the defence of the Nyogane at Isandhlwana. (*P. Hathorn*)

44. Sir Theophilus Shepstone and staff, Pretoria 1877. Back row standing: Sub Inspector F.L. Phillips (N.M.P.), M. Osborne, Colonel Brook and Captain James. Sitting: W.B. Morcom, J. Henderson, Sir T. Shepstone, Dr. Lyle, Frank Fynney. Reclining in foreground: Rider Haggard. (*From the George T. Smith Collection, courtesy Mr J. Young*)

45. General Sir Arthur Cunynghame, KCB, (1812-84). Commander-in-Chief, Imperial Forces in South Africa 1874-78. (*The Illustrated London News, 23rd March 1878*)

46. Lieutenant-General F.A. Thesiger (Lord Chelmsford) (1827-1905). Commander-in-Chief, Imperial Forces in South Africa 1878-79. (*The Illustrated London News, 2nd August 1879*)

47. *Left* Captain R. Younghusband (1844-79) commanded C Company 1/24th Regiment at Isandhlwana. (*The Illustrated London News, 29th March 1879*)

48. *Right* Captain G.V. Wardell (1840-79) commanded H Company, 1/24th Regiment, at Isandhlwana. (*The Illustrated London News, 29th March 1879*)

49. *Left* Captain R. Bradstreet (1838-79) Assistant Magistrate, Newcastle. Commanded Newcastle Mounted Rifle Volunteer corps; killed at Isandhlwana. (*The Graphic, 17th May 1879*)

50. *Right* Lieutenant and Adjutant T. Melvill, VC (1842-79) 24th Regiment. (*The Illustrated London News, 29th March 1879*)

51. *Left* Brevet Major F.B. Russell, RA commanded the Rocket Battery at Isandhlwana. (*The Illustrated London News, 5th April 1879*)
52. *Right* John R. Dunn (1833-95) white adviser to the Zulu kings, 1857-79. (*The Graphic, 26th April 1879*)

53. *Left* Colonel C.K. Pearson, 3rd Regiment of Foot, commanded the Natal Field Force in 1877 and No.1 or Coastal Column on 11th January 1879.
54. *Right* Captain James Lonsdale, Natal Native Contingent. KIA at Isandhlwana. (*The Graphic, 18th August 1879*)

55. *Left* Lieutenant F.W.D. Scott, Natal Carbineers. KIA at Isandhlwana. (*The Illustrated London News, 29th March 1879*)

56. *Right* Lieutenant-Colonel J.N. Crealock, 95th Regiment, Chelmsford's military secretary. (*The Illustrated London News, 27th December 1879*)

57. The east wall and tower of Fort Durnford, Estcourt, built 1874/75 according to Colonel A.W. Durnford's design. See the appendix for the details.

CHAPTER VI

'THE ROSEWATER REVOLUTION' AND THE NATAL FIELD FORCE, 1877

'I cannot feel any certainty about the Transvaal . . .'
(Durnford)

WHEN Durnford arrived in London in July 1876 he went to see a specialist, Prescott Hewitt, who suggested that the pain in his elbow might be eased by taking the mineral waters of the spa at Wildbad, a small village in the Black Forest in Baden, Germany. Hewitt impressed upon him that once he felt better he should ask to return to South Africa, for the dry climate there would be far more beneficial for the wound.

He left for Germany in August 1876 accompanied by his daughter, and although his arm benefited from the sulphates, he found Wildbad a hot and depressing place – 'halt, lame and blind all about,' he wrote. As his arm began to feel better he became restless. Although he complained of being 'idle from morning till night' he did keep himself occupied by writing 'an account of the present state of native affairs in the Cape Colony and Natal with remedial suggestions', which he intended sending to Lord Carnarvon. It is doubtful whether it was ever completed.

His brother Edward complained that Anthony Durnford was ordered to Cork in Ireland before he had fully recovered, but it is more than likely that Durnford had convinced himself and the military that he was well enough for active service again.

Ireland was cold and damp. He was given the responsibility of maintaining the three forts in Queenstown harbour. The work was dull and tedious, and by December 1876 he was weary of it:

I have been alone in the distant places of the earth, but I have never before felt like this. My life is one long slavery.

Not surprisingly his health deteriorated rapidly, and although he was buoyed up by visits to his old friends of the 75th Foot, who were stationed at the Curragh camp, these were not enough to make him want to stay. When, one morning, he fainted from pain and exhaustion after coming in from his morning rounds of duty, the staff-surgeon advised that he leave the climate of Cork. He returned to England where he took the opportunity to visit Charles Gordon in London while he was on three weeks' leave from his service in China. He asked Gordon to write to Sir Bartle Frere, the new High Commissioner for South-East Africa, and to Sir John Simmons, the Inspector-General of Fortifications at the War Office, to have him sent to the Cape. Gordon was impressed with Durnford's ambition 'to do great things' in South Africa. It is likely that the discussion at some stage touched Anglo-Zulu relations, which were strained at this time, and there was, most likely, an assessment of the fighting qualities of the blacks, both colonial and Zulu. Gordon recalled that Durnford had said to him: 'I and Shepstone are the only two men who understand native levies'. It seems that Gordon did indeed manage to secure Durnford's transfer to South Africa as a replacement for Lieutenant-Colonel Brooke, the same who had taken Durnford's place in early 1876. Durnford would return to his old job as officer commanding the Royal Engineers in Natal. Lieutenant-Colonel Brooke was to return home to Ireland for service at Cork, most probably inspecting the forts of Queenstown harbour!

Before he left for South Africa he spent some time with his parents. He was so ill that his father and brothers, Edward and Arthur, who saw him board the *Danube* at Southampton on 8 February 1877, did not expect him to survive the voyage. But the sea-air and the rest cured him, and when he disembarked at Algoa Bay he was his old self again. He made his way to King Williams Town on the eastern frontier, intending to ride through the trans-Kei territories to Natal, when word came to him that war with the Zulu seemed likely.

The denial by Cetshwayo of the *isicoco* or headring to men of marriageable age led to considerable stress and sometimes this boiled over into violence. In August 1876 the Zulu king had given permission for the regiment of 37–40 year olds to marry young girls but many of the latter refused and were put to death. On

3 October 1876 J. W. Shepstone, the acting Secretary for Native Affairs, sent two messengers to Cetshwayo to inquire into the reports. Cetshwayo was furious at what he considered to be uncalled for interference in his domestic affairs. In an outburst of anger Cetshwayo tactlessly replied:

> Did I ever tell Mr Shepstone I would not kill? Did he tell the white people I made such an arrangement? Because if he did he has deceived them. I do kill ... It is the custom of our Nation, and I shall not depart from it.

This sort of response was to put considerable strain on the good relationship between Natal and the Zulu.

Like most of the officers in South Africa not attached to one of the garrison regiments, Durnford hoped to be able to earn a brevet rank through service in one of England's little wars. He hastened to East London and caught the first ship leaving for Durban. When he arrived at Pietermaritzburg on 23 March 1877, he was disappointed to find that all was quiet.

The Zululand–Natal border was indeed quiet, but in the disputed land along the Blood River there was a great deal of uneasiness among both Boer and Zulu, and the simmering unrest there had now become of vital concern to the formulators of Imperial policy, for a conference held in mid-1876 in order to achieve a closer union of South African states had failed, and Carnarvon now toyed with the idea of annexing the Transvaal as a means of bringing about federation.

On 1 July 1876 Theophilus Shepstone had left for England once again, to participate in the conference on confederation. The conference was a failure because both the Cape Colony and the Orange Free State were opposed to federation. The Transvaal had not even sent a representative for in 1875 President MacMahon of France had arbitrated between Britain and Portugal over ownership of Delagoa Bay. The Portuguese retained ownership and shortly afterwards concluded an agreement with the Transvaal for the use of the Bay which would give them their long sought-after outlet to the sea and hopefully, economic independence. The Transvaal therefore had no reason to cooperate with Carnarvon.

News of the Transvaal's attack on Sekhukhune, the Pedi chief, whose lands straddled a likely route of the Transvaal-Delagoa Bay railway line, had reached England during the course of the conference, and Carnarvon had been greatly concerned lest unrest spread south to the Sotho and the Zulu. Both Shepstone and Barkly, the High Commissioner, believed that it would. When on 14 September 1876 Barkly notified the Colonial Office that the Boers had been repulsed by Sekhukhune and that the citizens of Lydenburg had petitioned the help of the British government, Carnarvon decided to use Shepstone to annex the Transvaal. He hoped that by taking control of the Transvaal, federation would be kept alive. The Colonial Office believed that the Orange Free State would not wish to be isolated, and a tighter regulation of Zulu affairs would strengthen the arguments of those at the Cape who favoured confederation. On 5 October 1876 Carnarvon ordered Shepstone to make preparations to go to the Transvaal. It was to be a fatal decision.

On 27 January 1877 the recently knighted Sir Theophilus Shepstone left Pietermaritzburg for Pretoria with nine wagons, a staff of twelve and an escort of twenty mounted police. On his passage through the Transvaal Shepstone received a number of enthusiastic welcomes largely from English-speaking residents, but on arrival at Pretoria the welcome was quite different and unexpected. Resistance to their presence made itself clear from the large number of armed burghers that had gathered. President T. F. Burgers, however, restrained his people, for he believed that he had already done enough to strengthen the Transvaal, if indeed there was any truth in the rumours that Shepstone's visit was a prelude to British annexation. The war with Sekhukhune had come to an end in December 1876 when the old chief had asked for peace; there was the prospect of loans from the Belgian and Portuguese governments for the construction of a rail-link between Pretoria and Delagoa Bay and Burgers still believed that his blueprint for constitutional reform would be accepted by the parliament or Volksraad.

Shepstone found an equally hostile Volksraad. The country was heavily in debt and the Zulus seemed to be a far greater threat than the Pedi, but the government remained implacably opposed to surrendering their independence. This was not to dissuade

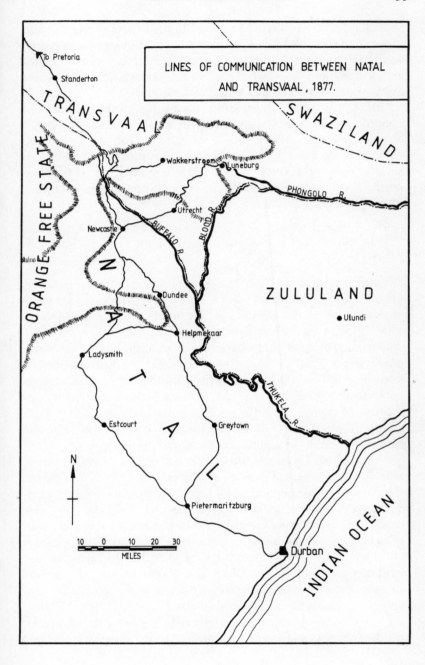

LINES OF COMMUNICATION BETWEEN NATAL
AND TRANSVAAL, 1877.

Shepstone who even had the gall to notify his superiors that the majority of the Boers favoured annexation! But fantasy and reality were two different worlds. He was not prepared to proclaim the annexation until he was assured that there would be sufficient military support close to the Transvaal border.

On 24 March 1877 the first five companies of the 1/13th Light Infantry arrived at Newcastle together with a mounted escort of twenty-five Natal Mounted Police under Major John Dartnell. Two companies of the 2/3rd Regt of Foot (The Buffs), the 80th Foot and the remainder of the 1/13th were also made ready to move north. This large-scale military activity confused the ever-vigilant *Natal Witness*:

> These troops are not being moved up to take the Transvaal . . . They are meant to occupy the border in the face of Kafir youth heated with war-fever.

Shepstone hoped that Zulu restlessness would mask the real purpose for the presence of troops. It certainly would do no harm of course, if, in the process, it discouraged any Zulu punitive action against the border farmers.

Durnford and Colonel Charles Pearson of the Buffs, the senior officer in the Natal garrison arrived in Newcastle on 10 April 1877. Both he and Pearson were surprised that Shepstone had not yet contacted them. Shepstone had sent instructions on 8 April for the troops to move to the border, but the orders had not yet arrived. On 9 April 1877 he had formally notified the Transvaal government that he would shortly annex the country.

Worried that communication with Pretoria had broken down, Durnford volunteered to ride post-haste to Shepstone to find out if the troops were needed. On 11 April, in the guise of a property speculator Durnford hastened along the Pretoria road. He reached the Transvaal capital on the morning of the 15th, four days later. Sir Theophilus confirmed his need for the troops, for although none of the Dutch appeared to be preparing to use violence, there were a number of influential men such as Paul Kruger, around whom opposition began to consolidate. It was sufficient for Shepstone to feel uneasy.

Pearson presumably received Shepstone's letter of 8 April, for on the way back Durnford met the advancing troops in Natal, ten miles from the border. He passed on Shepstone's request for the troops to proceed to Pretoria and continued on to Newcastle to organise the despatch of ammunition and supplies. At dawn on 19 April 1877 he had the whole camp up loading the wagons which were sent after the troops that afternoon. After a forced march through the night, the wagons caught up with the troops at Meek's Farm, 1½ miles into the Transvaal. Durnford accompanied the force as far as the next halt at Sandspruit – 40 miles from Standerton. The Boers in the area showed no animosity – indeed, were civil in their welcome. Durnford was nervous that there might be trouble but after a few drinks with some of the Boer men and entertainment for the women and children by the band of the 13th, he felt sufficiently at ease to leave Colonel Pearson and return with an escort of Natal Mounted Police to Pietermaritzburg which he reached on 26 April 1877.

Sir Theophilus Shepstone had, on 12 April 1877, felt sufficiently confident to proclaim the Transvaal a British colony. The President, Burgers, who may well have been a willing part of Shepstone's plans, issued a 'Protest' and urged those who opposed the annexation to allow a Boer deputation to speak for them when it left shortly for England. De Volksstem, a month later declared that the vast majority of the people obeyed 'under a sort of silent protest'. The Transvaal Argus was so surprised at the absence of Boer resistance that it dubbed the annexation 'the rosewater revolution'.

Durnford believed that annexation was necessary: compelled by Boer poverty and by their ill-treatment of the blacks which had resulted in a rebellion of the Pedi. He saw the role of Britain in simple terms: a just and strong nation taking control of the weak state in order to maintain the peace in South Africa. Furthermore, not only could the conflict between the Boers and the Pedi be resolved, but the boundary question in the disputed territory could be decided 'according to right and justice'.

In the absence of Pearson in the Transvaal, Durnford, as the most senior officer in Natal, assumed control of the remaining troops. 32 officers, 743 men (mainly of the 1/13th Light Infantry), two guns and 50 horses, were with Pearson in the Transvaal, and were due to arrive in Pretoria on 4 May 1877. This force was 380 miles or 25 days' march from reinforcements in Pietermaritzburg.

In Fort Napier there were 26 officers and 632 men (which included four companies of the 2/3rd Foot and one company of the 1/13th) and at Durban a further six officers and 289 men of the 80th Foot. Although trouble with the Transvaalers was not expected it would not be wise to have reinforcements at such a great distance. Assuming that it would take three days for an urgent message to reach Newcastle, troops stationed there could be in Pretoria in fourteen days. Durnford, aware of this factor, pressed Bulwer to allow a field force of 300 men and 2 field pieces to be sent to Newcastle.

Bulwer was reluctant at first, believing that such an act might precipitate conflict but Durnford finally convinced him of the necessity for such a step. Orders were sent to Lieutenant-Colonel C. F. Amiel at Durban to march his three companies of the 80th Foot with two field pieces to Newcastle. Durnford, on Cunynghame's instructions, mustered the advance force of forty men of the 24th Foot that had just arrived from King Williams Town on 28 April 1877 with a battery of artillery, and added some men of the 80th to bring the total to seventy-one, and proclaimed them his mounted infantry. Lieutenant F. Carrington of the 24th Foot was sent to the border districts near the Transvaal to purchase horses. There was to be a permanent camp at Newcastle for what was termed the Natal Field Force. Sir Arthur Cunynghame, Officer Commanding Her Majesty's Troops in Southern Africa, arrived from the Cape and took overall command.

Durnford himself raised and equipped 'a small corps of guides' from Hlubi's BaTlokwa Sotho. When Carrington returned with the horses he was given command of the new mounted detachment, which now bore his name and which was fitted out in Pietermaritzburg and then sent to Newcastle accompanied by some of Hlubi's men.

On 21 May 1877 150 men of the 80th were sent to reinforce the numbers already in the Transvaal. Cunynghame, with an escort of Natal Carbineers, hurried on ahead. Carrington's Horse replaced the Natal Mounted Police as Shepstone's bodyguard.

Durnford, possibly on Cunynghame's orders, commenced, on 18 June, a 'flying recce', as he termed it, of the borders of the disputed territory. He was ecstatic about the week-long ride. He wrote to his mother: 'I cannot tell you how I enjoyed it – rough as it was.'

He wrote a memorandum of his observations, in which he tried to be scrupulously fair to both Boer and Zulu.

He commenced his tour from the north, near the headwaters of the Phongolo. There he found a great deal of tension. Zulus living on the east bank of the river refused to pay hut tax to the Transvaal for fear of Cetshwayo's vengeance. When, in 1876, a forceful attempt had been made to collect the tax the Zulus called together an impi of 800. The officials prudently withdrew. Although there had not been any act of violence or of cattle-stealing, the villagers of the German settlement at Luneberg and the farming community around, lived in daily expectation of serious trouble. This led Durnford to note:

> The border situation is, to the farmer, at present intolerable. He owns land, either by right of birth or purchase, and yet cannot feed his cattle on his own! If he remains on his farm, he lives amongst Zulus who openly declare that the land is theirs . . .

Making his way toward the Intombe River he found that he was moving into territory controlled by the Zulus. Although whites occupied farms east of the Intombe, Durnford admitted, 'The Zulus are masters and the whites submit.' In this area and to the south, Mbilini, the Swazi emigré who had been given asylum in Zululand by Cetshwayo, terrorised Boer and Zulu alike. But, Durnford asserted, not all the blame should be placed on Mbilini: 'It seems very probable that many of these frontier Boers have worried the Zulus a good deal, encroaching on their lands and seizing their cattle.'

Durnford then travelled south along the Old Hunting Road which had been the western limit of Boer occupation. Between the White Mfolosi and Makatini Kop he found deserted Boer farms, some burnt, some simply abandoned. To the south and east of the Blood or Ncome River there were no white farmers to be seen, but on the western side of the river there were a great many, none of whom had yet been molested by the Zulus. The Boers claimed the land west and north of a line running from

Rorke's Drift in a north-easterly direction to Zuinguin's Nek and thence eastwards towards the Phongolo and the Lebombo mountains (see the map on page 139). The Zulus, Durnford stated, denied this claim, declaring that the land from east of the Lyn Spruit and Blood River appeared to be the boundary, but, he said, there needed to be some control. This should come from the British. He was sure that increasing encroachment, cattle-stealing, intimidation and the ever-present danger of Cetshwayo's impis falling upon the farmers, would draw the British into the role of arbiter anyway, so he offered these alternatives in his memorandum as a means of keeping the peace:

> Either at once draw in the border line in agreement with the Zulu king and *keep it*, or make use of the border question as one of battle, and annex the Zulu country altogether . . . From information obtained from fairly reliable sources, it would seem that the Zulu nation is divided against itself . . .

The idea that the Zulu kingdom was divided was common currency in 1877–78. In September 1877 F. B. Fynney was commissioned by Shepstone to report on the political situation in Zululand. Fynney was of the opinion that the Zulu army's loyalty would be in doubt in the event of a war with the British. Carnarvon agreed with this view. Although the support of one or two chiefs was uncertain – Hamu, for example – there was no proof that the kingdom was divided against itself. On the contrary, the long period of decentralisation from the latter years of Dingane's rule, was, since 1873, being reversed. Through the diplomatic skill of John Dunn, the white man who had become a Zulu chief and Cetshwayo's adviser, Cetshwayo consolidated his authority over potential rivals. The acquisition of firearms through Dunn enhanced Cetshwayo's military status. It was this strengthening of the monarchy in Zululand that led to Cetshwayo being able to channel his energies towards a settlement of the border dispute with the Boers.

Through 1873 to 1879 the process of strengthening Cetshwayo's control over his kingdom continued. It was not a simple process and many of the border chiefs, although they acknowledged Cetshwayo as their superior, pursued an independent line.

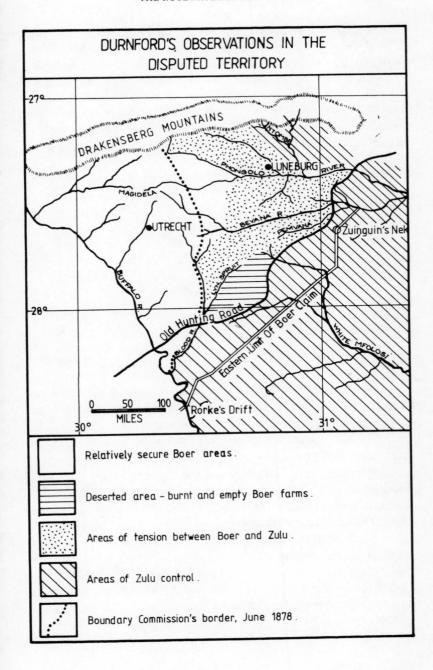

DURNFORD'S OBSERVATIONS IN THE
DISPUTED TERRITORY

DRAKENSBERG MOUNTAINS

MAGIDELA

PHONGOLO

NTOMBE

●LUNEBURG   RIVER

BEVANA R.

●UTRECHT

MVANA

Zuinguin's Nek

BUFFALO R.

VAL SPRUIT

Old Hunting Road

BLOOD R.

Eastern Limit Of Boer Claim

WHITE MFOLOSI

0   50   100
MILES

Rorke's Drift

Relatively secure Boer areas.

Deserted area – burnt and empty Boer farms.

Areas of tension between Boer and Zulu.

Areas of Zulu control.

Boundary Commission's border, June 1878.

Mbilini did much as he liked in the Phongolo district. Cetshwayo refused to be held responsible for Mbilini's fractious behaviour though it is possible that he turned a blind eye to his subject's activities, for Mbilini could be a useful counter to Boer encroachment in an area where Cetshwayo had not established an effective control. However, if he tacitly approved of Mbilini's acts, there was a limit to Cetshwayo's tolerance. When Boers protested at the bloodthirsty manner in which Mbilini had attacked Swazi kraals and killed a number of people, Cetshwayo gave permission to them to hunt him down. However, according to John Dunn, Mnyamana, the prime councillor, sent warning to Mbilini, who was able to escape. There is a strong possibility that the warning was sanctioned by the king.

It can be seen that although Durnford's memorandum endeavoured to be impartial, privately his sympathies lay with the Zulus. In a letter home the same month he submitted his memorandum, he noted that several Boer farmers had recently fled the disputed territory. He concluded: 'The way these border farmers treated the Zulus was so bad that they well deserved to be driven off.'

There is some evidence to lend weight to Durnford's private view. Cetshwayo, writing in 1881 to Sir Hercules Robinson, Governor of the Cape, recorded a number of instances where Boers had provoked the Zulus. He recalled notifying Shepstone of these incidents before he became administrator of the Transvaal in 1877, but although Shepstone told him that he would deal with these matters nothing was done.

It seems that Durnford preferred the defining of a border line which would favour Zulu claims, rather than the alternative of the annexation of Zululand. He declared: 'It were better that our little band of Englishmen in Pretoria should fall to a man by the hands of the Boers than that aught should be done by us to bring about a war of races.'

Durnford soon grew tired of the company in Pretoria. Apparently British rule seemed to have brought little improvement to the quality of life in the Transvaal.

Writing to his parents three months after annexation Durnford reminisced:

You have no idea of the lawless condition of the country and the utter confusion that exists. No revenue, no funds, no law, no honesty, nothing!

In a general sense Sir Henry Bartle Frere was later to substantiate this criticism of Shepstone's administration. In writing to Hicks Beach, Secretary of State for the Colonies, on 2 May 1879, Frere declared:

Unless I had seen it I could not have believed that in two years things could have drifted into such a mess ... [There was an] absence of all effort to devise or substitute a better system.

The imperialism which Durnford believed would provide all inhabitants with a just administration was not the same imperialism manipulated by Shepstone and later by Frere. There had been no hint that it would be different. The British government had already met, in some measure, Durnford's expectations in its counteraction of colonial injustice against Langalibalele's people and the Phutile. It has been pointed out that Durnford had had one of his firmest principles shaken, when in 1874 he was criticised for obeying an order without question. In March 1878 the continuation of the war by the British against Sekhukhune most likely forced him to examine closely his interpretation of imperialism. Initially he felt that there was no justification for the British, in annexing the Transvaal, 'to commit a series of wrongs towards the surrounding native tribes ... in order to pacify (and to gratify) our new subjects the Boers.'

He was distressed at the failure of the British administration to settle the problem of the disputed territory. Yet, although his distress may also have contributed to his desire to leave the Transvaal, he was not totally shaken in his commitment to British rule in the Transvaal. After consideration he seems rather to have adopted a pragmatic attitude, seeing British policy in the Transvaal as a necessary part of the wider framework of confederation. Perhaps the path to confederation might have to be a bloody one at times, necessitating in its fulfilment the sacrifice of not only the independence of the Transvaal Boers but of the Ngqika in the Cape, the Pedi in the Transvaal and probably the Zulu one day as well.

After tarrying to oversee the commencement of a fort and cantonment at Pretoria, he departed for Natal, arriving at Fort Napier on 12 August 1877. For the next two and a half months he travelled between Natal and the Transvaal in his two-wheeled cart, engaged on what appears to be a military survey. It most likely was of a secret nature, for there is no clue in his brother's biography, nor in the Colenso correspondence to show what he was doing. His frequent comings and goings between Fort Napier and Pretoria also indicate some appointed task. On 31 October 1877 he wrote from Fort Napier that he had just returned from escorting his superior, Colonel F. C. Hassard, CB, RE, the new commander of the Royal Engineers, South Africa. Perhaps there is some significance in the fact that he had shown Hassard the cantonments at Newcastle and Standerton and had most likely taken him to see the fort at Pretoria as well. Hassard remained in Pretoria for a very short time before making his way back to King Williams Town and the war against the Ngqika on the Eastern Frontier, much to Durnford's envy.

On 15 August 1877 Durnford wrote a confidential letter to Theophilus Shepstone in which he declared that: 'The annexation of Zululand seems a state necessity – supplementary to the taking of the Transvaal, and one that cannot be delayed.' He went on to ask Shepstone for the job of 'the commissioner for border affairs on the Zulu and Swazi line' with perhaps upon the annexation, the post of 'Resident'. For this he would be prepared 'to give up the military service of the Crown – if required.' What was Durnford's objective? One must be sceptical over his assertion that he was ready to devote his life to this new direction. Everything in this letter goes against the picture that one has of Durnford: a man true to his principles. The honesty of Durnford's assertions to Shepstone is contradicted by a recollection made by Frank Colenso, the bishop's son, only two weeks after Durnford had written this letter. Frank recalled that he had spent a most pleasant evening with Durnford 'who is a very agreeable companion, but is longing for a summons away to a European war!' One can only suspect that Durnford and the Bishop were desperate to retain some influence over the direction of Imperial policy towards the Zulus. If Durnford could secure the appointment of border commissioner he would be in a very influential position indeed.

The bishop's communication with the Zulus during this period had been, according to his daughter Harriette, 'effectually prevented' by Sir Henry Bulwer, so he most likely would have approved, and may have encouraged, Durnford's application.

Shepstone however, may well have suspected that Durnford was playing a devious game. In his reply a month later he agreed that the annexation of Zululand was 'an absolute necessity' but he could not recommend Durnford for an official position in the new administration. In a frank appraisal he went on to state:

> I believe you have many qualities that will exactly suit the position you wish to occupy, [but] at the same time . . . I should fear that your patience should not be equal to the strain that would be put on it by Zulu diplomacy. I do not know any position in Africa in which greater patience and skill are necessary than in the management of the Zulus . . .

Shepstone had put his finger on a weakness that Durnford was never able to curb – his impatience. He had gained a great deal for the Phutile people because he had been impatient and there was no doubt that Shepstone recalled those occasions in making his observations. It was a carefully worded letter. It must have been difficult for him to ask a favour of Shepstone and it is incredible that he now wished to associate himself with a policy – and it would most likely be Shepstone's policy that would be extended to Zululand – of which he had for so long been critical.

During the remainder of 1877 the major problem as far as Durnford was concerned was whether to move to the Transvaal or to remain in Natal. He had bought property in the Transvaal during the course of his 'tour' from August to October 1877, and on 31 December 1877 transfer of the following properties came through in his name: two 3,000 morgen farms, 'Boschmanspruit' and 'Palmietfontein' in the Standerton district, for which he paid £400 each, and two smaller farms, 'Doornhoek' and 'Klipfontein' in the Waterberg district, for which he paid £70 each. It appears that they were bought on speculation, for at no time did he ever indicate an interest in farming. They were still registered in his name at the time of his death in January 1879, and it was only in

1882 that the farms were sold and the money absorbed into his estate.

Although he contemplated residing in the Transvaal he finally decided at the end of 1877 that he would remain in Natal:

> I cannot feel any certainty about the Transvaal, and life here is more bearable than there. Here there is a certain amount of civilisation, there none.

After all, he could do what he enjoyed most without having to go to the Transvaal to do it:

> 'Chieftain' kindly allows me to ride him, and no one else ... Daily we wander together over wide plains and he stands like a rock if I dismount ... I have no dog, never having replaced my 'Prince' but I have serious thoughts of getting a lion cub from the Transvaal.

He never did of course, but perhaps he was simply jesting to his parents.

One gets the impression that his life was a lonely one – but that it had been his choice. He had few close friends. Nevertheless he did welcome and prolong the occasional acquaintanceship. His brother Edward recorded that 1877 was rounded off by the visit of a fellow officer of the Engineers, Major Moysey and his family, who stayed with him for a number of weeks into the new year. Moysey's daughter reminded him so much of his own daughter, Frances, that he became very attached to her.

The events of 1877 had left their mark on Durnford. Arriving in South African in anticipation of a Zulu war, he had channelled his enthusiasm into the activity associated with the extension of British imperialism into the Transvaal, but the reality of events had perhaps left him wondering what had happened to the paternal imperialist who was concerned with upholding the rights and freedom of tribes and individuals. The annexing of the Transvaal in 1877 had presented a new image of Imperialism. Under the new policy tribes and individuals were to be subordinated to the interests of the Empire. This had to be so if federation was to succeed. Perhaps Durnford had worked this out for himself.

CHAPTER VII

AN UNNECESSARY WAR: ZULULAND 1879

'I do kill ... It is the custom of our Nation and I
shall not depart from it.'
(King Cetshwayo to Bulwer, 2 November 1876)

THE Colonial Office had long considered the possibility of
a war with the Zulu. Sir Robert G. W. Herbert, permanent
undersecretary at the Colonial Office in 1873, believed that a war
with them was possible at any time after 1873. In 1875 Sir Garnet
Wolseley, fed with examples of Zulu bellicosity by Theophilus
Shepstone, urged Carnarvon to annex Zululand. Carnarvon would
have liked to do so and ordered Edward Fairfield, permanent
secretary at the Colonial Office, whose speciality was African
affairs, to prepare a memorandum on the Native Question in
South Africa. Fairfield, showing the unmistakeable influence of
Shepstonian thinking, recorded Cetshwayo as 'a bloodthirsty
tyrant who pays little practical heed to our counsels'. He concluded that 'the annexation of his kingdom presents itself as the
best ultimate security for Natal' but for the moment Cetshwayo
was a useful counter to Boer ambitions in the disputed territory.
It would therefore have been unwise at this stage to take action
against the Zulu.

However, after the annexation of the Transvaal the Colonial
Office left the annexation of Zululand an open-ended matter.
R. G. W. Herbert confided to Shepstone in June 1877 that the
Imperial government was 'rather nervous as to the probability
of their being pressed to take Zululand immediately'. He urged
Shepstone to delay matters for 'a year or so'. It was clear that the
decision to annex Zululand would be made when the time was
opportune. The mood in the Colonial Office was exemplified by
Herbert who minuted: 'It is certain that [Zululand] must before
long become British'.

Carnarvon resigned as Secretary of State for the Colonies on 25 January 1878 and was replaced by Sir Michael Hicks Beach who also believed that the annexation of Zululand was simply a matter of time. However events in Southern Africa were to be guided, not by the Secretary of State, but by the High Commissioner there.

Sir Henry Bartle Frere had been appointed High Commissioner on 13 October 1876 with the primary responsibility of carrying into effect Carnarvon's confederation scheme. Frere found on his arrival in South Africa that Shepstone's annexation of the Transvaal had brought with it a number of uncertainties, not least of which were the legacy of the disputed land along the Zulu border, and the prospect of an unfavourable reaction by both Boer and Zulu to the annexation. Many Natal colonists saw the annexation of Zululand as sequential to the annexation of the Transvaal. Frere decided that the Zulu and Transvaal 'problems' were interrelated and believed that the difficulties in the Transvaal toward federation could be overcome if Zulu militarism was destroyed. The rebellion of the Pedi in the Transvaal was widely believed to have been encouraged by Cetshwayo.

Both Frere and Shepstone proceeded to provide the Secretary of State with highly coloured accounts of trivial and sometimes unfortunate incidents that they believed, he could, with justification, present before Parliament as a *casus belli*. The most promising area of friction between Zulu and British administration worth exploiting was the disputed territory, but here they were to be frustrated by the decisions of a three-man boundary commission, one member of which would be Anthony Durnford.

The annexation of the Transvaal had brought the future of the disputed territory into sharp focus. The border issue was now a matter of dispute between the British administration in the Transvaal and the Zulus. Shepstone was in an unenviable position. It soon became clear that his first loyalty was to the Transvaal. Jeff Guy pointed out that this was to destroy 'the diplomatic link forged between Shepstone and Cetshwayo'.

The link was to be snapped at a meeting with Cetshwayo's chief counsellor, Mnyamana, and other indunas at the Blood River on 18 October 1877. They were not pleased to hear Shepstone announce that as a result of the annexation of the Transvaal the British and the Boers were all one *umuzi* or family, now.

At this meeting Shepstone proposed that the boundary line should be as far east as the Old Hunting Road that crossed the White Mfolozi and as far north as Inhlazatye. The Zulus rejected this. When pressed by Shepstone to lay down their claim the Zulus refused, though Mnyamana asserted Cetshwayo's right to the land west to the Drakensberg. Shepstone declared that this was asking for too much. The indunas thereupon insisted that the boundary dispute be settled by an independent arbitrator. They charged Shepstone with not 'settling matters for us' but favouring the Boers – 'the same men that trouble us and take our country from us'. Mnyamana accused him of wanting to deprive Zululand of its independence. 'Since you have taken the Boer country you have become a Boer.' The meeting broke up without an arrangement being satisfactorily worked out by the two parties. Shepstone's pride had been severely shaken. His own measure of influence over the Zulu had been greatly over-estimated, but he would not admit as much to his superiors.

The response of the Zulus to Shepstone's high-handedness was to bring considerable consternation to those who lived in the troubled area. The Zulus proceeded to clear the disputed territory of all settlers and missionaries and to construct a military fortification on the Phongolo near Luneburg. The settlers, alarmed, moved into laager and Shepstone ordered Lieutenant-Colonel R. B. Montgomery to prepare the cavalry at Standerton for a march to Newcastle. He asked Bulwer for the Newcastle garrison troops to be moved to Utrecht. When Zulu messengers tried to meet Shepstone near Utrecht in late November 1877 he refused to see them. They had come to impress upon Shepstone that all the measures taken by the king had been defensive and as an illustration of the king's desire for peace, the fortification on the Phongolo had been discontinued. But Shepstone was to deceive the Colonial Office. He declared that the Zulus were demanding territory that was impossible to give, and were totally uncompromising. To Frere he declared that the time to act against the Zulu was now most opportune. The newspapers rode the Frere–Shepstone bandwagon with considerable enthusiasm. On 7

December 1877 F. S. Statham, the new editor of the *Natal Witness*, declared:

> We have been all our lifetime subject to bondage ... by reason of this black shadow across the Tugela ... It can hardly be doubted that a deep disappointment will be felt if things maintain a peacable exterior ... The Zulu question must be settled.

Durnford scoffed at these reports of increasing tension in Natal: 'Things are very quiet here in Natal. The papers of course contain long yarns about the Zulus and Cetewayo.'

The request for the movement of troops from Newcastle to Utrecht brought Bulwer onto the stage. Bulwer, unlike Frere, was not convinced that the Zulu activity warranted the mailed fist, and he urged caution upon Shepstone. Nevertheless he sent a small detachment of the 80th Foot to Utrecht. He also expressed concern to both Frere and the Secretary of State that Shepstone was not helping toward the maintenance of peace with the Zulu.

Hicks Beach believed that the Zulu people would welcome British rule. He wanted no unnecessary conflict. Although Frere was given a great deal of independence by Hicks Beach he would still have to justify the need for a war. Consequently he was to resort to every verbal ploy he could devise to convince the Colonial Office that Zulu barbarism was an evil that had to be eradicated. He spoke of the need to 'civilise' the Zulu and listed the benefits that civilisation of this 'inferior race' would bring: peace and prosperity to their white neighbours – this in effect meant a large labour reserve for the whites – but while Cetshwayo and his military constitution held sway there was no likelihood of peace, prosperity or labour for the whites.

Frere and Shepstone were to find that Bulwer and the Colonial Office were not the only obstacles that had to be overcome; they also had opposition from Bishop Colenso and his friends, among whom was Anthony Durnford.

In November 1877 Pearson had returned from Pretoria to assume command of Her Majesty's troops in Natal. Durnford was able to spend a restful period amusing himself at Fort Napier by instructing the troops in military engineering. However he was soon embroiled in the colony's politics once again.

In December 1877 Durnford wrote to his mother that Cetsh-wayo had appointed Dr Walter Smith and Frank Colenso (the bishop's son) to act as his agents in settling differences between himself and his powerful white neighbours. No doubt he had in mind the issue of the disputed territory. Such a step threatened to complicate matters for Frere and Shepstone, and Durnford recorded that 'Shepstone is furious . . .'

Both Shepstone and Bulwer refused to accept the two men as Cetshwayo's agents, Bulwer because he could not possibly deal with the Zulu king through a third party, particularly one which was composed of British subjects.

Smith and Colenso found that the Colonial Office supported Shepstone and Bulwer. There would be no official recognition of the two men as Cetshwayo's agents in the boundary dispute.

The involvement of Smith and Colenso in Zulu affairs may well have been part of the bishop's counter-conspiracy to prevent an unnecessary war. Although the bishop himself denied it, it seems that he did involve himself in politics and was reprimanded by Bulwer for doing so. The injunction from the lieutenant-governor that he should not interfere hampered Colenso's activities, and his daughters Harriette and Frances took up the fight on his behalf. It was, no doubt, hoped by the latter that Durnford could become more actively involved, and it is possible that this issue was raised on the occasion of his visit to Bishopstowe in December 1877. It will be remembered that Durnford had, a few months earlier, been rebuffed by Shepstone in seeking employ-ment in Zululand. It was suggested that his object on that occasion was with a view to obstructing any devious Imperial act against the Zulu. Perhaps he could still do this, but in a different role. Frank Colenso was now persona non grata with the Natal govern-ment. Durnford would be a more than adequate replacement as a representative of Zulu interests. He may well have agreed to use his influence on behalf of the Zulus but it is most likely that he pointed out to the Colensos that Bulwer was considering the likelihood of Natal government arbitrating over the boundary dispute and that there was a possibility that the lieutenant-governor would ask him to sit on the commission. He could perhaps serve the interests of the Zulu more effectively as a com-

missioner. This might explain why Harriette wrote this hasty note
to her brother Frank shortly afterwards:

> *On no account* ... think of sending Colonel Durnford as your
> and Cetewayo's representative, *either now or for the arbi-
> tration.* I will tell you why when I see you.

It would not be in the interest of either the Colensos or Cetshwayo
to jeopardise Durnford's appointment as a Natal commissioner
by giving Bulwer cause to suspect that he, Durnford, might simply
be a tool of the Colensos.

The question of the boundary dispute was indeed going to be
in the hands of the lieutenant-governor of Natal. Bulwer, as anxi-
ous as Cetshwayo to avoid war, proposed arbitration by the Natal
government. Cetshwayo sent a deputation of indunas to indicate
his approval. At the same time they emphasised their distrust of
Shepstone: 'He wishes to cast Cetewayo off, he is no more a father
but a firebrand.'

In early February 1878 Bulwer selected the commissioners to
represent Natal government. It is significant that of the three
chosen, Durnford was the only one not a government official.
Perhaps the reason for this lay in the fact that Durnford had
written a memorandum on a tour of the disputed area in June
1877. Perhaps too he may have used influential friends to secure
the appointment. An interesting sideline on the composition of
the commission comes from a letter written by Lieutenant-
Colonel E. T. Brooke, RE, to Shepstone. Brooke, whose departure
from South Africa to Ireland had been delayed, had been serving
on Shepstone's staff in Pretoria. He wrote from Durban on 18
February 1878:

> There was some idea here that you would object to Colonel
> Durnford as one of the arbitrators. I hinted therefore to Mr
> Gallwey that I thought you would raise no objection to his
> appointment ...

It is unlikely that he would disapprove of a man who had already
declared to him that the annexation of Zululand was inevitable!
The other two members of the commission were the acting

Secretary for Native Affairs, J. W. Shepstone, and the Attorney-General, M. H. Gallwey. Gallwey was an excellent choice, for although the government of Natal 'was notoriously jealous of Transvaal claims to Zulu territory', according to historian De Kiewiet, Gallwey brought to the commission the clear incisive mind of the lawyer. His legal training allowed him to subject the Transvaal's documentary evidence to a strict scrutiny.

In January 1878 it seemed that the *pax Zululandia* might continue. One who was searching for a peaceful solution to the friction with Cetshwayo was Sir Henry Bulwer, who, although he was keen to put an end to the dispute over the Blood River territory, was not prepared to go to war over it. Durnford felt confident enough to notify his parents in late January 1878 that Cetshwayo wanted peace and that all was 'quiet on the Zulu border'. In mid-February the optimism was still there, 'all will be settled,' he wrote.

On 12 February 1878 Bulwer formally asked Cetshwayo to appoint three indunas to represent Zulu interests on the commission. Cetshwayo was pleased: 'I am very glad to hear what you say – I shall now be able to sleep.'

Sir Michael Hicks Beach, Carnarvon's successor, pressed on with 'confederation'. Frere wrote to Hicks Beach expressing his fear that if the commission accepted the Zulu claims to the disputed territory there would be trouble from the Boers, for Shepstone had promised to maintain the territorial integrity of the Transvaal.

Was Frere contemplating at this stage the possibility that he might have to overrule the recommendations of the commission? He gave his consent to Bulwer to the sitting of the commission presumably once he had convinced himself that the commission could come to no conclusion other than to one favourable to the Transvaal.

The representatives of the Transvaal, Henrique Shepstone, Secretary for Native Affairs in the Transvaal, Gert Rudolph, Land-drost of Utrecht, and prominent Utrecht farmer Petrus Uys, arrived at Rorke's Drift on the Buffalo River on 7 March 1878. The three Zulu representatives, Gebula, Mundula and Sihayo, were already there. The Natal commissioners, held up by the inclement weather, only arrived on 10 March 1878, and set up an imposing camp of

eighteen tents on the right bank of the river about a mile from the
drift. The escort of twenty mounted police under Sub-Inspector
F. A. Campbell, gave them an air of importance and dignity. Cetshwayo had also sent an *inceku* or body servant named Sintwangu to
watch proceedings on his behalf and to report back.

The commission was to be in session for about five weeks
during which time both Transvaal and Zulu claims were scruti-
nised with total impartiality. When the Transvaal delegates tried
to sit with the commissioners they were politely moved to a
position of equality with the Zulus before the commission.

The commission had to consider whether any of the territory
in dispute was ever ceded or sold by the Zulu. Evidence was
presented by the Transvaal in the form of the treaties of 1854 and
1861 made with Mpande, and in the subsequent beaconing of the
territory in 1864. The Boers claimed the 1864 line as their eastern
border although those who lived in the disputed territory
believed the Hunting Road that crossed the White Mfolosi to be
the boundary. The Zulus claimed all the land east of the Buffalo
River to its sources in the Drakensberg and then into the Transvaal
beyond the Oliphants River. It was a lot more than the Zulus had
claimed before.

Durnford endeavoured to be objective but he was disturbed
by the fact that Sir Theophilus Shepstone had publicly supported
the Transvaal claims. Perhaps he had read the *Natal Witness* of
5 March 1878, in which it was averred that Shepstone had visited
Utrecht and seen documents which proved that the Boers had a
strong claim to 'the line of 1864'. He daily expected the Transvaalers to show these documents but nothing but totally worthless
claims were put forward as evidence. In fact the picture became
a confused tangle of claims and counter-claims. Boundaries, when
they were defined on paper, simply could not be followed on the
terrain itself. There was a great number of contradictions not only
in the documents, but by witnesses called before the commission.

The commission finished hearing evidence on 11 April 1878.
On 4 June Durnford wrote home that the report of the commission was nearly ready 'and will please no-one except perhaps
Cetewayo'. Durnford drafted the report which was completed on
20 June 1878.

The commission did not award to the Zulus the full extent of their claims. The award was based on effective occupation. The disputed area was without doubt adjacent to the Utrecht district along the Blood River. The commissioners decided that the disputed area (marked B and C on the map on page 154) belonged to the Zulus. They felt justified in reaching this decision in that the Transvaal had, so it appeared, never exercised its authority there. The Transvaal documents laying claim to the area were declared worthless. In fact no land had ever been ceded by the Zulu nation to the Boers. The basis of the Boer claims to the area B (the treaty of 1861) was suspected of having been inveigled from the Zulu. Durnford aptly summed up the Boer methods of expansion:

> One thing is clear, that the white man wanted the black man's land – that he got leave from the black to graze cattle in the first instance, then came over and put up a shanty, then a house. Then more Boers came, and so on, until, as the Zulus told us, the Boers were like a toad that comes hopping and hopping until it hops right into the middle of the house.

The territory marked A on the map remained in the hands of the Boers. It was really the 'cession' of 1854 but although the documents laying claim to the area were of doubtful validity, the commission ruled that it was *effectively* occupied by the Boers.

The commissioners were not permitted to divulge the result to anybody until the High Commissioner had decided to make it public. However, Durnford could not resist hinting to his family at the satisfactory conclusion the commission had reached. He wrote on 24 June 1878: 'I think our views will be maintained – at least I hope so. You see we have gone in for "fair play".'

Very little is known about Durnford's influence over his fellow-commissioners, but it is probable that he argued in favour of the Zulu claim. Robinson, the editor of the *Natal Mercury*, reported a rumour that both Durnford and Gallwey had supported the Zulus whereas John Shepstone had opposed them. Certainly Durnford's observations would have been of use to the commission and one wonders to what extent he was responsible for the commission's suggestion for a fair boundary line. The commission's decision was that a line should run from the Blood

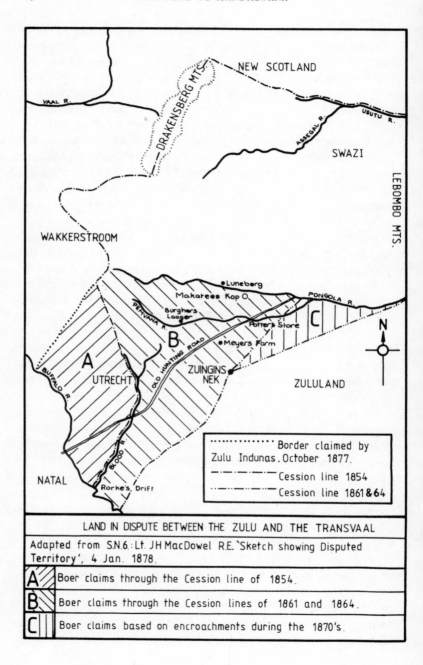

LAND IN DISPUTE BETWEEN THE ZULU AND THE TRANSVAAL

Adapted from S.N.6: Lt. JH MacDowel R.E. 'Sketch showing Disputed Territory', 4 Jan. 1878.

A — Boer claims through the Cession line of 1854.

B — Boer claims through the Cession lines of 1861 and 1864.

C — Boer claims based on encroachments during the 1870's.

River from its junction with the Buffalo, to its source in the Magidela mountains and from there in a direct line to 'the round hill between the two main sources of the Phongolo River in the Drakensberg.' It fits in neatly with Durnford's dividing line between the quiet areas and those where there was tension.

This award gave Cetshwayo more than he had expected even though it was less than he had claimed. (See map on page 154)

While the commission had been deliberating the claims of the Zulus and Transvaalers, Shepstone had been conspiring with a number of missionaries in Zululand to bring about a crisis. The missionaries, for years frustrated by Cetshwayo's restrictions, welcomed the possibility of being party to the overthrow of one whom they considered to be a tyrannical and godless monarch. Leading missionaries, such as Osmund Oftebro, Robert Robertson and Hans Schreuder, willingly provided examples of the Zulu king's 'barbarity' and contributed in large measure to exciting the feelings of alarm in the colony. In March 1878 Oftebro of the Norwegian Mission, in collusion with Shepstone, provoked a mass withdrawal of missionaries from Zululand in protest against persecution of Christianised Zulus and harassment by Cetshwayo's young soldiers. Whether there was any truth in the allegations is not material; they were believed to be true. Frere later informed Hicks Beach that all missionaries of all denominations had been 'terrified out of the [Zulu] country with a very serious loss of property.' Robertson, who had been one of the most active in inflaming the situation, indicated in a letter to Bishop Macrorie of Natal at the end of March 1878, that he had had hints of British intervention whispered to him:

> By the last post ... I received the mysterious communication 'The horses are coming in May. You understand?' Yes, I understand very well. All I hope for is, that there may be plenty of them.

The 'horses' were not to come in May, but behind the backs of the boundary commission and Bulwer the Frere–Shepstone conspiracy was shaping up for war. Hicks Beach expected trouble from one of the two parties disappointed by the award of the boundary commission and he would need Frere to restore order.

Sufficient troops were at hand to enforce whatever decision was approved by Frere. Hicks Beach was, in effect, loosening the restraints that bound Frere from annexing Zululand.

Durnford was unaware of the intrigue that was going on behind the backs of the commission. When news of the withdrawal of the missionaries reached the commission, Durnford wrote home:

> These missionaries are at the bottom of all evil. They want war so that we may take the Zulu country and thus give them homes in a good and pleasant land.

The direction that would be taken by the Imperial authorities was clearly signalled by the arrival in Durban on 7 August 1878, of Lieutenant-General F. A. Thesiger and his staff fresh from a successful conclusion to the Ninth Frontier War in the Cape. Colonels Pearson, Durnford and Orr, RA, were there to meet him, and accompanied him to Pietermaritzburg where he arrived on the 9th.

Aged fifty-one, Thesiger had had a distinguished career with the Grenadier Guards in the Crimea and with the 95th Regiment of Foot in the Indian Mutiny. He had served on Sir Robert Napier's staff during the Abyssinian campaign in the 1860s and had secured in 1868 the much-coveted appointment as aide-de-camp to Queen Victoria. In February 1878 he was sent to command British troops in the Eastern Cape in what came to be known as the Ninth Frontier War, which he brought to a speedy and successful conclusion within five months and earned himself a KCB. In October 1878 he was to succeed to the title of Lord Chelmsford on the death of his father.

Thesiger wasted little time in preparing for the conflict against the Zulus. As early as March 1878 Frere had convinced him that war was probable and Pearson, senior officer in Natal, was asked to make a survey of the prospective areas of operation along the Zulu border. The commander-in-chief obtained advice from colonists and Boers, including Paul Kruger, on fighting strategy, and F. B. Fynney, border agent for the Lower Thukela, drew up a profile on the Zulu army commanders and provided information on the structure of the Zulu army. His staff prepared a 'Precis of Information Concerning the Zulu Country with a Map', to which Durnford's contribution was considerable.

Thesiger would need to augment the number of his Imperial troops with colonial volunteers and African levies if he hoped to be able to overcome the 40,000 to 50,000 warriors that Fynney claimed Cetshwayo could mobilise.

The Natal government, perhaps affected by Wolseley's promise that Imperial troops would protect it, had done little to prepare itself for conflict with the Zulus. The Imperial campaigns against the Pedi, the Ngqika and the Gcaleka, appear to have had some effect upon this malaise, and the Defence Committee of the Executive Council, after being pressed by both Frere and Thesiger, began to take positive steps toward war preparations. The likelihood that Britain would send out no more troops to reinforce those already in South Africa may well have been a deciding factor.

In 1875 the Defence Committee had recommended that the colony maintain three separate forces: the one a permanently armed mounted force, the Natal Mounted Police, formed under Major John Dartnell in early 1874; the second a field force of white volunteers which could be readily assembled and moved wherever necessary; and the third a 'district force' which was only to be mobilised 'in cases of extreme emergency'. The organisation of this district force was, by the end of June 1878, overdue.

It had always been assumed that the government would, in the event of a conflict with the Zulus, expect assistance from its black population, but the question of arming them with guns had never been favourably considered. Black levies had been used during the Langalibalele affair with some success but the majority had not been given guns. Thesiger informed Frere on 21 June 1878 that nothing on the proposed native contingents had as yet even been committed to paper by the colonial government. Their policy appeared to be one of 'passive defence', for provision had been made for the 'building of a large number of defensible laagers'. He put pressure on Bulwer to get things moving.

Bulwer's announcement at the end of June that steps would be taken to divide Natal into seven defence districts was a step in the right direction. The organisation of Natal Colony's African population into a front line force and as a reserve was part of this district defence.

During the ensuing months defensive posts were sited; inventories of arms and ammunition were drawn up and a census of black and white forces was made. The final results were published as a Government Notice on 26 November 1878. It had not been achieved without some difficulty, for Bulwer had been, at that stage, still reluctant to give the Zulu any cause for unease.

Thesiger was irritated by Bulwer's pacifism and complained to Frere and the Duke of Cambridge, commander-in-chief of the British Army.

The activity in Natal towards what was preliminary preparation for war, was noted by Durnford with some alarm:

> There *is* a policy here to get up a Zulu row but it is not likely to succeed at present. I am not of course a negrophilist, and as a soldier I should delight in the war, but as a man I utterly condemn it.

This extract exemplifies the ambivalence of Durnford's attitude towards the Zulu. He hoped that there would be a war but there was the possibility that it would be against a people who might be the innocent victims of the new imperialism which he appears to have reluctantly accepted but continued to question till the day he left for the front. He could see that there was little if any cause for war against the Zulu. But he was desperate to satisfy his personal goals and the matter of innocence of the 'enemy' was to be thrust guiltily aside as the opportunity for battle approached.

This ambivalence is further illustrated by Durnford's preparation of a memorandum (on Thesiger's invitation) on the formation of an army of black levies to assist the Imperial forces in the event of war. At this time he was speaking out against war. He must have felt uncomfortable knowing that he was an active part of the preparations for war against the Zulu. Undoubtedly he *was* a negrophilist and there was no need to deny it. The contradiction in his language reflects the dilemma he faced: soldier or humanitarian? Could the two roles be merged? It was not possible. However, the two opposites as he saw them did provide him with an answer: whether there would be a war or not, he would be satisfied.

Nevertheless he did what he could to reduce the rising hysteria against the Zulus. When the Landdrost of Utrecht reported that

the Zulus were building a military kraal near Boer farms in the
Phongolo district, Durnford dismissed the report as alarmist. He
considered that if a kraal was being erected it was done so 'to
keep order among the Zulus residing there'. He went on to say:
'Cetewayo is far too wise a man to make a false move at present.'

Colonel Charles Pearson, who forwarded Durnford's remarks
to the High Commissioner, concurred with Durnford whom he
described as 'an officer who knows South Africa intimately ...
His opinions I consider always sound and intelligent.'

The balance between war and peace seemed to depend on
whether Bulwer could hold out against Frere. Durnford thought
that Bulwer had achieved a notable victory for the pacifists in
managing to 'cool down' Thesiger's desire for war shortly after
he had arrived. He wrote to his mother on 12 August 1878: 'I
assure you all is peace with the Zulus now, and will remain so if
the Governor can so keep it.' He certainly was not impressed
with Thesiger at his first meeting, calling him 'not a clever man'
but he seems to have found him to be an approachable and
friendly person – 'a pleasant man, a gentleman, and one can do
a great deal for a man of that type.' Over the months the two men
established a friendly but formal relationship.

Although in August 1878 Durnford was optimistic that Bulwer
could keep the peace, an unfortunate incident occurred which
was to add grist to the mill of the warmongers. In July 1878
runaway wives of Cetshwayo's induna, Sihayo, who lived near the
Natal border a few miles from Rorke's Drift, fled into Natal. They
were pursued by Sihayo's sons and murdered. Bulwer ordered
Cetshwayo to surrender those responsible for the murder. Cetshwayo was reluctant to do so and offered to pay a fine. Durnford
recorded that the raid had come at a most inopportune time,
but he was confident that Cetshwayo would give some form of
satisfactory compensation.

However it was not to be settled as simply as Durnford had
expected. When Frere arrived in Natal on 23 September 1878 he
saw in the incident a further opportunity to create an atmosphere
for war with the Zulu. He wrote to Hicks Beach a week later
suggesting that Cetshwayo should be sent an ultimatum that if he
did not surrender the murderers to the Natal authorities then war
should be declared upon him.

Hicks Beach, uncertain of events, and nervously awaiting news of the British punitive expedition against the Afghans, urged Frere 'to use every effort ... to avoid a Zulu war'. He reminded Frere on 21 November 1878 that Cetshwayo had 'expressed regret for the occurrence', and that his behaviour had not indicated otherwise.

The despatch arrived too late to stop Frere issuing his ultimatum, but it is doubtful whether Frere could have been halted anyway. Helped by the difficulties of communication – it took four to five weeks for a despatch to reach London – events in Natal and Zululand in those last crucial weeks of 1878 marched according to Frere's will. Hicks Beach, aware that events in South Africa were no longer under his control, frustratedly confided to Disraeli, his prime minister, in November 1878: 'I really cannot control [Frere] without a telegraph.' One result of this was eventually the establishment of a direct telegraphic link between Pietermaritzburg and London in December 1879; too late to prevent the Zulu war.

Frere used every opportunity to justify the drift to war. When two whites were manhandled by Zulu warriors for trespassing near the Middle Drift below Fort Buckingham on the Thukela in September 1878, Frere called the incident 'one of many instances of insult and threatening.' The irony was that the men were being employed by Thesiger on a military survey of the Drift as part of the preparations for war.

Nature too was having a hand in the drift to war. 1876 and 1877 had been years of severe drought in Zululand and there was a tendency for the Zulus to move into the fertile areas along the river banks. The overcrowding led to encroachment upon the Boer farms in the border areas. It was inevitable that an incident occur. On 21 September 1878, Gert Rudolph, the Landdrost of Utrecht, reported to Shepstone that Faku, a Zulu induna living near Luneburg, had, in the name of Cetshwayo, ordered the settlers of Luneburg to leave the area as it was now required by the Zulu. Many did move. Durnford believed that they fled 'in causeless panic'. It had also been reported to Rudolph that the failure of Colonel Hugh Rowlands's British force to capture Sekhukhune's stronghold in the Eastern Transvaal was giving Cetshwayo increasing confidence.

The failure of Rowlands and the refusal of Cetshwayo to offer adequate compensation for the murder of Sihayo's wives were to influence Hicks Beach in late November 1878 to send substantial reinforcements to Thesiger (now Lord Chelmsford) but the commander-in-chief was also urged to speed up the organisation of a Natal Native Contingent. Hicks Beach later reminded him that the reinforcements were to be used for defensive purposes only, but the despatch arrived after the invasion of Zululand had commenced.

The days of peace were drawing quickly to an end. On 7 October 1878 the northern area of Zululand was once again in ferment. Mbilini attacked Swazi kraals across the Phongolo. Because Cetshwayo had given Mbilini refuge in Zululand, the Zulu king was held responsible by Frere for Mbilini's activities. Mbilini was practically a law unto himself and it is well-known that, given the opportunity, he would attack the Boers in his district.

The report of the boundary commission had been presented to Bulwer in July 1878, but over five months passed before Frere released it. Frere had found the report an embarrassing hindrance to his plans. Frances Colenso most likely was correct when she declared that the commissioners had 'put him in a hole'. He reasoned that if he could delay the official release of the commissioners' decision the Zulus might, by chance, give him an excuse to destroy them. But there were a number of prerequisites: Bulwer's support was essential. Thesiger also needed additional time to organise his invasion force and preparation for the defence of Natal colony was still in its early stages.

Nevertheless the strategy of delay was simple to manipulate: Frere queried whether the report could in fact be a satisfactory basis for settlement, for it had confined itself to the disputed area between the Buffalo and the Phongolo, and had not included the troubled areas beyond. Bulwer believed that it could, but Frere continued to question its conclusions and raise totally unrelated problems. Despite Gallwey's presence on the commission Frere declared he was not satisfied that the Transvaal claims had been fairly considered. When the commissioners replied in detail to his queries he still prevaricated in an arrogant and disingenuous manner:

The documents produced by the Transvaal ... have certainly not been taken as evidence for the Transvaal claims, but they appear to have been allowed considerable weight in various ways in evidence against them. This course appears to me as of doubtful equity. As regards the documents themselves, it is hardly necessary that I should follow the commissioners through the analysis of their reasons in pages 2 to 16 for rejecting the documents as evidence of the Transvaal claims.

Durnford fought hard for the report and was prepared to meet Frere and discuss it with him. Edward Durnford recorded that his brother was quite exhausted after 'some hours close argument alone' with the High Commissioner. Frances Colenso believed the interview to have been 'rather stormy' and she declared that Durnford had 'had to make a firm stand to prevent Sir B[artle Frere] upsetting the whole.'

The time-wasting continued. Sir Theophilus Shepstone was asked for his opinion of the report. Although Shepstone's memorandum was ready by 17 October 1878, it was only sent back to Frere on the 31st. Further time was to be spent communicating Shepstone's views and objections to Bulwer and to the commissioners. Shepstone, facing increasing opposition from Boers against British rule in the Transvaal was a great deal more forthright in his criticism of the report than Frere had been. He deplored what he believed was 'the deprecatory tone in which everything Transvaal is spoken of in the report' and questioned whether it would be wise to publish it. But Frere found that he had in the meantime secured an unexpected ally in Bulwer.

Bulwer's response to the commissioners' report was most reassuring to Frere. The lieutenant-governor was losing patience with Cetshwayo. Frere was to use Bulwer's replies as a framework upon which to build an ultimatum, and by so doing firmly enmeshed the lieutenant-governor in his web of intrigue against the Zulu king. On 13 November 1878, five days before the commissioners' replies to his objections reached him, Frere had placed the draft of the ultimatum before Bulwer for his signature.

On 16 November 1878 Bulwer invited Cetshwayo to send a deputation to hear the decision of the boundary commission at the Lower Drift of the Natal side of the Thukela on 11 December

1878. Already steps had been taken to build Fort Pearson on a high promontory overlooking the drift and on 24 November 1878 a detachment of the Naval Brigade occupied the drift and prepared for both the meeting on 11 December and the intended invasion a further month away.

The 11 December 1878 broke fine and clear after heavy rains during the preceding two weeks had at last broken the two-year drought. The Thukela was running very full and strongly and the bluejackets had a difficult time working the boats to bring the Zulu delegates to the meeting place under a huge spreading fig at the base of Fort Pearson. The thirteen indunas led by Vumandaba and Gebula, together with 40–50 retainers and John Dunn, met the Natal delegation.

John Shepstone slowly read the boundary award while F. B. Fynney, the border agent, translated it into Zulu. Essentially the Zulu claims to sovereignty over the Blood River territory were upheld but Frere insisted that those Boers who lived there should have their land titles recognised by the Zulu monarch. Those Boers who wished to leave should be given compensation by the Zulu king. A British Resident would be appointed at Utrecht to see that this was done. The Zulus were not happy with these conditions. But the worst was still to come.

At lunch time an ox was killed and roasted and the Zulus were asked to reassemble after they had eaten. The proceedings of the afternoon were devoted to the reading of the ultimatum which left the Zulu delegation in considerable agitation. Cetshwayo was given twenty days to surrender the four responsible for the death of Sihayo's wives; pay a fine of 500 head of cattle for being uncooperative, and a further 100 head for the manhandling of the two white men at the Middle Drift. He was given a further ten days to surrender Mbilini for trial in the Transvaal; to disband his army and dismantle the present military structure and allow young men to marry when they reached maturity. Any crime committed by one of his subjects was to be heard by a jury of indunas, and the subject would also be given right of appeal to the king. Missionaries were to be allowed to return to Zululand and converts were not to be molested. A British Resident was to be permitted to reside in Zululand to ensure that these provisions were carried out. He would have the right to hear charges against Europeans in Zululand and could prevent the expulsion of Zulus from the kingdom.

The ultimatum was Frere's answer to the boundary award which threatened the fragile fabric of confederation. The loyalty of the Transvaal must surely be secured once the menace of the Zulu had been removed? Once the Zulu had been defeated Frere could rearrange the boundary to the advantage of the Transvaal.

For Durnford, 11 December 1878 was a memorable day; he received his brevet as a full colonel but it is likely that the satisfaction of receiving this promotion was diminished by the news of the ultimatum. His brother recalled:

> Amongst his fellows both military and official he seems to have stood absolutely alone in disapproval of the war policy, while a feeling of duty prevented his conversing freely with his friend the Bishop of Natal, upon the subject ... The good Bishop's last words to his soldier friend were: 'God bless you – do what is right.'

His reply to the bishop was sent as he made his way to the Zulu border at the end of December 1878:

> Believe me, all your interests in this sad business are mine. As a soldier I must do my very best, but I may have my own opinion.

But his brother Edward declared that now that war was imminent 'he laid aside his own opinions and threw himself heart and soul into the war preparations.'

The die was cast. He had made the choice.

CHAPTER VIII

THE MILITARY PREPARATIONS:
THE NATAL NATIVE CONTINGENTS

'Native levies may be employed ... with great
caution ...'
(Lt-General F. A. Thesiger, 27 August 1878)

DURNFORD had long been a supporter of the use of African
levies. When Thesiger, soon to be Lord Chelmsford, arrived
in August 1878 this issue was one of the first to be raised, for he
had made good use of black levies in the Ninth Frontier War. He
soon learnt of Durnford's enthusiasm for the idea and asked him
to prepare a confidential memorandum on it. This was hurriedly
completed by Durnford on 17 August 1878, possibly so that it
could be referred to by Chelmsford at the Mayor's dinner in
Pietermaritzburg on 23 August 1878, when he would make his
first official pronouncement regarding the use of black levies in
support of Imperial forces.

Durnford proposed a force of 5,500 men, 500 of which would
be mounted. Their role would be 'to lead every column, acting
as light troops'. At the top of the command structure there would
be a commandant with a staff officer and an interpreter. There
would be five assistant commandants and six medical officers.
Durnford recommended that all officers and non-commissioned
officers should be whites and that there should be five regiments
of infantry divided into ten companies of 100 men; each company
split further into ten sections of ten men each led by a white
man, which was 'necessary to efficiency where the Natal Zulu is
concerned'. The mounted men would be divided into five troops
of 100 men each, further divided into five sections of twenty men,
each with white officers. The total number of men in the Native

Contingent would then be the 5,500 black fighting men, 564 white officers including 14 staff officers, and 1,400 black auxiliaries to act as carriers of ammunition, of officers' accoutrements and of cooking utensils.

This rigid division of blacks along the lines of European armies was not to meet with the Natal government's wholehearted approval. John Shepstone, the acting Secretary for Native Affairs, when shown the scheme, was opposed to any 'new system or mode of warfare' among Natal's blacks and he, together with C. B. Mitchell, who had succeeded Napier Broome as Colonial Secretary, claimed that the existing organisation, namely that of keeping Natal's blacks in their tribal units, was the best system, even though these were of different strength according to the size of each tribe. Durnford claimed that his plan *did* make provision for clans to be kept together under their chief or headman and was flexible enough to be adapted to either system. The final decision would be Chelmsford's.

Durnford also suggested that each infantryman should be armed with Sniders (the cavalrymen would be issued with the Westley-Richards carbine) and sixty rounds of ammunition. A further forty-two rounds per man would be held in the regimental reserve. This was a particularly sensitive issue with the Natal government. They would not approve of every man being given a gun (there were not sufficient numbers of guns in the colony anyway) but they finally conceded that one in ten (generally the induna who would also be an NCO) would be issued with a rifle but he would be given only five rounds of ammunition. The mounted men, likely to be used in small numbers for scouting and to be in more frequent contact with the enemy, were not to be similarly treated; each would indeed be granted the use of a carbine.

In the matter of discipline Durnford recommended that it should be 'patriarchal – the only kind suitable'. The drill work would be adapted to the 'blacks' skirmishing ability: 'Shooting as steadily as possible – advancing – moving to the right and left – increasing and diminishing front.' This strategy could still be used even if the men were not issued with guns. The call-up of men would be left to the lieutenant-governor, who, as the Supreme Chief, was required by custom to do so. They would then be placed under the orders of the commandant. The recruitment of officers would be done by the latter who would contract suitable men for six months service.

Chelmsford was doubtful that there were sufficient numbers of whites in Natal Colony to meet Durnford's figures, but nevertheless approved of the scheme. Pay would be 2/6d per day for the mounted men and 1/- per day for the infantry. The cost to the government would be £28,667 per month. Durnford hoped to clothe the contingent in scarlet to impress the enemy and 'to ensure safety from the English side', but Chelmsford, concerned with keeping them mobile, preferred them to fight naked. This would indeed be the case, and many were the unfortunate accidents where the black levies were shot by the white troops in the belief that they were Zulus. It is significant that despite the fact that the fighting men would be paid a cash wage, Durnford wanted them to receive further rewards. He suggested that a proportion of the cattle captured should be given to them and that 'those who have displayed conspicuous valour should be decorated, native fashion, with the headring (the sign of manhood) and permitted to carry an assegai at all times.'

At the mayor's dinner Chelmsford, well aware of the touchy issue of a large armed black force in Natal, was guarded in his proposals:

We believe that to a certain extent native levies may be employed ... It must be with great caution and not with the view of relying on them as the principal part of the offensive force.

The public response was not favourable. One settler of thirty-five years in South Africa, reminded readers of the *Natal Witness* that the Hottentot levies of the Cape Mounted Rifles had deserted to the enemy in 1852/53, and the dreadful experience of the Indian Mutiny was something that could never be forgotten. Quite clearly the mobilising of black levies had to be delayed until the last possible moment.

It is possible that Durnford was responsible for selecting the invasion points along the Natal–Zululand border. On 23 August 1878 he presented Chelmsford with a memorandum on bridging the Thukela at three points: near its mouth (Lower Drift), below Kranskop (Middle Drift) and at Rorke's Drift. It is significant that on the next day Chelmsford drew up a provisional invasion plan which provided for an invading force of five columns operating from: Thukela mouth (No 1 Column), Middle Drift (No 2 Column), Rorke's Drift (No 3 Column), Blood River (No 4 Column) and the Phongolo River (No 5 Column). In command of No 1 Column would be the officer commanding the 24th Foot, Colonel R. T. Glyn; No 2 would be commanded by Colonel C. K. Pearson of the Buffs; No 3 by Lieutenant-Colonel H. J. Degacher of the 24th Foot; No 4 by Colonel Henry Evelyn Wood, and No 5 possibly by Colonel Hugh Rowlands, who had been fighting Sekhukhune. Chelmsford had understood from Bulwer that Natal's African population stood at 64,794 at the last census. From this number he hoped to be able to form a Natal Native Contingent of 15,000 men in three equal columns and placed under three separate commands. The structure of each command resembled that recommended by Durnford. No mention was made whether they would be used in an offensive or defensive role.

Chelmsford sent his proposed plan of invasion to the Secretary of State for War, pointing out that its successful execution depended upon much needed reinforcements being sent out. The War Office replied on 18 October 1878: no reinforcements could be sent. He had to make do with what troops he had in South Africa.

In his memorandum for bridging the Thukela, Durnford's greatest problem was to erect a bridge without giving the Zulus 'the appearance of hostile intent'. He decided that the only suitable type was the 'flying' one which could be prepared at Durban and carted by wagon to the selected sites. Essentially this bridge would be erected on the 'Indian principle' of stretching a wire or hemp cable across the river 'and making use of the current to swing or steer the "flying bridge" [which would simply be] one long wide shallow boat fitted with a lee board ... capable of taking one loaded wagon with 4 after-oxen at a time; to be worked by a trained detachment of seamen assisted by natives'.

Durnford estimated that six 'flying bridges' could be placed at the three drifts 'within thirty days' of a bridging department being organised – fifteen (at least) of those days being used to transport the material. However, it was first necessary to make improvements to the drifts, but Bulwer was opposed to this for it would give the impression that war was imminent.

The long drought of 1877/78 had most likely raised serious doubts among Chelmsford's staff that the Middle and Rorke's Drifts would be deep enough to use 'flying bridges'. Despite Bulwer's fears, Chelmsford asked two civilians, a surveyor with the Colonial Engineer's Department and a local trader, to inspect the Middle Drift and its approaches and report back. It was hoped that use of civilian rather than military personnel would not excite the Zulu. Most likely Durnford was party to this decision. Unfortunately the two men trespassed on to Zulu territory; were seized by the Zulus, interrogated and, after convincing the Zulus of the 'innocence' of their presence there, were released. As has been shown in the previous chapter, Frere was to make political capital out of the incident. The report on the drift, most likely given orally, would have confirmed that the drift was unsuitable for a 'flying bridge'. Only the Lower Drift near Fort Pearson was provided with a 'flying bridge'.

It can be seen that Durnford played a major role in Chelmsford's preparations. But his contribution did not end here for on 11 September 1878 he completed a memorandum on the raising and equipping of a force of black pioneers. According to this memorandum this force, 500-strong, would be divided among the five columns and would precede each column, repairing drifts and tracks in order to make them passable for artillery and wagons. The pioneers could also be used to throw up earthworks and to work 'the advanced bridge train' and to maintain the roads on the advance. Durnford recommended that, on his experience as colonial engineer, one white officer be appointed in proportion to seventeen pioneers. The uniform should be the scarlet serge, but only the officers should bear guns. The men would have their native weapons plus a tool, either pickaxe, shovel, spade, felling axe or crowbar. He pointed out that the colony could, after the war was over, also make use of these pioneers in the Engineer's department. But Bulwer, supported by his executive, rejected this argument, claiming that they would be 'a source of future embarrassment to the government'. As it was, such a call-up of men to work with the military engineers was, according to Bulwer, straining 'to the utmost any legal power I may have'. He was particularly reluctant to allow the pioneers to have military training. But after Chelmsford had complained to Frere about the lieutenant-governor's obstructionism, the issue was resolved and Captain A. H. Hime, the colonial engineer, was ordered to raise a pioneer force of 300 men to be divided among the three southern columns. Memories of the Langalibalele affair carried with them a legacy of distrust among white colonists of their fellow blacks. This attitude was neither understood nor tolerated by Chelmsford and his staff.

On 12 September 1878 Durnford presented yet a further memorandum to Chelmsford, outlining the necessity for an augmentation of the Royal Engineers in Natal in the event of a war with the Zulu. The establishment of the Royal Engineers was hopelessly inadequate, there being only nineteen NCOs and men in the colony. He recommended that two companies (240 men) be sent out. Both Frere and Chelmsford concurred with Durnford's request and a submission was accordingly made to the Duke of Cambridge, commander-in-chief of the British Army.

On or about 17 September 1878, Durnford joined the headquarters staff and would remain on it until Colonel F. Hassard, commanding Royal Engineers in South Africa, arrived in Natal. During September Durnford concluded work on a map of Zululand which he had drawn from the knowledge obtained on his various tours of the border area and, as he put it, from 'original sources' – Zulus and missionaries who gave him information on the heart of Zululand. This map was to be used by the British columns in the first invasion of Zululand in January 1879. Scaled at ½ inch to five miles, it indicated the major rivers and wagon tracks and showed the topography of the country. It was crudely drawn and lacked vital details in contour and distance, but under the circumstances it was a remarkable effort. It is likely that the tour of the border in October 1878 by Durnford and Chelmsford was with a view to familiarising themselves with the ground as shown on the map.

In order to understand the complexities of organisation that now took place in raising black levies, it is necessary to look first at what black units were in existence at the end of November 1878. It will be remembered that Natal would, for the purpose of defence, be divided into seven districts (see Appendix III). The blacks living in those districts would contribute to their own defence. Districts I, II, VI and VII adjoined the Zulu border. In these frontline districts a border guard or police, was raised in mid-November 1878 and placed under the command of border agents. These men had control over three 'lines' that approximated the three districts. The Lower Thukela line was to be controlled by Fynney; the Msinga as far as Rorke's Drift would be controlled by Fynn, and in the centre, the Mvoti or Kranskop line would be under the control of Fannin. In each of these lines there were sixty black guards armed with assegais and knobkerries, responsible to the border agents on their line. These border guards are not to be confused with the black police serving under the magistrates, from whom it seems, the border guards took over the responsibility of watching the Thukela border.

With regard to the Native Contingent: On 26 September 1878 Chelmsford had written to Bulwer that it was essential that the commander-in-chief have at his disposal 'an efficient force of native levies'. The colonial government had decided that, in the event of conflict, there would be two phases of call-up of black levies. The first contingent would be from the border districts and would be required by Lord Chelmsford to assist the Imperial forces. The second contingent would be called up to defend their district. This would also require a further call-up in the border districts; sixty border guards would be quite insufficient to protect these districts. The guards anyway were intended merely to warn the authorities of an impending Zulu attack in their area.

The role of black levies in the Imperial army was, by the end of November 1878, still not clearly formulated in Chelmsford's mind. Durnford in his memorandum had suggested that the duties of the black levies should be 'to lead every column acting as light troops' but Chelmsford did not seem to agree with that role. He did acknowledge that they should be employed in *some* manner, not necessarily with the invasion force. Chelmsford was able to defer a final decision, for Bulwer delayed the call-up of levies for the first contingent for as long as possible in the hope that differences with the Zulu might be solved without recourse to war. Furthermore, as the award of the boundary commission was awaiting the High Commissioner's decision, it did not seem wise or diplomatic to jeopardise the good faith of the Natal government by mobilising its forces.

Chelmsford had, in late September 1878, acknowledged that it was necessary that the border should be watched and guarded by an adequate force. It seems that he gave serious consideration to this as a role for the proposed Native Contingent. For this Chelmsford could quite safely reduce his black conscripts from 15,000 to 6,000 men: 2,000 for each of the three lines of the Lower Drift, Middle Drift and Rorke's Drift. These were to be organised into three regiments. Bulwer expressed doubt to Chelmsford as to the wisdom of disregarding the tribal system of call-up used by the Natal government, but Chelmsford acting on Durnford's advice was adamant. He claimed that the men were 'organised by companies tribally and had their own indunas; several chiefs also accompanying them', and he insisted on 'a strong white element' to control the levies.

The Natal Native Contingent then would be used as a defence force and would be backed up by the mounted patrols of the Natal Police. The 1st Regiment NNC was allocated to the middle line at Middle Drift, the 2nd Regiment to the Lower Drift and the 3rd to Rorke's Drift. Durnford was appointed to command the levies of the middle line. Mention was first made of this command by Durnford on 11 November 1878, although it seems that the appointment was made in October 1878. At that time he was still on the headquarters staff.

Most of the men earmarked for the 1st Regiment NNC came from the Bomvu, and although Durnford was pleased to have them, he preferred to have under his command men who had served with him before, or whom he knew. He was prepared to go to considerable lengths to get these men. Bulwer complained before the Defence Committee at the end of October 1878 that Durnford's preferences were leading to 'a great deal of confusion and difficulty'. John Shepstone, Secretary for Native Affairs, advised Bulwer to cooperate with Durnford. Permission was therefore given for Durnford to add to the 2,000 men allocated to the middle line. A further 1,000 men were chosen by Durnford from the magistracies of Ulundi, Weenen and Upper Thukela. The Bomvu were to be joined by 300 foot and 100 horsemen of Zikhali's clan; 300 Phutile footmen, 200 of Langalibalele's warriors and 50 of Hlubi's Hlongwe Sotho, his old friends who had ridden with him to the Bushman's Pass in 1873.

The three regiments were to be divided as follows:

1st Regiment under Durnford, of three battalions:
No 1 under Commandant A. N. Montgomery (ex 7th Fusiliers)
No 2 under Major H. M. Bengough (77th Regt of Foot)
No 3 under Captain C. E. LeM. Cherry (32nd Light Infantry)

2nd Regiment under Major Shapland Graves of the Buffs, of two battalions:
No 1 under Major Shapland Graves (2/3rd Regt of Foot)
No 2 under Commandant W. J. Nettleton

3rd Regiment under Commandant Rupert Lonsdale – ex 74th Highlanders, of two battalions:
No 1 under Commandant G. Hamilton-Browne
No 2 under Commandant A. W. Cooper.

Each battalion would have 95 white officers and non-commissioned officers. There would be ten companies per battalion divided up as follows:

1 captain			1 sergeant-major		
2 lieutenants	}	white	10 NCOs	}	black
6 NCOs			90 privates		

This would total 110, on average, per company. Chelmsford was true to his word – companies were organised where possible along tribal lines. By and large the final picture resembled Durnford's recommendations in his memorandum of September 1878. Chelmsford dismissed the major fear of the colonial government that the NNC, having been drilled and trained as soldiers, would constitute a potential threat to the security of the colony, by claiming that without the white officers the blacks would be 'unable to retain or reproduce the organisation under which they had gained success'.

There seems to be no verification of the claims held by some writers that Durnford was offered command of the entire Native Contingent and that Chelmsford's staff were envious of the size of his command and therefore prevailed upon their chief to offer him command of only one of the three units of levies. No doubt he would have liked to have been offered command of the entire Contingent but he had recommended the splitting of the NNC and Chelmsford had concurred. In any event he seemed pleased with his command when it was confirmed in early November 1878.

From the unfolding of events it appears that Chelmsford only decided at the beginning of November 1878 that a Natal Native Contingent would be used as part of the invasion force after all. On 2 November 1878 John Shepstone left Pietermaritzburg to make the necessary arrangements with the magistrates to provide Chelmsford with what Bulwer termed the Special Military Native Contingent or First Native Contingent. The absence of these men would leave a gap in Natal's frontier defence. Bulwer was not too alarmed, for in the three border districts that were supplying Chelmsford, he estimated that there remained a further 33,500 fighting men from which he would need only 10,000. Should there be a necessity to call out more, the four remaining districts (which had not been called upon to contribute any men) could provide a further 10,000. The first 10,000 would be referred to as the Frontier Defensive Native Contingent or Second Native Contingent. The overall command of levies in each district would be in the hands of the District Commandant who would have under him the two or three magistrates responsible for the divisions within the district. These magistrates would command the quota furnished by their division.

There was clearly no shortage of black manpower in Natal. The problem would be to find the requisite number of white officers. Chelmsford's fear that Natal Colony would not be able to supply the full complement for the NNC soon manifested itself, so he decided to contact ex-officers of the black levies that had fought in the Ninth Frontier War. He was only able to get hold of two of the six commanders who had helped him crush the Nqgika, and one of those was Rupert Lonsdale, who had commanded Mfengu levies. Through him the word was passed around to those whites who had served on the eastern frontier that the general wanted their services in Natal. Judging from the quick response (180 officers and NCOs arrived in Natal with Lonsdale on 23 November 1878) it appears that they were expecting the call.

On 9 November 1878 Bulwer recorded that a meeting was held between members of the Defence Committee and Chelmsford, at which the latter announced modifications to his plan of advance into Zululand. It was now decided that the column at Middle Drift should consist solely of black levies. One hundred mounted blacks would be placed with each of the three southern columns. The five columns would now be as follows:

No 1 or Coastal Column at the Lower Drift under the command of Colonel C. K. Pearson.

No 2 at the Middle Drift (Fort Buckingham) under Lieutenant-Colonel A. W. Durnford.

No 3 or Centre Column at Rorke's Drift under Colonel R. T. Glyn, 24th Foot.

No 4 at Utrecht under Colonel H. Evelyn Wood.

No 5 at the Phongolo under Colonel H. Rowlands.

Bulwer gave his blessing to the new plan. Durnford was pleased. On 11 November 1878 he wrote to his parents:

The Governor has been pleased to express his confidence in me ... I shall have some 3000 men, infantry, cavalry and a rocket battery, so the command is at least a respectable one for a Lieutenant-Colonel.

On 15 November 1878 the lieutenant-governor thought it prudent to prepare the Frontier Defensive Native Contingent or Second Native Contingent. The division of the colony into its seven districts was proclaimed on 20 November 1878, and the next day some of the district commandants were selected. The three districts on the Zulu border were each to be put under the command of a senior officer who would be taking an active part in the invasion of Zululand: Durnford was to be appointed district commandant to District VII, the Mvoti District; Major Graves was to be district commandant of the VI or North Coast District, and Major Dartnell of the Natal Mounted Police, was to be commandant of District I or Klip River District. They were to be responsible for the defence of the district until it was placed under direct military command, and were to send in regular reports to the Defence Committee in Pietermaritzburg. On 27 November 1878 official letters of appointment were sent to the district commandants of the seven districts. Durnford, Graves and Dartnell were relieved of their district commandantships because

Chelmsford no doubt felt that it was simply not possible for them to serve two masters; their first responsibility was to Chelmsford as the commander-in-chief. On 2 December 1878, W. Wheelwright was appointed acting commandant of District VII.

Shortly after this, on 4 December 1878, Bulwer informed his Colonial Secretary that only 6,000 of the Frontier Defensive Native Contingent (the Second Contingent) would be called up. Only the three districts bordering on the Thukela and Buffalo rivers (I, VI and VII) would be provided with a frontier defence force. There would be 1,000 men at Helpmekaar, 1,000 men in the Sandspruit valley to cover the area from Rorke's Drift to the junction of the Thukela and Buffalo rivers, and 2,000 to guard the Lower Thukela border from Mvoti County to the sea. Bulwer instructed his Colonial Secretary to contact the magistrates and tell them that they should call up the men only when Bulwer gave the order. There only remained the furnishing of the various defence posts with arms and ammunition, for Natal to be ready for war. On 7 December 1878 this was completed, and Frere, was, no doubt, given further encouragement to present his ultimatum four days later.

There was a great deal to encourage Frere. On 25 November 1878 the Secretary of State for War notified Chelmsford that the 2/4th, 99th, two companies of Engineers, and drafts for the 13th, 24th and 88th Foot, in all a total of 1948 infantrymen and 240 Engineers, would be leaving England for South Africa on 2 December 1878. They would arrive in time to join the invading columns on 11 January 1879. Colonial volunteers, by 30 November 1878, were already on their way to their mustering points.[1]

Throughout November and early December 1878 the officering

[1] *Natal Witness*, 30 November 1878. By 2 December 1878 the troops, both Imperial and colonial were assembled at the following places:
  a) At the Lower Drift was a detachment of the 3rd Foot (The Buffs).
  b) The remainder of the Buffs and the 24th Foot were at Greytown and Helpmekaar. The Natal Carbineers, Buffalo Border Guard and the Newcastle Mounted Rifles were also at Helpmekaar.
  c) At Thring's Farm near Mapumulo, the Stanger Mounted Rifles and the Victorian Mounted Rifles awaited orders to proceed to Stanger.
  d) The Durban Mounted Rifles, Alexandra Mounted Rifles and the Natal Hussars were camped at Pott's Spruit, a farm between Fort Buckingham and Hermannsburg.
  e) The rest of the Imperial Troops – the 80th, 90th and 13th Foot, were on the north-western border together with the Frontier Light Horse.

of the Natal Native Contingent continued. Advertisements were placed in the newspapers calling for applications for both officers and NCOs to be made to Chelmsford's assistant military secretary, Lt-Colonel John North Crealock. Military experience was no longer deemed by Chelmsford as a prerequisite, and a great number of ruffians were enrolled. For those who had had no experience commanding black levies Chelmsford, possibly with Durnford's assistance, drew up a list of instructions 'for the management of natives', which patronisingly declared that the Natal Zulu was but an 'intelligent, precocious boy with the physical strength of a man' who preferred 'a firm, kind rule'. An officer was never to use 'epithets of contempt' nor 'passionate language' and was not to nag. Much practice would be required to drill the levies, so a great deal of patience was necessary.

The call-up of the black levies was a slow process. Despite the attraction of a free blanket and meat rations, the men were reluctant to serve, and it was necessary for the magistrates to get the chiefs to fine the men if they refused to report for duty. The men originally selected for Durnford's 1st Regiment were as slow in coming forward as those assembling for the remaining two regiments. They did not know him as intimately as the tribes Durnford had chosen to serve with him. The response from the latter tribes was magnificent. The Phutile and Hlubi people, together with Zikhali's Ngwane, were given two weeks to assemble at Greytown after Christmas Day 1878. By 8 January 1879 Durnford was only five short of the 300 Phutile called for, and four of these had appeared by the 11 January. Of the 400 Ngwane, all were present but Durnford horsed 157 thus leaving himself short in Ngwane infantry. Both Hlubi's Sotho and the Christians from Edendale Mission had sent more than was asked for. Only 200 had been levied from Langalibalele's people and Faku's Mabaso. The response from this duo was quite unexpected: 227 turned up.

Bulwer's delay in calling out the levies made matters most difficult for the commandants of the three Native Contingent regiments. They had barely a month to get them assembled, officered and trained. Matters such as the uniform worn by officers, were left to the commandants themselves. Durnford selected an unusual garb for himself. He described it thus:

Boots, spurs, dark cord breeches, serge patrol jacket, broad belt over the shoulders and one round the waist – to the former a revolver and to the latter a hunting knife and ammunition pouch. A wide-awake soft felt hat with wide brim, one side turned up and a crimson turban wound around the hat – very like a stage brigand!

George Shepstone, who had served with him in 1874, was appointed his political assistant which, when the rank of captain was given to him, in effect meant that he was Durnford's principal staff officer. George Shepstone was energetic and efficient and had an uncanny anticipation of Durnford's requirements. He was a son of Sir Theophilus Shepstone, who viewed with some concern George's desire to serve under Durnford, and later made these reflections:

It is strange but it is true that when I heard he [George] had been appointed to serve with Colonel Durnford, I felt as if I had heard his death warrant. I had no confidence in Durnford's prudence or capacity to suit himself to the circumstances in which he might be suddenly placed.

On 12 December 1878 the correspondent of the *Natal Mercury* with Wood's column at Utrecht, reported that black scouts had uncovered the news that the Zulu army had been ordered to assemble at Ondini, the king's principal kraal, at the next new moon. It was the first indication that the Zulus were willing to fight.

From 15 to 18 December 1878 the three NNC regiments began to take shape as each commandant received lists from the Natal government of the numbers that each chief would be sending to assist the Imperial forces. Some were to fail to meet their promise; others exceeded their quota. Durnford's 1st Regiment was made up of conscripts from fifteen clans. His headquarters on the Middle line was to be at Dalmaine's Farm, about 3½ miles on the Greytown side of Kranskop. J. E. Fannin, the border agent for this part of the line, waited at Dalmaine's for the NNC to assemble. Supplies for them began arriving there on 21 December 1878. That same day Durnford, who was at Fort Napier, sent off Zikhali's

Horse and Major Francis Russell's 9-pounder rocket battery to Greytown, destined for Dalmaine's. The departure of those infantrymen of the 1st Regiment that had assembled in Pietermaritzburg, was delayed until their tents had arrived on 23 December 1878. Durnford followed the next day with the stragglers and late-comers.

For some reason that is not clear Durnford had acquired a reputation of being a martinet, and the young officers that reported for duty to him in Pietermaritzburg went, according to one, 'not without some fear and trembling', but 'his kind and genial manner' soon put them at ease. However, he was not one to relax military responsibilities or discipline and Captain Dymes of the 1/1 NNC, the young officer mentioned above, recorded this example of Durnford's insistence on discipline, when, a few days later they were at the camp at Dalmaine's:

One one occasion we were commanded by our senior Captain [Hay] and we (the officers of the 1/1 NNC) made up our mind to attend parade on foot, giving our horses a holiday. When day broke and Colonel Durnford rode down our line he stopped, and calling out our senior officer, asked him, 'Where is your horse, Captain Hay?' 'Well, Sir,' was the rather hesitating answer, 'the fact is – my horse is not well this morning.' 'Oh! Indeed' replied the Colonel, 'I am sorry to hear that; and are all the officers' horses ill this morning?' 'Yes, Sir,' said our senior, reassured by his quiet manner, 'the fact is that they are all on the sick list.' 'Oh! Very good,' assented the Colonel, and said no more. We went through our usual morning drill, and the others thought it was allright, and that we should hear no more of our breach of discipline, which it certainly was, as the orders were distinctly that every officer should be mounted on parade. I, however, was not quite easy in my mind ... I was not mistaken, for, after a while, he said in his quietest manner: 'Now gentlemen, I think we will do a little skirmishing.' Our faces fell, for we knew what this meant ... He kept us at it for two hours, skirmishing over some very rough ground ... All the drill was done at the double. I can honestly say that, what with the pace, and the encumbrance of my arms and accoutrements – not to mention the rough ground, and the tumbles into antbear holes, etc – I felt thoroughly knocked up when the drill was over. At the end of it Colonel Durnford remarked to our senior Captain: 'I hope your horse will be fit for work tomorrow morning, Captain Hay.' I need scarcely say that we never again appeared on parade dismounted.

At Sandspruit Rupert Lonsdale's 3rd Regiment was nearly at full strength. By 31 December 1878 there was only 300 of Mganu's Tembu people from the Klip River magistracy outstanding.[1] The 3rd Regiment could see the tents of the Imperial and Colonial troops at Helpmekaar. The proposed invasion point at Rorke's Drift lay 12 miles away. There the Native Pioneers under Captain Nolan were busy improving the drift. On 30 December 1878 the Natal Carbineers, Newcastle Mounted Rifles and the Buffalo Border Guard moved down to the drift.

[1] Lonsdale's 2nd Battalion was made up of Cunu, Bele, Tembu and isiXosa. Pakade's Cunu provided enough men to fill six of the ten companies. In the 1st Battalion there were four companies of Tembu under Ngwane, and three companies of isiXosa under Mkungu, a half-brother of Cetshwayo. A single company under the chief Ndomba was also assigned to the 1st Battalion. (CSO 674, Lonsdale to Crealock, 23 December 1878.)

CHAPTER IX

ORDERS, ORDERS, ORDERS...

'I well remember the look of disgust that crossed
his countenance as he read the order.'
(Captain Dymes, NNC, recollection of Durnford,
14 January 1879)

O N 23 December 1878 Chelmsford issued to his column commanders instructions regarding the invasion of Zululand.
The main objective would be the king's kraal at Ulundi. The
advance was to be undertaken by three main columns: right,
centre and left. The right column under Colonel C. K. Pearson
would cross the Lower Drift of the Thukela river near its mouth,
with its first objective as Ekowe, some 15 miles to the north. The
centre column under Colonel R. T. Glyn would leave from
Rorke's Drift and move eastwards, whilst the left column, under
Colonel H. Evelyn Wood, would march south-east from the direction of Utrecht. The three columns would converge on Cetshwayo's capital. The role he assigned to the NNC is of particular
interest: they would, it was noted, have the duty of 'protecting
the flanks [of the column] and of helping the wagons when in
difficulties'. In the event of a Zulu attack the best formation,
Chelmsford decided, would be this deployment:

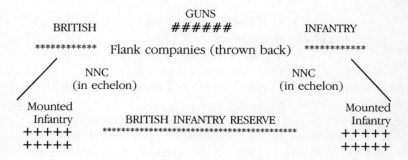

```
                        GUNS
        BRITISH         ######            INFANTRY
    ***********  Flank companies (thrown back)  ***********

   /          NNC                      NNC          \
  /         (in echelon)            (in echelon)     \
 Mounted                                           Mounted
 Infantry      BRITISH INFANTRY RESERVE           Infantry
 +++++    ************************************    +++++
 +++++                                            +++++
```

It can be seen that, although the square could be formed, the initial formation would be frontal – an extended line. The infantry were to open fire on the enemy at 600 yards. These instructions were to have an important bearing on the formation of the British defence at Isandhlwana. Why this disposition should have been recommended by Chelmsford after the successful use of the square at Quintana against the Nqgika in the Ninth Frontier War in 1878, is a mystery. Perhaps the square invited the Zulu to complete its traditional strategy of encircling the enemy with the horns and chest formation. This disposition would be more effective in preventing encirclement.

The march of the first conscripts of the 1st Regiment NNC to Greytown had been accompanied by appalling weather and probably explains why Durnford's column was delayed in its march to Dalmaine's farm. On 31 December 1878, while still at Greytown, Durnford wrote to Crealock to ask for his second thousand men. The invasion was only eleven days away and Durnford's force was only at one-third of its total strength. Fortunately, C. B. H. Mitchell, the Colonial Secretary, attended to his needs personally. Wheelwright, the resident magistrate, had anticipated the call, for the chiefs had already been contacted. Durnford would receive the men by 6 January 1879.

On 31 December 1878 Chelmsford had informed Pearson that he had to remain at Eshowe until Glyn's column had made some progress. Furthermore he decided that Durnford's column would be used to consolidate the gains made by Pearson's Coastal Column, by making sure that no large body of Zulus existed between Entumeni (Bishop Schreuder's mission station in Zululand) and the Middle Drift. Durnford would then take his column to Entumeni.

Over the new year Durnford's infantry began to assemble at Dalmaine's farm. By 2 January 1879 there were 1,300 levies of the 1st Regiment there. The rain continued to fall.

Durnford received fresh orders on 1 January 1879. In the space of twenty-four hours Chelmsford had changed his mind. Pearson would now be responsible for clearing the area between Entumeni and Middle Drift. Durnford would remain at the Middle Drift until the general advance on 11 January 1879, when he was to send a battalion to Thring's Post, and from there it would aid

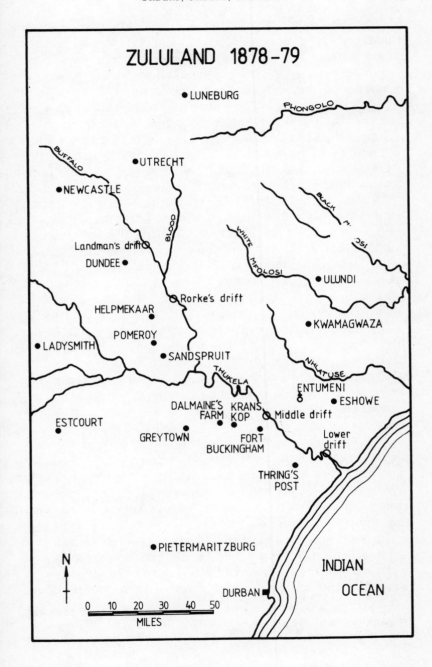

ZULULAND 1878–79

Pearson. The rest of Durnford's column would cross the Lower Thukela when Pearson had reached the road where it branched off to Entumeni. Durnford would then march his column to Entumeni where he was to open communications with Glyn near the headwaters of the Mhlatuze River. Durnford was ordered not to engage a large force of Zulus unless supported by British troops. Pearson would then move to Kwamagwaza, but Durnford would remain at the Mhlatuze until Glyn had reached the Upper Mhlatuze and Wood had reached Inhlazatye Mountain.

On arrival at Dalmaine's Durnford had had to make preparations for ten days' stay. When his column would finally leave, the frontier defence would be left to the Natal government's Second Native Contingent and to Fannin's sixty border guards (which were finally assembled on 3 January 1879 at Kranskop). Shortly after Durnford arrived, one company of the 1st Regiment under Captain Smythe was stationed at Kranskop on outpost duty, and a company under Lieutenant Vetch was sent to work on the road between Kranskop and the river. There were four companies of the 2/1st and five companies of the 1/1st NNC at Dalmaine's.

The Zulus watched preparations from the other side of the river. During the night of 2 January the rain stopped and by 4 January the river began to fall and became fordable at the drift, which under normal conditions was about 40 yards across and 18 inches to 2 feet deep. On 4 January the 2nd Battalion of the 1st Regiment was ordered to march down to the drift to join Vetch's company.

Over the following three days Durnford's 1st Regiment was augmented by a further 636 men. On 8 January 1879 Durnford reported to Crealock that he had 2,610 levies.[1] A week later only 164 more had joined, and the invasion was already under way. He was still 276 men short of the total promised by the Natal government.

Durnford was most satisfied with the behaviour of his black levies. When Chelmsford visited the NNC he too was impressed with their good spirit. Durnford was no easy taskmaster. Troops were up at 2.30 a.m. and on 'Alert parade' at 3 a.m. They remained

---

[1] This total was made from 1310 from R. M. Mvoti, 400 from R. M. Upper Thukela, 700 from Weenen County, 50 from R. M. Mgeni, 40 from R. M. Ixopo and 100 from R. M. Mkomanzi (R. M. = Resident Magistracy).

under orders till 4 a.m., then there was drilling for three hours until breakfast. Durnford took the mounted men under his care. He enjoyed working with them and proudly announced to his mother: 'My Horse are my old friends the Basutos under their chief Hlubi, who sends 50 [men]; Sikali 150; Christians from Edendale send 50, led by John Zulu, brother of Langalibalele; Jantje 50 – all full of ardour.' During the day there were garrison duties and more drill (Smythe's company at Kranskop was supplemented by a further company on 6 January 1879) and shooting practice for the Native Horse, of which the Edendale contingent was adjudged by the correspondent of the *Natal Mercury* as the best shots.

Durnford himself had his day generally taken up with 'deputations and business'. He might have added 'communication' with Fannin's and Schreuder's black messengers, who through family contact, were able to keep their masters informed of Zulu dispositions across the border and of rumours of the situation at the king's kraal. Bishop Schreuder no longer was at Entumeni; he was now housed close to Dalmaine's and Durnford saw quite a lot of him. He had first met the bishop when he had been on Theophilus Shepstone's staff during the expedition to crown Cetshwayo in 1873. He spoke most highly of him and was deeply appreciative of the many kindnesses he performed for him during these days at Dalmaine's. He had either forgiven or forgotten about Schreuder's role in the Imperial conspiracy against Cetshwayo.

Durnford's energy and enthusiasm were admirable. Captain Dymes of the 2nd Battalion recorded that 'He was a slave to duty and expected everybody who served under his command to be the same, but he never gave an order involving hardship or fatigue to the column without himself sharing the fatigue and hardship.'

Chelmsford was equally energetic. On 4 January 1879 he arrived at Helpmekaar to inspect the encampments. From there a stream of directives went out to his column commanders: Wood was to move in the direction of Sihayo's from Bemba's Kop on 11 January and to link up with Glyn's column. As Chelmsford feared a Zulu inroad into Natal when the invasion commenced, Durnford was ordered to send his two strongest battalions to Sandspruit valley to stop possible raids across the Buffalo River into the populated Msinga district. These two battalions could also be used to cooperate with Glyn if necessary. The rest of Durnford's force would only move over the border once Pearson had occupied Eshowe. However, he did grant Durnford the option to move across the Buffalo if he considered it necessary in order to prevent a Zulu attack, but he had to return to Natal after the action. Fifty Horse, possibly Jantje's, would be left at Middle Drift; the rest of the Native Horse would join the two battalions at Sandspruit. Durnford was also told that Glyn's column would be clearing Zulus from the border to the south-east of Rorke's Drift. Further instructions would be sent once the border was cleared. It is likely that Chelmsford handed Durnford these instructions personally, for he visited Durnford at Kranskop the same day.

Earlier in the day two of Bishop Schreuder's messengers arrived at Kranskop to report that they had visited Cetshwayo and he had said that he was willing to abide by the terms of the ultimatum and hand over Sihayo's sons, but that everything was happening too quickly. They also reported that there was considerable confusion amongst the Zulu, and the loyalty of many clans was in doubt.[1] It is likely that Durnford repeated the substance of the interview to Chelmsford that evening. The next morning Chelmsford returned to Helpmekaar. Glyn's column was already on the march to Rorke's Drift where they were expected to arrive in the afternoon.

It is not known whether Durnford had any qualms of conscience over Cetshwayo's reported willingness to comply with the terms of the ultimatum. If he did there was no reference made in his last letters home. Perhaps he expected Cetshwayo not to resist. There is such a suggestion in this letter he wrote shortly before he moved to Isandhlwana:

I am very well, and this life suits me down to the ground. My

[1] John Dunn had written to Frere on Cetshwayo's behalf on 18 December 1878, agreeing to give up Sihayo's sons and pay the fine in cattle, but asking for more time in order to comply. (The letter only reached John Shepstone on 30 January 1879, nineteen days after the invasion had commenced and a week after the disaster at Isandhlwana!) But Frere would permit no extension of time.

horses are all well, and I am well mounted too; all in this life is enjoyable, and I think we are just going to make a 'military promenade' in Zululand.

On the coast the Naval Brigade at Fort Pearson, had, on 6 January 1879, laid a 300-yard wire hawser across the Lower Drift for the purpose of putting into operation the 'flying bridge' recommended by Durnford in September 1878. Three days later they mounted a permanent guard on the huge anchor of HMS *Tenedos* which had been removed from the ship to be used to hold the hawser. The river was shallow at the proposed point of crossing but there was a strong current.

Imperial reinforcements had arrived in Durban in the second week of January 1879, and within a week were on their way to supplement the troops preparing to move into Zululand. The weather continued to be wet and windy, and the losses in oxen were appalling. On 10 January Chelmsford moved to Rorke's Drift to attach himself to Glyn's column. At 3 a.m. the next morning he assisted Glyn in supervising the crossing of the Buffalo in 'a thick fog'. That afternoon Durnford visited him at the camp at the drift to report that all Zulus of military age had (according, most likely, to Schreuder's spies) gone away from the border to the king's kraal. Chelmsford appears to have accepted the possibility that this was indeed so, but announced to Frere that he would still make sure that as he advanced he would not leave 'any large [Zulu] force' in his rear.

The Natal government's plans to defend the frontier were well under way by the time the invasion commenced. Fannin reported on 4 January 1879 that all the blacks along the Thukela had been called up. On 6 January 1879 when John Dunn arrived at the Lower Drift with his people to seek protection from the British, he offered Lucas, the District Commandant, 300 armed men for border defence. Bulwer refused the offer, declaring that they were to be treated as refugees and that they had to surrender their arms. Dunn and his people were finally settled on Bishop Colenso's mission lands on both sides of the Nonoti river near Doornkop.

It is likely that the plan initiated by William Beaumont, commandant of District I, who established six garrisons in his district, provided the blueprint for defence in the other districts. Each garrison was furnished with 100 men and a further reserve of 1,200 for each was available on short notice.

The correspondent of the *Natal Mercury* reported that the Zulu regiments were waiting opposite the British columns: the Ngobamakosi and Mcijo were near the Lower Drift, the uDududu, Nokenke and Mbonambi were waiting in the Nkandla bush opposite Durnford's column; the uDhkloko and Ndlondhlo were in northern Zululand watching Wood, and Sihayo, believed to have 9,000 men, was in his stronghold opposite Glyn's column.

Chelmsford paid no attention to the newspaper report on the Zulu dispositions. The objective for the columns remained Ulundi. Chelmsford wrote to Wood on 16 January 1879: 'We must try and push everyone slowly before us towards the king's kraal, or otherwise disarm the tribes and take their chiefs and some of their headmen as hostages.' It was also hoped that there would be a great number of chiefs who would not support Cetshwayo, and Chelmsford instructed his column commanders to use every effort to encourage these leaders to seek British protection for their tribes. Among those whom it was believed would ask for protection was Gamdana, brother of Sihayo, and Matyana ka Mondisa, who lived to the east of Gamdana.

It was believed by Chelmsford that the fighting strength of the Zulu was approximately 40,000 men, and that their mode of attack was likely to be the Shakan method of 'chest and encircling horns', which in simple terms meant that the enemy would be drawn on to the chest or centre of the Zulu force; horns or wings would be thrown out on either side and the enemy would then be surrounded by the joining together of the enveloping horns. In a circular to officers in November 1878 Chelmsford had recommended that the forming of a laager and partial entrenchment around the camp would counter this mode of attack yet, a month later he had amended this strategy, for the expected brief halts and the continual need for the wagons to bring on supplies, made such an instruction impracticable.

On 12 January 1879, the day after the invasion, contact was made with Zulu tribesmen of Chief Sihayo, near the Batshe River, and a brief skirmish was fought in the rocky fastness of his stronghold. Sihayo's main kraal was burnt; there were thirty Zulus and two infantrymen of the NNC killed. It was a successful start, for the Natal Native Contingent did all that was asked of it.

No 3 Column then returned to Rorke's Drift camp, for progress had to be delayed for a few days while the Native Pioneers and road parties toiled on making a road through the Batshe valley. Chelmsford rode out of Rorke's Drift camp on the 17th and selected a fresh camp site for the next stage of his operations. The place he chose was Isandhlwana mountain, nine and a half miles from Sihayo's stronghold.

Sphinx-shaped, Isandhlwana stood at its highest point 500 feet above the plain, solitary and bastion-like. The plain stretching away to the south-east was intersected by a series of dongas and dry river beds. The two most noticeable features in this plain were a conical hill, Amatutshane, which rose 190 feet above the plain and was about 1½ miles from Isandhlwana, and Qwabe, a ridge of red soil a further 3½ miles away. The plain was flanked on the north by the Nyoni ridge which was approximately the same height as Isandhlwana, and which opened out on to the Nqutu plateau which stretched away to the Amanzimnyama River to the north-north-west and the Ngwebeni River in the north, the latter about four to five miles from Isandhlwana. The Nyoni forked out into a spur to the north of the mountain about 1,000 yards away. Here along this latter point, lay the camp's great weakness, for the Zulus could only be seen when they reached the spur.

Towards the east the Nyoni dipped into what Donald Morris in his *Washing of the Spears* aptly refers to as a 'notch' where serious erosion of the Nyanga River had formed a deep ravine and left a long donga with many arms reaching out on its left and right on the slopes below. Next to the 'notch' was iTusi, six feet higher than Isandhlwana and giving a commanding view of the whole plain before and of the plateau behind. Its broken cliffs and hanging rocks blend well with its name of 'the frowning one'. Looking towards the east the Nyoni fell away to the Slutshane, a 1,000 foot mountain-bastion in the left hand corner of the plain.

Across the front lay the heights leading to the Mangeni River. On the right was the massive wall of the Malakatas dominated by the Hlazakazi, 5,000 feet above sea-level. The only other feature above 5,000 feet in the vicinity was Isipezi Hill which was behind Slutshane, 15 miles away. Here, close by, was the stronghold of the Matyanas, a powerful Zulu family whose chief, according to one Zulu source, hoped to be Commander-in-Chief of the Zulu Army.

While the skirmish against Sihayo was taking place, Durnford was waiting impatiently at Kranskop. The last orders he had received had been on 8 January 1879, when he was told to send two of his strongest battalions to Sandspruit to protect the Msinga district from possible Zulu attack. He was also told to wait for Pearson to occupy Eshowe before he moved across the border with the remainder of his force. But the orders also gave him the discretion to move across the Buffalo if he considered it necessary to prevent a Zulu attack. Once he had completed this action he was, however, to return immediately to Natal. Chelmsford also had suggested that the force at Sandspruit could be used to support Glyn. Further orders regarding the movements of Durnford's force would be sent once the border area was cleared of Zulus.

Rumours flew. Perhaps Durnford had read the report in the *Natal Mercury* of 10 January 1879 that there were three Zulu regiments believed to be in the Nkandla bush opposing his force at the Middle Drift. It does appear however that a letter written by Bishop Schreuder reached Durnford on 13 January 1879, reporting that a Zulu impi was assembling near the drift with a view to fording it to invade Natal, and brought him back to Dalmaine's with some haste. Durnford, recalling the latitude given him by Chelmsford in his memorandum of instructions of 8 January 1879, acted quickly, perhaps too quickly, for a closer inspection of the drift would have shown that, as a result of the heavy rains, the river had risen to a level that would have made an invasion a risky affair. It seems that Durnford arrived at Dalmaine's in the twilight of 13 January and was unable to see the water's level at the drift. The rivers in Natal and Zululand rise in a matter of hours after heavy rains.

Durnford sent a message to Chelmsford notifying him of the course he intended to pursue. At 2 a.m. on the morning of the 14th he was ordering his men to be prepared to march to the Middle Drift at 4 a.m., their objective being to break up the Zulu invasion at that point. His force, which had not yet lost the two battalions to Sandspruit, was at the summit of Kranskop preparing to descend the valley to the drift, when a mounted orderly arrived from Chelmsford with a message. Captain Dymes, aide-de-camp to Commandant Montgomery of the 1st Battalion, was sitting on his horse close by Durnford when it was delivered. He recalled:

> I saw a change in his face at once. Suddenly he gave the word to retrace our way to camp and I well remember the look of disgust that crossed his countenance as he read the order.

Chelmsford had never intended Durnford to have as much independence of movement as he was arrogating for himself, and when he received Durnford's note he was greatly annoyed, and once again was to write things that were to have an important bearing on later events. In view of the seriousness of the charge of misconduct that Durnford was later to be burdened with after Isandhlwana battle, it is necessary to record what Chelmsford wrote:

> Unless you carry out the instructions I give you, it will be my unpleasant duty to remove you from your command and to substitute another officer for the command of No 2 Column. When a column is acting SEPARATELY in an enemy's country I am quite ready to give its commander every latitude and would certainly expect him to disobey any orders he might receive from me, if information which he obtained showed that it would be injurious to the interests of the column under his command. Your neglecting to obey the instructions in the present instance has no excuse ... If movements ordered are to be delayed because report hints at a chance of an invasion of Natal, it will be impossible for me to carry out my plan of campaign. I trust you will understand this plain speaking and not give me any further occasion to write in a style which is distasteful to me.

The rebuke was justified, but the significant words are those that draw attention to the situation when a commander *would* be allowed to disobey orders.

The day after the incident Durnford was given instructions to move towards Rorke's Drift with a battalion of infantry, the rocket battery and the Natal Native Horse. He was to leave two weak battalions, the 1st and 3rd under Captain C. E. Cherry at Kranskop. Donald Morris sees these instructions as an indication that Chelmsford was determined to keep an eye on Durnford and thus to subordinate him to Glyn. This is unlikely, for Chelmsford had indicated previously that Durnford's men might be required to work with Glyn, and the actions against Sihayo may have convinced him that the Zulu army lay along the route of the Central Column and not near Pearson. Furthermore, the mobility of the Zulus had made it essential that Glyn's column be supplemented with mounted men. Certainly Durnford's independence of command was in existence on the morning of 23 January 1879, for Major C. F. Clery recalled in a private letter to a friend, that when Chelmsford ordered him to call up Durnford to reinforce the camp at Isandhlwana, Lt-Colonel J. N. Crealock, Chelmsford's assistant military secretary, was acting as deputy adjutant general, overheard the order and asked 'very properly, I think', declared Clery, 'Is Major Clery to issue orders to Colonel Durnford?' for Durnford's was an independent command hitherto – so the General said [to Crealock] 'No, I let you do it.'

The incident had undoubtedly strained the good relationship between Chelmsford and Durnford, and might well have contributed to Chelmsford's deterioration in health shortly before 23 January 1879, making him tired and forgetful. This was later to have serious consequences on the clarity of orders for Durnford. However, once again Durnford's impulsiveness and impatience had driven him to commit an act which could have an adverse effect on his reputation. Chelmsford, aware of Durnford's valuable contribution to his war preparations, had treated him leniently.

On 16 January 1879 Chelmsford wrote to Wood that he intended to move to Isandhlwana and from there clear the Qudeni forest of Matyana's people, moving between Isipezi Hill and Mhlabamkhosi in the direction of the Little Itala where he hoped 'to establish Durnford's Column'. All three columns, namely Glyn's, Durnford's and Pearson's, would then clear the country up to the Mhlatuze River before moving across it towards Ulundi. 'By this plan,' he declared, 'we shall oblige Cetewayo to keep his force together when it will suffer from want of food, and become thoroughly discontented, or we shall oblige him to attack, which will save us going to find him.'

It should be noted that Durnford was not told of this new plan. That same day Durnford's column left Kranskop. The next day Durnford (who was at Burrup's Farm) ordered three companies of the 1/1st NNC, the whole of Bengough's 2/1st, the rocket battery and the Natal Native Horse, to be ready to join the Central Column. The three companies of the 1st Battalion were Zikhali's Ngwane under Captains Nourse, Stafford and Hay. However, Hay had to remain behind as paymaster, and his company (which, it will be remembered, was most likely under strength) was split between Stafford and Nourse.

The men marched all day and well into the night, arriving at Sandspruit at 3 a.m. in the morning of the 18th, thoroughly exhausted. Durnford recalled the occasion with immense pleasure:

You would have been pleased [he wrote to his mother] at seeing us in the night, marching, dark night, 'watercourse' roads, self leading, with an orderly and a lantern then cavalry, each man leading his own horse, rocket battery next, then infantry, the wagon train straggling over some five miles of road. Crossing rivers in large boats in the night, horses swimming, then cattle killing, cooking on the red embers, horses feeding, men eating and sleeping etc. All the sights and sounds of camp life which I love.

The 19 January 1879 was wet and cold, and since the 13th the rivers were running fast and full. Wheelwright, together with his levies of the Second Native Contingent, was now watching the seven drifts in his district, and reported as early as the 13th that, in his opinion, the river was impassable while the rains continued.

As the rain had not abated since the 13th it was unlikely that there could be an invasion by the Zulus at the Middle Drift, so there was no longer any need to garrison the area with a large number of troops. Cherry's battalion would remain at Kranskop, but there would be two companies of the 24th Foot under Major Upcher at Helpmekaar, and further reinforcements at Greytown, should a threat arise at the Middle Drift. On the 19th Chelmsford wrote to Durnford, who was at Vermaak's Farm:

No 3 Column leaves tomorrow [for] Isandhlwana hill and from there as soon as possible to a spot about 10 miles nearer to the Qudeni forest. From that point I intend to operate against the two Matyanas if they refuse to surrender ... I have sent you an order to cross the [Buffalo] river at Rorke's Drift tomorrow with the force you have ... I shall want you to cooperate against the Matyanas but will send you fresh instructions on this subject.

The order was delivered by Major Spalding, the deputy assistant adjutant general, the same day. Durnford was instructed to take his mounted men, Zikhali's infantry and the rocket battery, and camp on the Zulu side of the Buffalo, about half a mile from the drift. Bengough was also to move down to the Buffalo, and be ready to cross on 22 January 1879.

The 20 January 1879 dawned fine for the troops. The force at Isandhlwana had laid out a camp on the eastern slope by late afternoon. There was no laager and no entrenchment despite the warnings of prominent Boers and colonists, and his own directive to column commanders two months previously. However, it should be said that Chelmsford did not intend to stay long at Isandhlwana mountain; within forty-eight hours he was to select the next halt in his advance. The wagons were required to transport supplies and could not be immobilised. An entrenchment would have been wasted effort, for the ground was hard and stony. When later it became necessary to bury the bodies at Isandhlwana, it was decided to heap stones on them instead.

Natal Native Contingent pickets were placed close to the camp. Captain Edward Erskine's No 4 Company, 2/3rd NNC was on Mkwene Hill 1,500 yards to the north, and Captain James Lonsdale's No 9 Company, 1/3rd NNC was placed on a high point along the Nyoni about a mile to the east of Mkwene and due north-east of the camp. A mounted reconnaissance had scouted the area as far as Isipezi Hill on 15 January 1879 and reported no Zulu army in sight.

It appears that they had not seen the Ngwebeni valley. It is not surprising, for the slopes leading to the lip are strewn with stones thus making horseriding a hazardous affair. They most likely followed the low ground on the plateau, along what is now the main

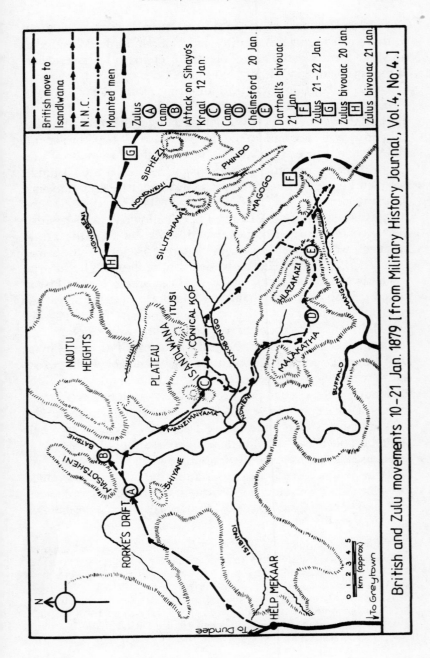

British and Zulu movements 10–21 Jan. 1879 [from Military History Journal, Vol.4, No.4.]

road. When Chelmsford departed on the afternoon of the 20th with a small mounted escort to examine Ngaba ka Mazungeni (the high ground at the end of the plain, ten to twelve miles away to the south-east) he too saw no Zulus.

It is true that there was no Zulu army in the vicinity on the 15th, but on the 20th, as the British force began to set up their tents in a neat line 150 yards from the base of the mountain, the Zulu army was moving into the deep horseshoe-shaped valley of the Ngwebeni River[1] four to five miles to the north-east of the camp. Eight regiments[2] – some 20,000 men – had left Ulundi two days before. In overall command were Mavumengwane and Tshingwayo.

By the evening of the 21st most of the army had assembled at the Ngwebeni. Further parties would be expected on the 22nd. An attack would be made on the camp at Isandhlwana on the 23rd. The 22nd was believed to be a day of ill-omen because it was a day when the 'moon was dead' because there would be a partial eclipse of the sun, and it would not please the spirits to fight on such a day.

At the British camp on the morning of the 21st, Chelmsford, apparently sure that his northern flank was not threatened by a Zulu army, turned his attention to his southern flank. He ordered out sixteen companies of the 1st and 2nd Battalions of the 3rd Regiment NNC, under Rupert Lonsdale to scour the western side of the Malakatas to the south. He also sent out two mounted scouting parties: one under Major Dartnell, composed of Natal Mounted Police and Volunteers, in the direction of the Mangeni River; and another composed of mounted infantry under Lieutenant Browne to scout the area around Isipezi Hill. The three units had some success: Lieutenant Browne returned to report contact with numbers of Zulu; Commandant Lonsdale's NNC battalions

---

[1] Colenso and Durnford, pp. 345–8: Account of Isandhlwana by Uguku of the Mcijo. See also G. S. Swinney (trans.), *A Zulu Boy's reminiscences of the Zulu War*. This is the only area within a few miles of Isandhlwana in which 20,000 men could have remained undetected.

[2] The Mcijo (which included the Mhlanga and nKandampemvu); the Ngobamakosi (which included the uVe); the Nokenke; the Thulwana; the uDhloko; the Mbonambi; the Nodwengu (which included the Mkhulutshane) and the Isangqu.

saw a lot of cattle but no Zulus. Major Dartnell, however, reported numbers of Zulu moving north-east.

The sequence of events is well known. Zulus began to congregate in increasing numbers and Dartnell induced Chelmsford to respond to his call for assistance. The general decided in the early hours of the 22nd to take out half his force at the camp to support Dartnell.

At 3 a.m. a message was sent with Lieutenant Horace Smith-Dorrien to order Durnford to bring his men to reinforce the camp at Isandhlwana. Lieutenant-Colonel H. B. Pulleine of the 1/24th was left in command of the camp. He had left under him A, C, E, F and H Companies of the 1/24th – 15 officers and 403 men (approximately 3 officers and 80 men per company); G Company 2/24th – 6 officers and 178 men; two of the six 7-pounders of N battery, 5th Brigade, RA and 70 artillerymen, 50 of whom were not attached to the guns; 4 companies of the 3rd Regiment NNC (No 4 and 5 of the 2nd Battalion and Nos 6 and 9 of the 1st) totalling 19 white officers and 391 men; 110 mounted men (details from No 1 Squadron Mounted Infantry, Natal Mounted Police, Natal Carbineers, Newcastle Mounted Rifles and Buffalo Border Guard). A number of Royal Engineers, bandsmen of the 24th, and men of the Army Service Corps and Army Hospital Corps, Native Pioneers and various staff officers of the column, bringing the total to 1,155 men. The addition of Durnford's force would bring the numbers at the camp to 1,661.

Durnford had arrived at Rorke's Drift with his force at dusk on 20 January 1879 and wasted little time in setting up camp where he had been instructed. He could still see Otto Witt's Swedish Mission station at the foot of the Oscarberg at Rorke's Drift. At that moment Witt's house was being used as a hospital, and the church as a storehouse for the 3rd Column's supplies. Durnford wrote to Chelmsford to report his arrival and asked for further orders. He then penned a letter home – a letter which clearly indicated the reason why he believed his force had been called to follow Glyn's column: 'My movements are to operate against the two Matyanas and if they won't submit, make them.'

This note is in perfect accord with Chelmsford's note to him on 19 January 1879. Durnford, though, most likely could not understand why, if he was needed in the sweep against the

Matyanas, he had been ordered to *camp* at Rorke's Drift. He wrote a postscript in the same letter: 'I am "down" because I'm left behind, but we shall see.'

At 7 a.m. on 22 January 1879 Durnford was out with a detachment of mounted men trying to purchase wagons from the farmers on the Biggarsberg when Lieutenant Smith-Dorrien brought him Chelmsford's message that he should take his men to Isandhlwana. Lieutenant W. Cochrane, his transport officer, recalled that on reading the note Durnford remarked:

> Just what I thought. We are to proceed at once to Isandhlwana camp. There is an impi about 8 miles from the camp which the General moves out to attack at daybreak.

The contents of the note were ambiguous. As it is a vital piece of evidence in the tragic misunderstanding that in some measure led to the massacre of British troops at Isandhlwana, it is necessary to reproduce it in full:

> 22nd, Wednesday, 2.a.m.
> You are to march to this camp at once with all the force you have with you of No 2 Column.
>   Major Bengough's battalion is to move to Rorke's Drift as ordered yesterday. 2/24th, Artillery and mounted men with the General and Colonel Glyn move off at once to attack a Zulu force about 10 miles distant.
>
> J. N. C.

It was signed by Crealock.

It is reasonable to assume that Chelmsford had something in mind for Durnford other than a defensive role. The decision to bring on mounted men who were better suited to reconnaissance and rapid movement, instead of calling for the two infantry companies of the 24th at Helpmekaar under Major Upcher, indicated a need for mobility rather than stability. The reinforcements provided by No 2 Column comprised five excellent mounted units: the Edendale Horse and the BaSotho Horse, both containing many old friends who had ridden with Durnford as guides to the Bushman's Pass in 1873, and there were three troops of Zikhali's mounted men, who came from the foothills of the Drakensberg and were quite at home on horseback. Also from Zikhali's Ngwane were two infantry companies of the 1st Battalion, 1st Regiment, NNC.[1]

Although Durnford was deficient in infantry he nevertheless had the services of Major Francis Russell's rocket battery, the personnel of which consisted of a bombardier, RA, and eight soldiers detailed from the 1/24th Foot. The battery was armed with three rocket troughs, each with 62 × 9-pounder rockets. Their maximum range was about 1,000 yards but they were awkward to fire. The rocket, about 15 inches in length and three inches in width, was propelled by a hand-lit charge from a trough which balanced on a pair of metal legs. The rockets were generally inaccurate, for sighting was determined on angle of elevation, but it was hoped that their piercing shriek might terrify the Zulus and cause them to scatter.

Durnford impatiently hastened on ahead with his mounted men, leaving the rocket battery, his wagons and the two Ngwane infantry companies to follow. A quarter of a mile from Isandhlwana he met Lieutenant John Chard of the Royal Engineers who was returning to Rorke's Drift. Chard informed him that the Zulus had been seen on the hills to the north in some considerable number. He asked Chard to tell Stafford, commanding E Company 1/1 NNC to remain to escort the Column's wagons, and for Russell and Nourse's D Company to hasten on to Isandhlwana.

[1] Durnford's force had lost Bengough's 2nd Battalion, which had been left behind at Sandspruit, and the 3rd Battalion under Captain Cherry which was left at Middle Drift with the remaining six infantry companies of the 1st Battalion.

CHAPTER X

WEDNESDAY, 22 JANUARY 1879

'There are not enough tears to mourn for the dead'
(King Cetshwayo)

AFTER Chelmsford's departure at about 4 a.m., the camp continued to bustle with activity. He had left orders for Lieutenant-Colonel H. B. Pulleine to draw in his line of defence about the camp; to pull his infantry pickets closer in and keep his cavalry vedettes well out. Accordingly those mounted men who had been left behind and were fit to ride provided vedettes for the high ground, three to six miles away to the north-east and the south-east. There is no evidence to indicate that infantry pickets were brought closer to the camp but it must be assumed that this was done.

At the wagon park on the *nek* between Isandhlwana and Mahlabamkhosi (Black's Kopje), forty-five wagons, standing with their oxen to lumber back to Rorke's Drift for another load of supplies, were awaiting the return of the transport officer, Lieutenant Horace Smith-Dorrien, who had been sent to summon Colonel Durnford's force from Rorke's Drift.

The cavalry vedettes caught sight of the Zulus soon after sunrise. Captain Edward Erskine's No 4 Company of the 2/3rd NNC, on outlying picket on the hills to the north of the camp, had been relieved during the night by Captain A. T. Barry's No 5 Company. Barry's pickets confirmed the presence of numbers of Zulus to their front. Erskine's Company joined Captain R. Krohn's No 6 Company of the 1/3rd NNC near their tents where they were to remain in reserve for most of the forthcoming battle.

Pulleine ordered the 'Fall-in', and with the exception of those companies on picket duty, the troops lined up in front of their tents. When, during the next two hours, further reports of Zulus

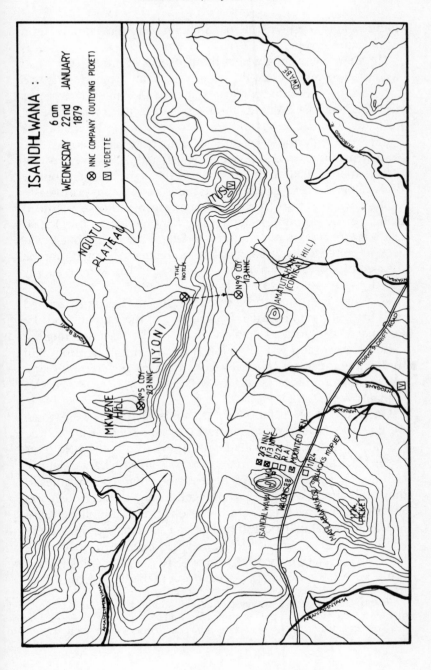

ISANDHLWANA :

WEDNESDAY 6 am   JANUARY
           22nd   1879

⊗ NNC COMPANY (OUTLYING PICKET)
⊠ VEDETTE

in the vicinity reached Pulleine, the men were moved in column to the camp's front.

The men were delighted at the prospect of a fight. They had no reason to suspect that the camp was in any danger, for it was believed that the Zulu army was ten to twelve miles away on or near the Malakatas. Already the sounds of battle could be heard from that direction. But unknown to the camp, the sounds of battle were only those of brushes with Matyana's people. The Zulu army, numbered at between 20,000 and 25,000 men, was at that moment squatting in the valley of the Ngwebeni, a tributary of the Nondweni River, about five miles away to the north-east.

More wagons were prepared for a return to Rorke's Drift to bring on the column's supplies. Pulleine and his officers had taken the necessary precautions to defend the camp, but it was also imperative that the invasion of Zululand should not be delayed by a breakdown in the commissariat. The wagons simply could not be used to form a laager.

At a time estimated to be just after 10 a.m. Durnford arrived with his 250 mounted men. D Company of the 1st Battalion, 1st Regiment, NNC, under Captain C. R. A. Nourse, was escorting the rocket battery, and was about an hour and a half behind.[1] Still further behind were his ten wagons carrying his column's supplies and ammunition escorted by E Company 1/1st NNC under Captain W. Stafford.

On arrival at the camp Durnford's mounted men were given the order to 'Front form troop' near the centre of the camp, while Durnford made his way to Pulleine. At the rear of the NNC tents he met Brickhill the interpreter, who had in his charge eight of Gamdana's people, who lived beneath the Phindo, a few miles to the south-west. Gamdana had pledged loyalty to the British and as a sign of goodwill had sent in eleven guns to the officer commanding the camp. Brickhill had taken Gamdana's people to the column's office where, it seems, they had been detained for the last hour or so. Convinced that they were not Zulu spies, as was rumoured about the camp, he had brought them to Durnford for

[1] The rocket battery left the camp after a 15 minute wait. Lt Davis claimed that Durnford's force left half an hour after Zikhali's men had been sent to the Nqutu plateau at about 11.15 a.m. The rocket battery most likely arrived at about 11.30 a.m.

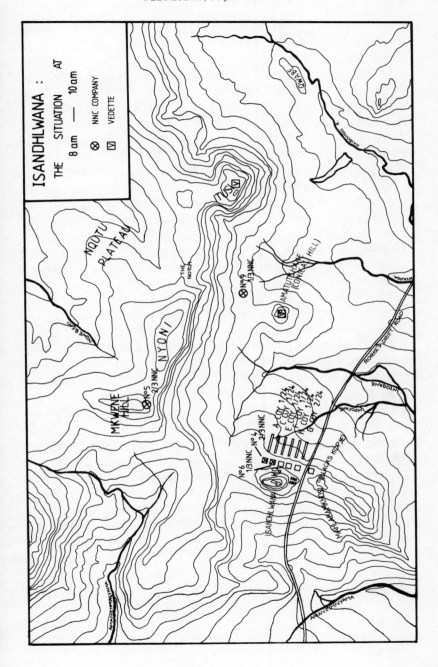

ISANDHLWANA :

THE   SITUATION   AT

8 am — 10 am

⊗   NNC COMPANY

Ⅴ   VEDETTE

NQUTU PLATEAU

MKWENE BEN ?

THE NOTCH

NYONI

ITUSI

No 9
1/3 NNC

AMATUTSHANE
(CONICAL HILL)

NGWEBENI

'K CHANGE'

QWABE

No 5
2/3 NNC

MKWENE HILL

No 4
2/3 NNC

No 6
1/3 NNC

A COY 1/24
E COY 1/24
C COY 1/24
F COY 1/24
G COY 2/24

ISANDHL WANA

MPOFANE

RORKE'S DRIFT ROAD

NYANGA

MABASO

AMANZAKANYAMA

AMANZAKANYAMA

MHLABAMKHOSI (BLACK'S KOPPE)

his verdict. Durnford accepted Brickhill's judgement and let them leave the camp to collect their cattle which was grazing on the Hlazakazi.

Durnford's orders had been to march to the camp at once with all his men. Was he to relieve Pulleine or was he required for a supporting role to the Chelmsford's forces on the Mangeni? He had written off to the general the day before to ask for instructions. He must have expected to find clarification at Isandhlwana. But there were no further orders waiting for him with Pulleine who presumably could give him little information on what the general had in mind for him to do.

Pulleine gave Durnford an account of the state of the troops in the camp and emphasised that *his* orders from Chelmsford were to 'defend the camp'. It was the custom that a senior officer arriving at a situation such as this would not only take over command but would also be responsible for carrying out whatever orders had been left by the commanding officer. There also seemed to be an accepted practice that the man on the spot could use his discretion if the situation warranted it. However, if he miscalculated, he was solely responsible for the consequences.

The frequency of reports from the pickets and vedettes was increasing. One such report was that the enemy were in force behind the hills on the left. A further report came in that the enemy were in three columns, and then a little later that the columns were separating and that one was moving to the left rear and one towards Chelmsford.

Fearing that the enemy might overwhelm his baggage guard of NNC escorting his wagons, Durnford sent back Lieutenant R. W. Vause with No 3 Troop, Zikhali's Horse, as a reinforcement. Then as the officers began an early lunch, came a report that the Zulus were retiring in all directions but presumably this did not refer to the column which was still believed to be moving towards the general.

Durnford could have remained in camp, but he was now in possession of information that a Zulu force was moving to threaten the general's rear and cut off his line of communication with the camp. According to Cochrane, he decided to use his force 'to prevent the one Zulu column joining the impi ... engaged with the troops under the General.' In this respect he felt quite justified. The general had, in his rebuke to Durnford on the 14th, declared that he would expect a commander 'to disobey any orders ... if information which he obtained showed that it would be injurious to the interests of the column under his command.' Although it was Chelmsford's force threatened (both its rear and its lines of communication with the camp and Rorke's Drift) the circumstances appeared to be similar.

If he took his force on a wide sweep of the Nqutu plateau and of the plain below and cleared the general's rear he could then link up with him and be in a position to cooperate with the force operating on the Malakatas. The general *had* indicated three days earlier that that was why he was wanted. In so far as the force at the camp was concerned, it appeared that the immediate threat was past; there was no need for the mounted men, and even six companies of Imperial infantry and four companies of NNC seemed more than necessary for the defence of the camp. Two companies of the 1st Battalion, 1st Regiment NNC, of his column would be in the camp within the hour.

It seems relevant at this point to raise the question of who had command at the camp – a question which appears not to have been clearly settled by either Durnford or Pulleine. Chelmsford had not ordered Durnford to *remain* at the camp and from the latter's behaviour it seems as if he believed that he was not bound to. And yet Durnford had already, by his release of Gamdana's people, assumed the responsibility of command and it is clear from Lieutenant Cochrane's evidence that Pulleine accepted it outside the framework of the orders left him by Chelmsford. But 'defence' of a position can be widely interpreted and Pulleine was distressed when Durnford wanted to position two Imperial companies beyond the inlying pickets. It is inconceivable that he wished to take the two companies with him – they would have been more of a hindrance than a help. It seems likely that he wished to both strengthen the weak position to the north and protect the rear of his mounted men who would be operating on the Nqutu plateau.

Pulleine's distress was shared by his officers who felt that a relocation of such a large part of the camp's force was not what Chelmsford had allowed. Cochrane recalled that Lieutenant T. Melvill, the adjutant of the 1/24th, approached Durnford and said:

'Colonel, I really do not think Colonel Pulleine would be doing right to send any men out of camp when his orders are "to defend the camp".' Durnford replied: 'Very well, it does not much matter. We will not take them.' He could do without them, although it must have been clear to the officers of the 24th that the northern aspect was a blind spot in the camp's defences. As a result two companies of the 1/24th were indeed later sent on to the spur to the north and although the order might be traced back to Durnford, Pulleine quite clearly had the final say in the timing of their despatch.

It was later believed by Chelmsford's staff that Durnford and Pulleine had had harsh words over the issue of taking Imperial troops from the camp, but Cochrane, who was present, denied that this was so. Durnford's request had been 'persuasive' rather than 'peremptory'.

The lunch was soon over and according to Cochrane, Durnford, restless for action, said almost as an afterthought as he left Pulleine: 'If you see us in difficulties you must send and support us.' Historian David Jackson declares that Durnford had no right to give this order. While Durnford was out of the camp there was no confusion over command, but what would happen on his return? We shall see later what serious effects the failure to delimit the areas of command would have on the course of the battle for the camp.

Durnford now set his plan into action: the remaining two troops of Zikhali's Horse, under the command of Lieutenants Charles Raw and J. A. Roberts, were sent under Captain Barton, who had been attached to Durnford's column for General Duties, to the hills to the north to sweep away those Zulus who could be seen there about two miles off. Barton accompanied Roberts, and George Shepstone, Durnford's staff officer, went with Raw. The numbers of Zulu on the hills were estimated at little more than 600. The time was about 11.15 a.m.

At about 11.30 a.m. the rocket battery arrived and Durnford hurried down from the 1/24th tents and gave them orders to be prepared to move out of camp in fifteen minutes.

At 11.45 a.m. Durnford hastened out of camp. He took with him Lieutenant Harry Davis's fifty-two Edendale and Lieutenant Alfred Henderson's fifty-two BaSotho mounted men and the

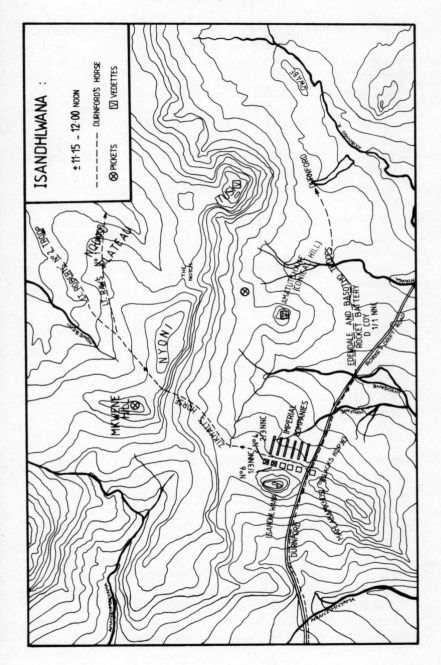

rocket battery under Major F. Russell supported by D Company, 1/1st NNC under Captain Nourse. His wagons bringing his ammunition and supplies had not yet arrived, but he must have been confident that the Zulus would scatter before him. The worst he could expect might be a short skirmish. Each black trooper was armed with a carbine and most likely forty rounds of ammunition.

Captain Penn Symons of the 2/24th later reconstructed the course of the battle from survivors' accounts, possibly with the object of refuting charges by Lord Chelmsford and the English press that the 24th had offered little resistance. Symons focussed blame for the loss of the camp on the Engineer, Durnford:

> Unable to see the proper tactics to be pursued, burning and impatient for the fray, and fretting at the curbing and restraining nature of the orders transmitted to him, he left both the camp and the direction of affairs. He was the senior and responsible officer, and it was not given to him to see the danger, or save the camp and many, very many precious lives.

A number of Symons's charges will be shown to be groundless. Was Durnford 'unable to see the proper tactics' to use? In order to invalidate this charge it is necessary to analyse his proposed strategy. In the absence of a means of communication every plan must work from a base of fundamental assumptions. Durnford *assumed* that there was no Zulu army in the vicinity of the camp. Precautions were taken nevertheless. He *assumed* that the small Zulu column reported to be moving toward the rear of the general's forces would have been undetected by the general, and posed a threat to him. He also *assumed* that the earlier intention that his column work with the general against Matyana still stood. His plan therefore was simple and straightforward: to clear the rear of the general and link up with him. These were the proper tactics. As it turned out, his left column discovered the Zulus and in so doing, although it failed to save the camp, made the Zulu price of victory a high one, for there was some measure of defence to meet the onrushing hordes.

It is true that Durnford was 'impatient for the fray' but certainly not true that he was 'fretting at the restraining nature of the orders transmitted to him'. Of course Penn Symons had ignored or was unaware of so many vital factors: previous orders, immediate danger to the general and his line of communication with the camp, and the failure of Chelmsford to have had the area effectively scouted. Durnford must have been informed that the area in close proximity to the camp had been reconnoitred. If not he would have taken it for granted, for Chelmsford had certainly been most thorough in all his preparations.

Soon after they had moved into the hills on the left, Zikhali's horsemen came into contact with elements of the Mcijo and opened fire upon them. These elements had heard firing from the direction of the Malakatas where Chelmsford was operating five miles away to the south-east, and believed that the Ngobamakosi, bivouacked out of sight further down the Ngwebeni valley, had become engaged with the British. Such was the keen rivalry between the Zulu regiments that the Mcijo had risen to their feet and made their way to the lip of the Nqutu plateau to investigate. The Ngobamakosi had in fact not moved, though a few had been detailed to collect mealies for lunch.

These men of the Mcijo now found themselves face to face with the Natal Native Horse led by Lieutenant Raw. The rest of the Mcijo rose immediately and scrambled towards the Nqutu plateau. Their induna, Vumandaba, was unable to restrain them. Their action now drew on the whole Zulu army. The indunas of the Ngobamakosi regiment, Tumopu and Mkosana, ordered their regiment to forego lunch, for the Mcijo were already engaged, firing off their assorted weaponry at the retreating Native Horse. The Ngobamakosi hurried out of the valley and on to the plateau and swung into line with the Mcijo.

The Zulu army was in chaos. What discipline there was was provided by regimental commanders, who, unable or unwilling to stop the determined rush toward the British camp, now gave their men some direction. The reckless warriors in the van were left alone. They were to be the first to fall to the disciplined volley firing from the carbines of the mounted men and from the long-barrelled Martini-Henry rifles of the British infantry.

On 21 January 1879 the regiments had been allotted an order of encampment which presumably would be the order of battle. On the right were the Nodwengu, Nokenke and Mcijo; the centre was formed by the Ngobamakosi, uVe and Mbonambi, and the left by the Undi corps and the uDhloko regiment. The precipitate action of the Mcijo changed all this. The commanders-in-chief, Mavumengwana and Tshingwayo, were only able to hold back the Undi corps and the uDhloko. This resulted in the right and centre regiments being extended to provide for the absence of a left horn. The left horn (such as it was) was formed by a portion of the Ngobamakosi,[1] approximately 1,500 men, striking off to the south to the left of iTusi toward Qwabe, the ridge of reddish soil that overlooked the Nxibongo River about five miles from Isandhlwana. The uVe, together with the rest of the Ngobamakosi and the Mbonambi formed the left centre of the chest and swept to the west of iTusi hill and into the neck between the Nyoni and the Conical Hill (Amatutshane). Most of the Ngobamakosi were eventually to make their way round the eastern side of Amatutsh-ane and join their branch that had come down the plain. The heart of the chest was made up of the Mcijo, Mhlanga, Nkandem-pemvu and Ngakamatye regiments. On the right centre were the Nokenke and uDududu regiments. The right horn was the Nodwengu, Mkhulutshane and Isangqu regiments.[2] The Undi corps (Thulwana and Ndluyengwe regiments) and the uDhloko, 4,000 strong, followed in the wake of the commanders and were kept in reserve until a late stage of the battle when an opportunity arose to send them after the fugitives. At that stage, after detaching the Ndluyengwe and sending them along the Amanzimnyama, Dabulamanzi, the commander of this corps decided to move on to Rorke's Drift to attack the garrison there.

The mounted men, white and black, were fighting a strategic withdrawal along the plateau of the Nqutu. Captain George Shep-stone left Raw to control the retreat, and together with James Hamer, a civilian friend who was serving as a transport officer in Durnford's column, rode back to camp to report to Pulleine that the Zulu army was on the plateau and was moving rapidly toward the camp.

[1] The Ngobamakosi with 6,000 warriors could have been split. The other two regiments, the uVe (1,000 men) and Mbonambi (2,000), were too small. Mehlokazulu claimed that he commanded one wing of the Ngobamakosi.
[2] Davis mentioned that he was attacked 400 yards in rear of the camp by Zulus wearing a headdress of a single red feather. The Isangqu were the only regiment that fit this description.

WEDNESDAY, 22 JANUARY 1879

At the headquarters tent Shepstone met Captain Alan Gardner who had just brought an order from Chelmsford for Pulleine to send on camp equipment and supplies to the Mangeni, and for the moment to remain at Isandhlwana and entrench it! The time was about 12 noon.

At about this time firing was heard from the direction of the spur to the north of the camp. Two companies of British troops there were firing at Zulu moving left across their front about 800 yards away.

Pulleine was nonplussed when he received the news from Shepstone that the Zulu *army* was on the plateau. Shepstone tried to bring himself under control:

I am not an alarmist, Sir, but the Zulus are in such black masses over there, such long black lines, that you will have to give us all the assistance you can. They are fast driving our men this way.

Gardner advised Pulleine that under the circumstances he should ignore Chelmsford's order. Pulleine immediately sent a note off to Chelmsford (which only reached him at about 2 p.m.): 'Staff Officer. Heavy firing to the left of our camp. Cannot move camp at present.' It was not sufficiently informative so Gardner penned his own message and sent it by a second mounted man:

Heavy firing near left of camp. Shepstone has come in for reinforcements and reports that Zulus are falling back. The whole force at camp turned out and fighting about one mile to left flank.

It is not known where Gardner had got the idea that the Zulus were falling back. Both messages were treated by Chelmsford with little concern. The force at the camp, he believed, was well able to hold its own against the small numbers of Zulu believed to be around the camp.

Soon after Gardner had sent off his message, Zikhali's men came tumbling over the lip of the Nqutu plateau. Raw's and Roberts's men had been joined by Captain Barry's company of NNC infantry, but the latter were fast deserting the front, leaving

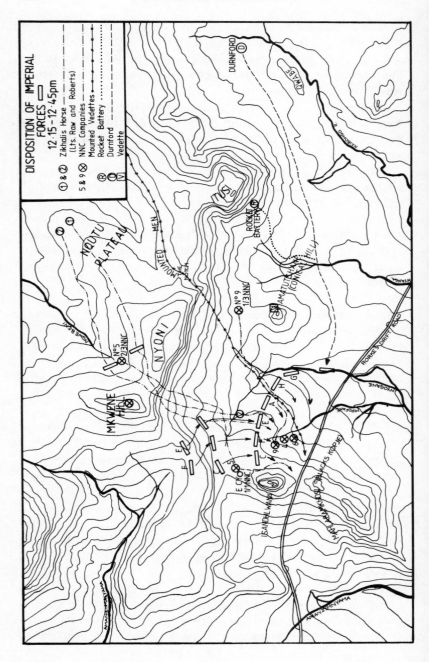

their officers fighting with the mounted men and retiring back to camp.

The mounted men were now augmented by Vause's No 3 Troop, Zikhali's Horse, which had recently arrived with Durnford's wagons, and by Stafford's company of the 1/1st NNC. The enemy was driven back over the Nyoni. But it was clear to Pulleine that the position of the Imperial companies on the spur could become precarious. Lieutenant Melvill was sent with orders to withdraw these companies. The men fell back, hard pressed by the Zulus, to a line some 300 yards from the NNC tents. The rest of the Zulu army had caught up with its exuberant van. The entire ridge to the north was covered with dense numbers of warriors, who now drove forward toward the British line, but the volley firing of the infantry had a devastating effect on the close-packed ranks. The Zulus, seeking protection, crawled along in the grass until they could go no further. They searched for safety in the folds of the ground and in a number of huts at the foot of the Nyoni ridge. The attack had been held.

The NNC still in the line should have been instructed to join the NNC companies in reserve in front of the tents. It is hardly possible that the flight of Barry's company from the spur had escaped Pulleine's attention and it can be reasonably assumed that while the Zulu drive appeared to have faltered, Pulleine should have brought all the NNC into reserve – their reliability and firepower being severely limited. It must be remembered that only one in ten of the black infantrymen were issued with firearms and once the Imperial troops were unable to keep the Zulus at a distance it was unlikely that the NNC would be able to stop them. However, from the scant information available it appears that Pulleine had, at these early stages of the battle, placed the Native infantry and mounted men on the flanks of the Imperial infantry. This strategy had been advised in a circular to commanders dated 23 December 1878. Reference is made by a number of survivors, of the NNC being part of the British line on the left, and certainly the Native Horse was there, but there is no evidence to support the commonly held view that the NNC were on the knuckle or centre of the line at the time of the collapse, or that they were a cause of that collapse. The origin of these views may be found in the poor sketch of the troop dispositions submitted by Captain Essex to the court of inquiry. On closer inspection of this map it can be seen that he puts them on the right flank but also admits that he was not certain where they were. This evidence was used by Captain W. Penn Symons in his defence of the honour of the 24th Regiment. He placed the NNC in the centre of the British line which is where it was believed that the Zulu broke through. This charge was echoed in the official account of the battle prepared by the Intelligence Branch of the Quarter Master General's department of the War Office in 1881.

The six Imperial companies stood facing the left front where the attacks were expected. They covered the line from the base of Isandhlwana to the Nyogane riverbed. This was extending the camp perimeter and thinning the defence – there was probably as much as 300 yards between each company – but it seems that if this had not been done the Zulus could have sheltered in the large donga formed by the Nyogane River and in the broken ground overlooked by a low ridge that ran north to south about a mile from the camp. Furthermore, covering fire had to be given to enable the vedettes and other mounted men to withdraw from the upper reaches of this donga, from which they had been firing at the Zulus pouring down the 'notch' on their left front. When the infantry arrived, the mounted men, by this time running short of ammunition withdrew to the camp to their respective ammunition wagons. By this time all the vedettes had returned to camp.

The three troops of Zikhali's Horse ended up in camp in a most confused state. Raw's No 1 Troop became mixed up with Cavaye's E Company, 1/24th, and finally ended up in a donga 800 yards to the north of the NNC camp. No 2 Troop left some of its men, including its lieutenant, in a stone-walled cattle kraal where they were inadvertently shelled by one of the 7-pounders. No 3 Troop, under Vause, rode back to their ammunition wagons to replenish their stocks[1] or collect their reserve supply. As it turned out, they were not going to be given time to return to the front.

What of Durnford's movements during this last hour? Approaching Qwabe ridge, five miles from the camp, he was with

---

[1] This troop must have gone to the front without its reserve ammunition. It also failed to notify the remainder of Durnford's Horse of the location of the column's ammunition wagons in the park.

CAPTAIN EDWARD ESSEX'S MAP OF ISANDHLWANA MADE IN RESPONSE TO THE
REQUEST OF THE COURT OF INQUIRY INTO THE FALL OF THE CAMP

[Redrawn as a copy from the map contained in the Chelmsford Papers
(ref.6807/386/8, file 26) National Army Museum, London]

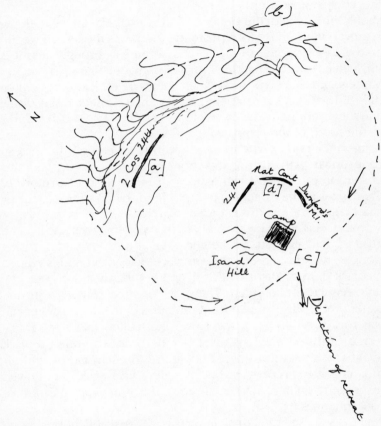

Essex's explanation of the map:
(a) Position occupied by 2 companies 1/24th at commencement of action.
(b) Hill behind which the Zulu army appeared to have concentrated; where
    it was first seen; and from whence the extension began. The direction is
    shewn by arrows.
(c) Neck where the [two(crossed out)] extremities of the Zulu army met.
Underneath was written by Essex: "I cannot be certain that the position (d)
which may be said to have been assumed at 1 p.m. is strictly accurate as
regards the right, nor am I able to fix the place where the guns came into
action. The north point is only approximate as regards direction."

his two troops of Native Horse, and struggling along behind him was the rocket battery with its escort of Zikhali's infantry. Why the battery had to be accompanied by the slow-moving infantry, is a mystery, for they were undoubtedly a liability. But taken in the context that Durnford was under the impression that he should link up with the General's forces on the Mangeni then the removal of his *entire* force from the camp was the logical step to take. If one is going to follow this argument through then it is likely that Durnford had left instructions with Pulleine to send on Vause's and Stafford's men when they arrived. However, when they did arrive at the camp the situation had changed dramatically and they were immediately put to use reinforcing Zikhali's Horse to the north of the camp.

Just after noon two Carbineers who had been on the plateau rode down with instructions from Lieutenant Scott, who was posted on the Conical Hill (Amatutshane), to warn Durnford of the danger to the camp and to himself, for by now the Zulu army had been alerted and was on the march.

In the meantime the rocket battery, struggling over the broken ground, had got left far behind. The three 9-pounder rocket troughs, rockets and equipment, were carried on mules tended by black drivers. Major F. Russell and Bombardier Goff were the only regular artillerymen. The eight or nine privates with the battery were all seconded from the ranks of the 24th. The terrain was rocky and progress was slow. The rockets had to be trans-ferred from the fractious mules to the backs of Nourse's black infantrymen. Durnford could not afford to delay and he and his mounted men were soon out of sight. Once again he allowed his force to splinter into small units, this time with unfortunate consequences.

Francis Russell took the battery toward iTusi Hill, hoping poss-ibly to get through the 'notch' there and thus avoid the dongas and broken ground, and link up with Zikhali's men on the plateau. He met Troopers Hawkins and Barker of the Natal Carbineers who warned him that the Zulus were advancing toward iTusi and that within half an hour they would be there. Russell could not have believed them for he nevertheless felt that the short cut would be justified (he would be linking up with Raw and Roberts later anyway) and proceeded up towards the 'notch'. But the

Zulus were there sooner than expected; the over-anxious young hot-bloods of the Zulu left, the Ngobamakosi, uVe and Mbonambi, poured over the lip of the Nyoni ridge close to iTusi hill, driving the mounted vedettes into the Nyogane riverbed. This advance was soon halted by the firepower of the mounted units and James Lonsdale's NNC Company and the shrapnel fired by one of the 7-pounders. Many of the Zulu sought refuge in the ravine which runs into a deep donga, the Nyanga, from the Nyoni close to iTusi. These men worked their way down the many tributaries of this donga and found dead ground behind the Conical Hill. It was probably they who surprised the rocket battery which was only about 100 yards away making its way along the contour of iTusi and unable to see the activity in the 'notch'. There was only time to fire one rocket when the Zulus appeared and fired a volley, killing Major Russell and five of the battery. The mules stampeded. Those of the Native Contingent with guns fired a few shots but were unable to reload – empty cartridge cases jamming in the breech. They turned and fled with their fellows, black and white, who were already streaming back to camp, leaving only five of their company who resolutely stood by Captain Nourse and kept the Zulus, who were not in great numbers, at bay. There were only four survivors of the rocket battery, two of whom made their way to the mounted men in the donga, the other two making their way with three of the battery horses back to camp.[1]

When the two Carbineers reached Durnford near Qwabe, they passed on Lieutenant Scott's message that it would be advisable to return as the enemy were fast surrounding them. Durnford was surprised: 'The enemy can't surround us, and if they do we will cut our way through them.' But maybe he could not have been as confident as he appeared for he told the Carbineers to return to Scott and instruct him to be ready to support him. Whitelaw, one of the Carbineers, told Durnford that this would not be possible because Scott was under Pulleine's orders not to leave his post. Durnford replied: 'I am Colonel Pulleine's senior; you will please tell Lieutenant Scott to do as I tell him.'

Assuming that this was indeed Durnford's response – and it

---

[1] Bombardier Goff, Privates Grant, Trainer and Johnson survived. Johnson and Trainer went to the donga.

does have that measure of impatience in it that stamps it as authentic – then Durnford is at the least guilty of discourtesy for failing to have Pulleine notified of his proposed use of his vedettes, although the vague injunction that Pulleine should support him if he were in difficulty did give him some excuse to use the vedettes. The failure to delineate the measure of command was not to be put to the test on this occasion, for Durnford was to be driven back to the perimeter of the camp and Scott appears to have left the Conical Hill before the return of Whitelaw and his companion.

At the moment the Carbineers left Durnford, his scouts appeared to report Zulus on the left front, and soon afterwards the enemy could be seen 'in great numbers, about 1,500, steadily advancing and firing' at them. Lieutenant Henderson later indicated on an Intelligence department map printed in 1880 for the War Office, that this force which Lieutenant Cochrane described as '10 to 12 deep with supports close behind' was both the uVe and the Ngobamakosi. None of the Zulu accounts of the battle can assist in identifying the regiment comprising this force. Circumstances however seem to indicate that there had been a split in the Ngobamakosi. Both uVe and Mbonambi can be located with some measure of confidence as coming down the 'notch'.

The Zulus opened fire with their assorted guns at about 800 yards. Durnford ordered the men to hold their fire until the Zulus were 400 yards from them. Henderson's and Davis's troops were extended in open line and ordered to fire and retire alternately toward the camp. The Zulus pressed on; the mounted men giving way slowly. At the dry Nyanga River, which the rocket battery had followed to the base of iTusi, they picked up more of their scouts and chased off Zulu skirmishers fighting against Nourse and his few men. They fought for a while from the Nyanga but as more Zulus were beginning to threaten them from their left rear Durnford ordered his force to withdraw into the lower reaches of the Nyogane, the upper reaches of which had so recently been held by the mounted vedettes. The Nyogane at this point was a deep watercourse thirty or forty feet across in parts and gave protection to the horses. The men dismounted and prepared to hold the Zulus back. One of the 7-pounders was now giving valuable assistance and shelling the Zulus as they came round the Conical Hill and raced across the mile or more of open plain toward the British right. Shrapnel was being fired, though as the numbers of Zulu increased, a few rounds of case were fired too. The Zulus tried to find cover in a kraal but were driven out by the accuracy of the artillery piece.

But the gunners themselves were now under fire from sharpshooters hidden in the broken ground at the foot of the Nyoni Ridge. The Artillery commander, Major Stuart Smith, was wounded in the arm, one man was killed and two others wounded. There was no time to attend to them. Their replacements had been detailed for other duties and could not be found.

When the Ngobamakosi swept around the Conical Hill to join the rest of their regiment in the attack on Durnford's mounted men, Captain Gardner obtained Pulleine's permission to take thirty to forty white mounted troops in the camp to help them. This may, of course, have been prompted by Durnford's order to the Carbineers to come and support his retirement on the camp. Gardner arrived at the Nyogane just about the time of the arrival of Durnford's Horse. When it could be seen that the Zulu left had also been checked, Gardner left Captain Bradstreet of the Newcastle Mounted Rifles in command and rode back to Pulleine who wanted his services. In the meantime Durnford had also ridden back into camp and collected the remainder of the mounted men, possibly as many as sixty to seventy, and sent them to the Nyogane.

The Zulu attacks on both the British left and right had been held. A lull had descended on the battle, although Zulu sharpshooters were still active.

Durnford's return to camp was critical to its survival. It most likely placed Pulleine in an awkward situation, for the former would now assume overall command, but it appears that in the excitement of the moment Durnford either failed or deliberately avoided to clarify this issue with Pulleine. The vital decision to draw in the line of defence was left when it was too late. It would have been imprudent of Pulleine to act independently of Durnford and order a move which at this stage would have isolated Durnford on the right. It is possible that Durnford had considered such an order, but, no doubt most satisfied with the fact that his small force was holding the Zulu left, gave no thought to the danger to the camp as a whole. There seemed to be an

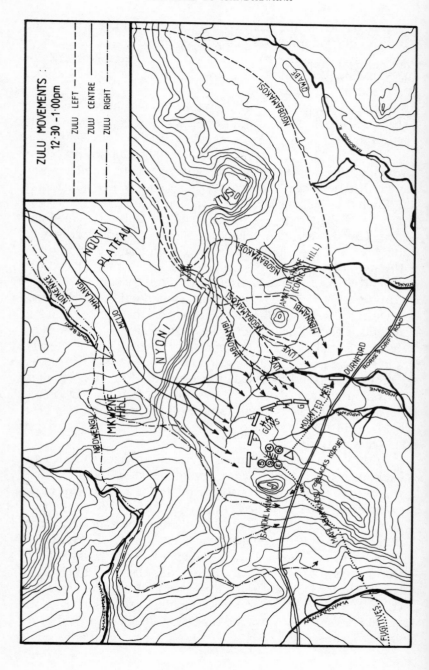

appalling lack of communication between the two colonels, and no cooperation. It was Captain Gardner, not Pulleine, who saw the need to reinforce the right, and Durnford himself came into the camp, not to assume overall command as was his duty, but to gather more reinforcements and to return with them to the Nyogane.

One must pause to examine Durnford's leadership qualities up to this vital stage of the battle. He has shown faultless control of his own small unit, but faced with the responsibility of the entire camp's forces, he appeared to falter; indeed, to avoid the responsibility. One gets the impression that he merely wished to return to his own front and that the remainder of the camp's defences should be Pulleine's responsibility. Had Pulleine and his officers not already emphasised to Durnford that *their* responsibility was to *defend the camp*? Durnford no doubt had considerable confidence in the Imperial officer, and most, if not all, of the officers of the 24th and the Artillery had had campaign experience.

An order probably from Pulleine went out to bring the men in closer to the camp. Durnford had already returned to the Nyogane. As the men were retiring the Zulu commanders saw an opportunity. A sub-chief of the Mcijo ran down below Mkwene Hill, and rallied the wavering warriors. They urged each other on by a great shout of '*Usutu!*'; rose as one and charged the soldiers while they were in the process of retiring. The sub-chief was shot dead but the weight of numbers told and the Mcijo were soon among the soldiers hacking and stabbing with their assegais. On Amatutshane, Ndhlaka, a sub-chief with the Ngobamakosi, called out to the young men on the Zulu left:

> Never did his Majesty the king give you the command to lie upon the ground. He told us to toss [the enemy] into Pieter-maritzburg!

The warriors responded and drove forward once again. For about twenty to thirty minutes Durnford's 200 men[1] held the Zulu left

---

[1] Davis lost only two troopers at Isandhlwana; Henderson lost about the same. This would add 100 to the total of mounted men.

horn, which by now probably numbered as many as 5,000.[1] The Zulus could get no closer than 200 yards. The galling accuracy of the mounted men with their short-barrelled Westley Richards carbines called for a suicidal bravery. The open plain in front of the Nyogane gave no cover and the attempts to outflank the British by way of Nkonyane Hill to the south were, at this stage, unsuccessful. It was an excellent position. Durnford was in his element. One of his Edendale troopers recalled that he rode up and down the line calling 'Fire, my boys!' in a cheery voice. On occasions he became quite euphoric and stood on the lip of the donga where there was no cover whatsoever and urged on his men. Lieutenant Henderson was sure he had lost his head, and had serious doubts whether he was capable of commanding. He had behaved in an over-excited manner on the Bushman's Pass in 1873, and, it will be recalled, some of the men lost confidence in him there too.

The mounted troops soon began to worry about a shortage in ammunition and some of them began to leave the donga to go and fetch some more. Unfortunately they could not locate their wagons, and their attempts to beg ammunition off Pullen, the quartermaster of the 1/24th, were unsuccessful. They returned to the donga empty-handed.

The time would have been close to 1 p.m. Lieutenant Henderson was now sent back by Durnford to collect ammunition. Lieutenant Harry Davis took fifteen Edendale men with him to collect some for his troop, leaving his sergeant-major, Simeon Kambule, in command of the rest of the Edendale men. After hunting around unsuccessfully for the wagons which Vause had brought into camp, Davis eventually found 200 rounds in a box in the Carbineers' camp, and was preparing to return with it when the left flank of the British line was seen to be penetrated, and the Zulus were soon fighting among the tents of the NNC.

It appears that the order, which presumably came from Pulleine, possibly after communication with Durnford, to draw in the left closer to the tents because of the difficulties of supplying the

---

[1] Stalker: Trooper Barker's account of Isandhlwana. The Ngobamakosi alone numbered about 6,000. It is possible that uVe and Mbonambi also fought on the left as well as in the centre.

men with ammunition was ill-timed. Captain Younghusband's C Company on the extreme left, having expended less ammunition than E and F Companies, was still a formidable fighting unit, led by a resolute and competent officer. The remaining two companies on the left would have been concerned about their reserve stocks. They had been in action perhaps for half an hour longer than the remainder of the regiment – they had been posted on the spur near Mkwene Hill – and it is possible that there was a shortage in the ranks.[1] One difficulty had been to stop the bullets falling from the pouches while the men were running from position to position. No doubt this had contributed largely to the shortage.

The organisation of ammunition supply to the firing line was hopelessly inadequately. The 1st Battalion 24th Foot reserve stocks were a mile away on the southern side of the camp. The wooden boxes each containing 600 rounds of ball cartridges for the Martini-Henry rifles, would be opened by the quartermaster, then transferred to mule-carts – a slow and cumbersome procedure.[2] From the mule-carts the ammunition was emptied into haversacks which were then taken to the various platoons by those deputed to act as carriers. It seems that there was not a sufficient number of the latter appointed, for both Essex and Smith-Dorrien, who were officers, found it necessary to collect all those who were inactive and employ them in this task.

The lids of the boxes[3] were secured by only one screw and although one was at a disadvantage if one did not have a screw-

[1] Although recent research has indicated that it is unlikely that the men in the front line ran out of ammunition (see Jackson, 'The First Battalion Twenty Fourth Regiment, marches to Isandhlwana' from the Zulu War Centenary publication of the Victorian Military Society, February 1979) there still exists the statement by one of the survivors, Private J. Williams, Colonel Glyn's groom, that he fired off his ammunition (70 rounds?) in very quick time – within an hour. (See WO 32/7726/079/1588)

[2] *The Times*, 2 April 1879: Captain E. Essex's account of Isandhlwana.

[3] The ammunition boxes were most likely the Mark V series of January 1876. The wooden box was lined with tin-plate and reinforced by two copper straps each secured by 13 screws. A sliding 'tongue in groove' lid was held down by a single 2″ screw covered by a tin seal which was removed by pulling at a ring attached to it. The box weighed 79lb 4oz when full.

driver there were a number of tools such as axes, hammers and crowbars which were standard baggage for all companies, and which could be used to smash open a box in an emergency. It is therefore doubtful whether the design of the boxes had anything to do with the delay of the despatch of reserve ammunition to the front.

It is highly unlikely that Quartermaster Pullen had not prepared adequate stocks of reserve ammunition for despatch but it was most unfortunate that the 1/24th ammunition wagons were to be so far from the 1/24th companies. Lieutenant Smith-Dorrien became so frustrated at the tardiness with which troops in the front line were being supplied that he went in person to the 2nd Battalion (at least 300 yards closer to the firing line) where he found that only a limited number of boxes had been opened – there being only one company from the 2nd Battalion in the camp. When he began to break open the boxes, Quartermaster Bloomfield was horrified, and insisted that he take ammunition required by the 1st Battalion from the 1st Battalion reserves. Smith-Dorrien refused and hastened back to the line to find that he was too late: the Zulus had broken through the left and were forcing the soldiers back towards the tents.

At the rear of the camp the Zulu right horn threatened to encircle the defenders and cut off the Rorke's Drift road. Durnford's principal staff officer, Captain George Shepstone, saw the danger and calling most likely for a fresh company from the NNC (the only reserves available) took possibly Captain Edward Erskine's amaCunu company to hold the Nodwengu back. The likelihood that Erskine's company went with Shepstone is given some credence by the fact that, in 1883, when A. Boast was employed by the colonial authorities to re-inter the bodies at Isandhlwana, he found it necessary to dig approximately thirty graves near Shepstone's last position. Unfortunately Boast left no exact figures other than the fact that each grave contained two to four bodies. It seems that there were a larger number with Shepstone than is generally believed. It also seems relevant to mention that colonial records show that there were no survivors of Erskine's company. This does seem to indicate the likelihood of heavy fighting rather than a harassment during flight, the pattern

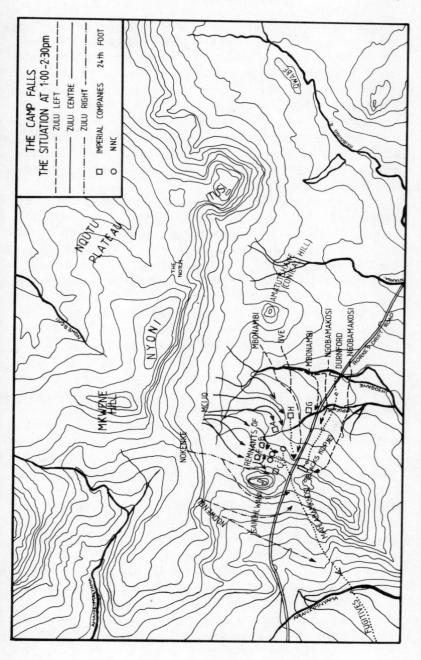

that fits the fortunes of the remainder of the NNC. Shepstone's resistance prevented the right horn from getting into the camp earlier but he could do nothing to prevent the fugitives being attacked. Once he was overwhelmed the Zulu cordon drew tighter round the camp.

The guns had begun to limber up on the order to retire. Hardly had they done so when the foremost Zulus were upon them. The guns dashed for the road but were brought to a halt by a deep donga which branched off the Amanzimnyama River. The Zulu right horn cut them off and killed the gunners and horses before the guns could be spiked.

Zikhali's Horse began to leave earlier than other units. Captain Barton had ridden back to camp in haste in order to collect ammunition for Raw's and Roberts's troops. He had been unable to locate the wagons Vause had brought in so most likely went to the 1/24th camp where Pullen refused to supply him, presumably insisting that he get his requirements from his own reserves. Barton returned to the front empty-handed. There was now no good reason why Zikhali's Horse should remain, but it was possibly at the moment of Barton's return to his troops that a bugle blew the retirement and shortly thereafter the horsemen availed themselves of this opportunity to leave the camp.

Criticism has been levelled at Pulleine for failing to order 'Form Square' but the Zulus were in among them too soon for them to be able to do so. The companies facing the front were caught completely by surprise. Having held off the Zulu left centre with little difficulty they were in fact least threatened and had retired in good order from the ridge overlooking the Nyogane to near the Mpofane and seem to have had adequate stocks of ammunition. Lieutenant Pope's G Company, 2/24th, was detached and sent to assist the mounted men who at this time were beginning to return to the camp for ammunition. The NNC, in reserve, should have been ordered into the breach, estimated at about 600 yards, but nothing seems to have been done. This appears to have had serious consequences, for the Mbonambi, driving across the face of Porteous's A and Wardell's H companies 100 to 150 yards away and braving the volley firing made for the gap. It is possible that Wardell saw the threat and tried to rush his company toward the 1/24th camp in order to cut the Zulus off. Pope's company most likely had to check and then enfilade the Mbonambi, thus giving Wardell and his company precious time to get across the Mpofane. Pope's G Company now became isolated from the remainder of the line.

The sight of Zikhali's mounted men leaving the camp, and then the close proximity of the Zulus, were too much for the NNC, who despite the curses and threats of their officers, threw down their arms and ran.

Durnford had, only shortly before, arrived in the camp himself. He had ordered his mounted men to fall back on the camp when it could be seen that the Zulus had crossed the Nyogane on either side of his force and were working their way towards his rear. Captain Gardner was surprised to see the mounted men retire. On being told by Captain Bradstreet that Durnford had ordered it, he thereupon sought out Durnford who was looking for Pulleine. Although the withdrawal of the mounted men exposed Pulleine's right flank there was little that could be done to avoid such a step. He told Gardner that it would be necessary now to draw in the defence perimeter. In the centre of the camp Durnford met Captain Essex still supervising the supply of ammunition. He ordered him to collect as many men as possible in order to hold back the right horn which was threatening the rear of the camp. The small force collected by George Shepstone for this purpose, was most likely in the process of being overwhelmed at this time. But Essex was not going to have the time to be able to do this, for the British left had crumbled. Durnford rushed back to his men without, apparently, having seen Pulleine. The position on the British right was now critical.

The Ngobamakosi had followed hard on the heels of the mounted men and now Pope's men, about 400 yards from the camp, found themselves hard-pressed and had to turn to face this new threat. This gave the Mbonambi their opportunity. In concert with the momentum of the right centre they thrust aside the remnants of the NNC and drove towards Wardell's company which had possibly just reached its battalion tents. Wardell's left was unprotected and it is possible that Quartermaster Pullen saw the danger and collected some soldiers retreating past the wagons and took them down there, where, it seems, they were soon brushed aside.

The Zulu right, although it had broken through the British line, nevertheless still found considerable resistance: Younghusband's C Company was able to retire unimpeded as a unit across the face of Isandhlwana, and in ranks of four, were enfilading the Nokenke and Mcijo as they chased E and F Companies through the tents. These two companies had dissolved into a running, fighting mass among the Zulus and the tents. This slowed up the Zulu advance here and probably explains why it was decided among the Zulus afterwards that the honour of breaking into the camp first should go to the Mbonambi.

The Edendale and Hlubi contingents that had ridden in to collect ammunition were supplied by Lieutenant Henderson who had finally located the ammunition wagons, but it was clear to them from the stream of refugees from the left and front that they could do nothing more, so they too began to leave the camp. They had lost contact with Durnford, who had been searching for Pulleine.

The position was now hopeless. Porteous's A Company was cut off from the camp. The men closed in on each other and resorted to the bayonet. About twenty-five bodies were later found at the spot where A Company were believed to have been.

Wardell's H Company was driven into the 1st Battalion tents where Wardell and most of his company, fought shoulder to shoulder, until they were overwhelmed.

Fugitives had been leaving the camp before 1 p.m. Zikhali's Horse were able to warn the garrison at Rorke's Drift that the Zulus were on their way there. They then dispersed to their kraals.

The Rorke's Drift road was soon cut by the Zulus, possibly by the Ndluyengwe regiment, which had been held in reserve up to this point. In fact the closing of the horns was poorly executed, and a large gap was to be left for some time enabling a large number of the British force to escape from the camp precincts. The Nodwengu and elements of the Nokenke finally joined the Ndluyengwe and attacked the British forces in the *nek* and along what was to be known as the 'Fugitives' Trail', a line toward the Buffalo River six miles away in a south-westerly direction from the camp.

The gap was to be kept open by a number of gallant defenders. Near the tents of the 1/24th Durnford had rallied most of the white

mounted men who were still fighting, and possibly remnants of
Pope's G Company, about thirty men who had been detached
from their company which had re-formed on the *nek* for the
purpose of fighting off elements of the Zulu right horn, which
was possibly more intent on chasing fugitives than in completing
the circle around the camp.

A large square was formed on the shelf below the southern end
of Isandhlwana, under Captain Younghusband who had brought
C Company to this spot and had also attracted numbers from
other companies. Sixty-eight bodies were later found here.

The two major units of resistance under Durnford and
Younghusband prevented the horns from closing up, according
to Mehlokazulu, who led one wing of the Ngobamakosi, and
allowed those who were escaping to get through to the Fugitives'
Trail.

Durnford was magnificent. According to a Zulu source, he had
the men in good order and took the wounded with him. Identifi-
able from his arm being in a sling, he killed four warriors with
his revolver. It seems that he had been driven up among the
rocks on the slopes of the stony kopje (Mahlabamkhosi – Black's
kopje), near the right hand corner of the 1/24th camp. With him
were fifteen Natal Carbineers, under Lieutenant Scott, twenty
Natal Mounted Police, a number of Newcastle Mounted Rifles and
Buffalo Border Guard, Imperial infantry and even some black
infantry. The men fought from the rocks holding the Ngobamakosi and the Mbonambi back. It seems that Durnford tried to
make this area a centre of resistance. Behind the officers' tents of
the 1/24th over seventy dead, mostly infantrymen, probably of
Wardell's company, were found when Lieutenant-Colonel W.
Black visited Isandhlwana five months later. It seemed to him that
the soldiers had been gravitating toward where Durnford had
drawn up his defence.

By 1.45 p.m. Wardell's company and Pope's men had been
overwhelmed. It was not long before Durnford's survivors were
surrounded. They fought on till their ammunition was exhausted
at which stage they then fought with bayonet, clubbed rifle, knife,
stones – any weapon they could lay their hands on. They were
finally overwhelmed by a determined charge. During the course
of the final conflict, as the ranks thinned, numbers tried to join

Younghusband's square further up the *nek* but they were killed before they could reach it.

According to the *Natal Almanac* for 1879 the partial eclipse of the sun began at about 1.10 p.m. and experienced its greatest phase at 2.29 p.m. (Pietermaritzburg time) and ended at 3.50 p.m. Durnford's party lasted until, according to a Zulu with the Mcijo, 'the afternoon was well spent', though it seems unlikely that they could have held on for much longer than an hour – which would put their demise at approximately 2 p.m. Norris-Newman, the correspondent for the *London Standard*, who was with Chelmsford, recorded that Commandant Rupert Lonsdale rode into the camp at about 2.30 p.m. to find that the Zulus were already looting the camp. However, according to Edward Durnford, his brother's smashed watch, which was later recovered from the body, had stopped at 3 p.m.

Younghusband's party lasted a little longer, possibly as much as half an hour. The last man to be killed at Isandhlwana, said a Zulu account, was a soldier holed up in a small crevice on the slope and who had kept his foes at bay for a considerable length of time. 'The shadows were long on the hills' when he was finally shot by Zulu sharpshooters. The only activity at the camp was to be that of the executioners and the looters.

When the killing stopped at the Buffalo late that afternoon, 858 white and 471 black soldiers and non-combatants lay dead, strewn along the banks of the river, along the Fugitives' Trail, and in the perimeter of the camp. The Zulu dead were estimated at between 1,000 and 4,000. They were buried in grain silos in two nearby kraals, and in the many dongas. There was no burial ritual. When Cetshwayo was told of the battles of that day he was reported to have said: 'There are not enough tears to mourn for the dead.'

Durnford's last moments are not clear. He was believed to have been shot through the heart but his body was also found to be covered with assegai wounds. He lay on his back – for some reason the Zulus had not stripped off any of his clothes – on the *nek* close to the stony kopje, probably close to the Rorke's Drift road. Around the fallen colonel was a most poignant scene. Lieutenant Durrant Scott and fourteen of his fellow Carbineers, Natal Mounted Police, Buffalo Border Guardsmen, Newcastle Mounted Riflemen, Imperial and black infantry lay scattered around him.

This sight led a Carbineer with the burial party to declare: 'What struck everyone on the field was the way in which the Carbineers who fell stuck ... to Durnford, of all men!' The issues of his leadership and the clarity of Chelmsford's orders were to be an integral part of the investigation ordered by Chelmsford into the fall of the camp.

CHAPTER XI

AFTERMATH

'Poor Durnford's misfortune'
(Sir Henry Bartle Frere on Isandhlwana)

A T about 12.30 p.m. when the camp's defences were cracking,
Lord Chelmsford, near the Mangeni River waterfall, eleven
miles from Isandhlwana, listened to the sound of artillery fire
coming from the direction of the camp. A mounted black orderly
rode in from Commandant Hamilton-Browne who was on the
road to the camp, and reported heavy firing at Isandhlwana.
Hamilton-Browne's 1/3rd NNC had seen large bodies of Zulu
passing by Isipezi on their way to attack the camp. He had pressed
down into the plain and moved toward the Nxibongo River on
to a rocky ridge close by, but three large bodies of Zulu appeared
to be moving toward him so he retired in the direction of the
Mangeni, and sent off mounted orderlies to inform the general.

Chelmsford and his staff rode toward the neck that led from
the plain to the Mangeni gorge and examined the camp through
field glasses. The time was about 1.15 p.m. There seemed to be
nothing amiss. The tents could be seen and men were moving
about.

Captain Develin, one of Hamilton-Browne's orderlies, met
Lieutenant-Colonel Arthur Harness and his guns and informed
him that the camp was in desperate straits. Harness ordered his
guns and their escort to start back. Major Gosset, Chelmsford's
aide-de-camp, who was with Harness, rode back to inform the
General. Chelmsford, well aware of the news, believed that there
was no cause for alarm and ordered Gosset to call Harness back
and move instead to the new camp site.

But the sounds of fighting no doubt disturbed the General so
at about 2 p.m. he decided to ride back to camp with the Volunteers and find out what had happened.

Shortly after starting, Chelmsford met Lieutenant-Colonel Cecil Russell and his mounted infantry. Russell had received Pulleine's second note addressed to Chelmsford that Durnford was engaged with Zulus to his front. If Chelmsford had had any doubts about the Zulu attack on the camp these were dispelled and Russell's mounted infantry now joined the general on his return to the camp. Hamilton-Browne's men were picked up on the way. Four and a half miles from the camp they met Lonsdale who breathlessly told the General that the camp was taken. Chelmsford halted his small force.

The situation was serious. Apart from half the column being in the camp, the entire stock of reserve ammunition was there too.[1] Gosset was sent to the Mangeni to ask Glyn to bring the remainder of the force. Russell and the mounted men rode on to investigate while Chelmsford waited for Glyn. Russell soon returned to confirm that the camp appeared to have been taken, but according to Captain Theophilus (Offy) Shepstone, commanding the Natal Carbineers, there was still firing going on but it must have been the final stages of resistance.

It was only at 4 p.m. that afternoon that all the troops finally assembled, and despite the haste they only reached Lord Chelmsford at 6.30 p.m. On the darkening skyline on the right Zulus could be seen retiring. At 7.45 p.m. the force was half a mile from the camp. It was now dark. Fires could be seen burning there and the wagons appeared to be scattered in such a way as to resemble a barricade. The four remaining 7-pounders of Harness's battery were ordered to fire some shrapnel into the camp, and the 24th, drawn into line, fired a few volleys. There was no reply. Lt-Colonel W. Black took three companies of the 24th with fixed bayonets and stormed on to the kopje to the left of the nek. The Zulus had gone. The rest of the force, stumbling over bodies and debris, moved into the camp.

The men bivouacked on the nek for the rest of the night. Although Chelmsford wanted the men to stay awake sleep was fitfully snatched as Zulu signal fires burned on the hills around

[1] 102 wagons, 1,000 oxen, 2 × 7 pounders, 400 shot/shell, 1,000 rifles, 250,000 rounds of ammunition, and 60,000 lbs of commissariat stores were lost according to Reuter's telegram, 27 January 1879, published in *The Times*, 11 February 1879.

them. Early next morning when the men awoke they could not fail to see in the half-light the carnage in the camp. Numbers of bodies, many of them mutilated, were no doubt identified. Durnford's was discovered by a Doctor Thrupp. It was lying near the hospital tent on the nek. Thrupp removed Durnford's watch and later handed it to Bishop Colenso.

Chelmsford, short of ammunition, perturbed that the dismal scene might erode morale and concerned at the fate of the garrison at Rorke's Drift (from which firing could be heard during the night), quickly assembled the men and at 4 a.m. marched toward the base camp at the drift. The bodies of the fallen were left unburied for four months among the broken wagons, the scattered burnt stores and the debris of battle.

Not until 21 May 1879 did a strong force under Major-General Marshall arrive from Rorke's Drift for the purpose of recovering the wagons that were so desperately needed for the second invasion. A number of journalists accompanied the force. Melton Prior wrote in the *Illustrated London News* alongside his sketch of the distressing scene, that the skeletons of the men lay in the long grass

> mixed up with the skeletons of oxen and horses ... bleaching under a tropical sun ... The individuals could only be recognised by such things as a patched boot, a ring on the finger bone, a particular button, or coloured shirt or a pair of socks ...

Archibald Forbes, writing in the *Daily News*, described the discovery of Durnford:

> In a patch of long grass, near the right flank of the camp lay Durnford's body, the long moustache still clinging to the withered skin of the face. Captain Shepstone recognised him at once, and identified him yet further by rings on the finger and a knife with a name on it in the pocket, which relics were brought away. Durnford had died hard – a central figure of a knot of brave men who had fought it out around their chief to the bitter end. A stalwart Zulu, covered by his shield, lay at the Colonel's feet. Around him, almost in a ring, lay about a dozen

men, half being Natal Carbineers, riddled by assegai stabs. These gallant fellows were easily identified by their comrades who accompanied the column. Poor Lieutenant Scott was hardly at all decayed. Clearly they had rallied round Durnford in a last despairing attempt to cover the flank of the camp, and had stood fast from choice when they might have essayed to fly for their horses.

Theophilus Shepstone, Jnr, had the body wrapped in canvas and buried under a cairn of stones.[1] The Volunteers were able to bury their dead but the dead of the 24th Foot were only to be put to rest in late June 1879.

Durnford's horse Chieftain was a survivor. He was ridden by Durnford's servant (also a survivor) to the Colensos. There Agnes, Nell's sister, looked after him until he died in 1883. Durnford's portmanteau with his private papers was recovered from his wagon by Trooper A. Pearse of the Carbineers, but these papers were only returned to the Durnford family in 1885.

On 27 January 1879 Chelmsford ordered that a court of inquiry into the fall of the camp at Isandhlwana assemble in Helpmekaar. Its purpose was to collect evidence for Chelmsford's own information. The members of the court were Colonel F. C. Hassard, RE, Lieutenant-Colonel F. T. A. Law, RA, and Lieutenant-Colonel A. Harness, RA. It was at this stage a preliminary inquiry – all the Imperial officers that had escaped, plus Captain Nourse, Colonel Glyn and Major Clery, gave statements. Chelmsford sent the report of the court to the Secretary of State for War. Aware that the inquiry left much of what had happened at Isandhlwana shrouded in mystery, Chelmsford assured Stanley that over the next few months evidence would be taken from others in an effort to clarify the picture.

The inquiry was an extraordinary one. According to Harness, the statements of many men were taken that day but most of them were rejected. It seems that only the officers (six of whom were escapees from Isandhlwana) gave statements – a total of 8 men.

[1] Norris-Newman said it was placed in a ditch (see p. 183). This is doubtful as there were no ditches on the nek. Alfred Davis who wrote under 'Another visit to Isandhlwana by a correspondent' in the *Natal Witness*, 27 May 1879, watched stones being heaped on the body.

REFERENCES.

The Contours are numbered with reference to a
Datum Level of 2000 feet. Rorke's Drift has been
arbitrarily fixed at this level, and all contours are
referable to it. The main points on this Plan are
taken from the Triangulation made by Capt. Anstey R.E.
and Lieut. Porter R.E.

O   Burnt Kraals.
E.   Left bank of Spruit strewn with Cartridge-cases.
F.   Cartridge-cases lying thickly behind the boulders.
Ò   Vedete.

Contours at 100 feet vertical intervals.

MILITARY SURVEY
of the
BATTLE-FIELD OF ISANDHLWANA

B

Scale 1:15840 or 4 inches to a mile.

Yards 100 50 0 100 200 300 400 500   1000   1500   2000 Yards

to Matyana's Country

This 'Military Survey of the Battlefield of Isandhlwana' was published in the *Narrative of the Field Operations Connected with the Zulu War of 1879* and shows the location of the NNC at the centre of the British line as well as in reserve. (A is Mkwene Hill, B is iTusi. See page 214 for further reference.)

When one looks at the paucity of information in the evidence there is simply not enough to help the court decide what caused the fall of the camp. Later statements taken from other survivors gave a clearer picture. The full statements of Interpreter Brickhill and the officers of the Natal Native Horse were invaluable; so too were the Imperial survivors of the rocket battery. As an indication of the pressing nature of the court to find some quick explanation, Captain Essex, Lieutenant Cochrane, Lieutenant Smith-Dorrien and Captain Gardner, all added considerably new material to the picture at a later stage in letters to newspapers or to family.

None of the later statements was given before a court; there was no cross-examination; each was deposited with the deputy adjutant general or the most senior staff officer with the nearest garrison. Why then was it necessary to have three men listening to (but not examining) a select number of statements? Was the object behind this hasty exercise simply to look for a scapegoat in the camp for its fall? As an example of the carelessness in its scrutiny of statements, Essex's rough map (a copy of which is shown on page 215) resulted in a false charge against the black levies for the collapse of the British line of defence. The map shows the location of the Native Contingent on the knuckle of the British position which he drew with some uncertainty and stated so! Colonel William Bellairs, the deputy adjutant general, in reporting the proceedings of the court to Chelmsford, no doubt believed that the inquiry had served its purpose when he declared:

> From the statements made before the court ... it may be clearly gathered that the cause of the reverse sustained at Isandhlwana was that Lt. Col. Durnford, as senior officer, over-ruled the orders which Lt. Col. Pulleine had received to defend the camp, and directed that the troops should be moved into the open, in support of a portion of the Native Contingent which he had brought up and which was engaging with the enemy.

Bellairs's conclusions are mere supposition; it was not possible to gauge from the evidence that Durnford ordered Imperial troops to move into the open. Yet, Chelmsford believed too that it was Durnford's disregard of the orders left with Pulleine that had led to the disaster. The Duke of Cambridge, Commander-in-Chief of the British Army, acknowledged later that Durnford was duty-bound to obey those orders left for Pulleine. But the Duke was not aware of the circumstances leading up to Durnford's arrival at the camp. Previous orders from Chelmsford to Durnford had confused rather than clarified matters. Even the orders to Pulleine were born out of confusion. Pulleine might not have had those orders if Clery, Chelmsford's aide-de-camp, had not had his wits about him on the morning of the 22nd. The general had forgotten to order Pulleine to defend the camp so Clery did so in his name. Even the message to Durnford that he was to come to the camp to reinforce it was left to Crealock who missed the early (and vital) part of the General's conversation with Clery, and was therefore not so well acquainted with the general's plans.

The result of this was that Crealock made a number of errors. He ordered up the whole of Durnford's force, when only the mounted men were required; he did not tell Durnford that he was to reinforce the camp and he did not tell Durnford that he was to take command. Furthermore he made no reference to any previous order. The misunderstanding that arose in Durnford's mind has been discussed in the previous chapter. Chelmsford, in explaining to the War Office why no further orders were sent to Durnford, later declared that he 'refrained from sending any fresh instructions [because they] might only have caused confusion'.

The failure of Chelmsford to ensure that Crealock properly understood what was required of Durnford's force was an appalling error that had its repercussions years after the battle itself. The breakdown in the relaying of orders might have had even more serious repercussions if the defence of Rorke's Drift had not been successful. One (Rainforth's) of the two companies of the 24th at Helpmekaar had been ordered by Chelmsford on the morning of the 20th January to protect the pont and the drift at Rorke's, but the orders (under name of the DAAG, Major Spalding) did not reach the garrison until Spalding himself arrived on the 22nd. Both companies under Major Upcher were then sent to the drift but on the way were met by survivors of the fight at Isandhlwana. They were told of the attack on the hospital at Rorke's, so turned back, arriving at Helpmekaar late that night, nervous at the prospect of what they believed was an imminent Zulu assault.

Crealock's role in the tarnishing of Durnford's reputation was far from over. He later made a statement to Bellairs regarding the order to Durnford. This order had been copied into an order book which had been lost at Isandhlwana. Crealock tried to recall what he had written. His memory though, turned out to be grievously unfair to Durnford, for he declared that he had ordered Durnford up to Isandhlwana at once with all his mounted men and told him to take command of the camp. In explaining why he believed Durnford had been ordered up, Crealock proffered the opinion that 'the presence of an officer of Colonel Durnford's rank and corps would prove of value in the defence of a camp if it should be attacked'.

If it was expected that the camp might be attacked why then were no orders left with either Durnford or Pulleine to prepare the defences? What would be expected of Durnford once he had arrived at the camp? Inspector George Mansel of the Natal Mounted Police was certain that Crealock was responsible for having the blame for the disaster put on to Durnford. This suggestion was certainly not new. The *Natal Witness* of 29 May 1879, reported that it was well known that 'certain members of Lord Chelmsford's staff . . . came down to 'Maritzburg after the disaster, prepared to make Colonel Durnford bear the whole responsibility, and it was upon their representations that the High Commissioner's telegram about "poor Durnford's misfortune" was sent'.

Edward Durnford tried to get Chelmsford to clarify certain comments made by him and published in parliamentary blue-books but Chelmsford would not. In fact his position becomes clear when one studies the content of a memorandum which Major Gerald French, Chelmsford's biographer, declared was written to refute the 'calumnies' of Chelmsford's critics. This memorandum was quite revealing in so far as the apportioning of blame for the loss of the camp was concerned. Being a private memorandum it reveals a great deal about Chelmsford:

I consider that there never was a position where a small force could have made a better defensive stand . . . The ground was too rocky to throw up a shelter trench but the wagons which were ready inspanned at 10 a.m. could, if thought necessary, have been formed into a laager.

Major Clery ... repeated [the instructions regarding] the defence of the camp to Lt. Col. Pulleine...

[When Durnford left the camp with his mounted troops] no idea had been formed regarding the probable strength of the enemy's force ... At the same time that Col. Durnford left the camp a company of the 1/24th under Lieut. Cavaye was sent out on picket to a hill to the north of the camp about 2000 yards distant. This was done at Col. Durnford's order.

Col. Durnford cantered with the two troops of natives for about 5–6 miles leaving the rocket battery to follow on as best it could ... About noon ... Captain G. Shepstone arrived in camp ... and said that he had been sent by Colonel Durnford for reinforcements as the mounted men were heavily engaged on the hills to the left. Lt. Col. Pulleine sent out first Captain Anstey's company and a little later Captain Younghusband, so that half his force of British infantry were sent away about one mile from the extreme left of the camp.

The distressing aspect of this memorandum is the large amount of conjecture stated as fact. The carping criticisms of Durnford are grossly unfair. The irony of Chelmsford's self-exoneration can perhaps best be seen in a principle laid down by him on 18 April 1879 when, shortly before the second invasion of Zululand, he left orders how the Natal border was to be defended. One wonders whether the image of Durnford was present when he penned these words:

If a force placed on the defensive ... content itself with remaining on the passive defensive without endeavouring by means of scouting in small bodies or by raiding in large ones, to discover what the enemy is doing in its immediate front, it deserves to be surprised and overpowered.

When the news of the disaster reached England in the second week in February 1879 there was very little criticism of Durnford in the press. Frere and Chelmsford were the two that received the wrath of the armchair generals and editors. Both Queen Victoria and the Commander-in-Chief of the British Army, the Duke of Cambridge, sent messages of support to Chelmsford, but the public outcry soon forced the Duke to reconsider. In March 1879 when the subject came for debate before both Houses of Parliament, Frere and Chelmsford were heavily criticised. Attempts were made in both Houses to have Frere censured and although the vote in the Lords was overwhelmingly against such a step, the motion in the Commons was only defeated by 60 votes in 552.

Frere had anticipated the outcry. He and Chelmsford had their scapegoat in Colonel Durnford. In a letter to Queen Victoria on 10 February 1879 he declared that the orders left for Pulleine to defend the camp 'were not obeyed, owing apparently to Colonel Durnford . . . coming up and either taking command of the camp or inducing Colonel Pulleine to divide his forces'.

However, faced with increasing public misgivings of Chelmsford's role, the Duke of Cambridge discreetly pressed Chelmsford to answer a number of questions regarding his command on the 20 and 21 January, 1879. Chelmsford's replies were far from convincing. Perhaps the Duke had already decided that Garnet Wolseley would be sent to replace Chelmsford, for he had no kind words for his commander. He apportioned a large measure of blame to Chelmsford for the fall of the camp. He was highly critical of the failure of Lieutenant Browne's reconnaissance to discover the presence of the Zulus, and questioned why, after Dartnell had reported Zulus to his front, no attempt was made to laager the wagons not required for transporting supplies. Furthermore, he pointed out the contradiction in Chelmsford's report that Milne had seen nothing in the camp to warrant any alarm and yet it was deemed necessary to send Commandant Hamilton-Browne's NNC back to camp to investigate Pulleine's message. Cambridge's assessment of the cause of defeat at Isandhlwana differed markedly from Bellairs's. He ascribed 'the primary cause' to the underestimation of the Zulu military strength and prowess. He criticised the division of the column into two; deplored the absence of a laager or redoubt; was amazed at the defenceless nature of the camp and condemned the lack of an effective reconnaissance. The only criticism he had of someone other than Chelmsford, was of the officer (he did not mention him by name) responsible for the splitting of the camp's force at the time the attack was being made, instead of massing the troops into square.

Cambridge's remarks were written in the margin of a letter addressed to C. H. Ellice, the Adjutant-General, in April 1879, and passed on to the Duke for his information. His Lordship's comments were confidential and were never published. When the correspondence relating to the disaster was published in the parliamentary bluebooks, Bellairs's letter, Frere's despatch of 3 February 1879 (both of which charged Durnford with not obeying orders) and the publication of the proceedings of the court of inquiry in March 1879 turned attention to Durnford's role. The legacy of this correspondence resulted in secondary sources per-petuating the same charge against Durnford, and the official view-point was never corrected. The Duke never deigned to involve himself in the defence of Durnford and it appears that once he had secured Wolseley's appointment in the place of Chelmsford, he left the controversy to the politicians and the public.

An interesting example of how the official viewpoint was twisted by Chelmsford's friends in the War Office can be seen in a comparison of the confidential draft of the battle of Isandhlwana made by the Intelligence Branch of the Quartermaster General's department, dated 21 March 1879, with the *Narrative of Field Operations* which was the final publication by the Quartermaster General and came out under date 1881. In the draft no mention is made of Cavaye (E Company 1/24th) being ordered to the ridge by Durnford, yet in the *Narrative* Durnford is named as having ordered him. The case against Durnford was given added weight when Chelmsford, in a speech in the House of Lords on 19 August 1880, focussed on Durnford's role in the fall of the camp, and declared that in the final analysis it was Durnford's disregard of orders that had brought about its destruction.

Edward Durnford challenged Chelmsford's charge in a pam-phlet entitled *Isandhlwana – Lord Chelmsford's statements com-pared with the evidence*, and argued that there was 'not one word in the orders proved to have been given either Colonels Durnford or Pulleine to warrant Lord Chelmsford's statement'. Despite pointing out the discrepancies between Chelmsford's statements to the Lords and the evidence of those officers who contributed to the inquiry into Isandhlwana as well as Lord Chelmsford's own despatches, his attempts to clear his brother's name came against the unyielding wall of the military establishment. His correspondence with Chelmsford and the Secretary of State for War was unproductive; neither was prepared to allow the question to become an official inquiry. It was necessary to find conclusive evidence if any admission of misjudgement or negligence was to be drawn from Chelmsford.

In the latter half of 1880 word reached Edward Durnford from Veterinary Surgeon S. Longhurst of the King's Dragoon Guards that on 21 May 1879 he had seen Captain Theophilus (Offy) Shepstone remove papers from Durnford's body. Edward Durnford decided that this was a line of inquiry well worth following. These 'papers' might well have contained an order that Durnford was to bring his force to assist Chelmsford on the Malakatas.

Edward Durnford contacted Offy Shepstone through the Colensos. Shepstone denied taking papers from Anthony Durnford's body. He had recovered private papers from his brother George and these may well have been what he had had in his hand when he was bending over Durnford. Both the bishop and Edward Durnford believed Offy Shepstone's claims of innocence. Edward Durnford apologised for having suspected him of any dishonourable action. But Frances Colenso, cherishing the memory of Anthony Durnford, and heartbroken that he had been held responsible for the fall of the camp at Isandhlwana, refused to accept Offy's word and for the next four years doggedly built up a case against Offy who, she believed, 'had abstracted [the papers] under the direction of Lord Chelmsford or some other member of his staff in order that Lord Chelmsford might safely lay the blame of the disaster upon Colonel Durnford'.

In 1882 Edward Durnford had published *A Soldier's Life and Work in South Africa* to which Frances Colenso contributed. In its latter chapters it became a blow by blow attempt to restore the good name of Anthony Durnford. The book lacks balance and tempo because Anthony Durnford's correspondence, carefully selected and edited by Edward, is simply pasted together with a brief linking commentary. There is, of course, in the correspondence a great deal of valuable historical material on Natal and Zululand. It is regrettable that the major concern of Edward was over his brother's reputation, with the result that he omits any controversial item that might detract from this goal. There is no explanation for the break-up in his marriage; no mention of his relationship with Frances Colenso; very little information on his private life other than inconsequential titbits such as life in Trincomalee; no indication of the crisis that occurred on 14 January 1879 when he received a note from Chelmsford threatening him with the loss of his command if he did not do as he was told; no acceptance that his brother might have had any weakness, despite his being labelled impetuous.

Edward presented his brother as a man wronged: by colonial and Imperial authorities, by colonists and by the military establishment. He emphasised Anthony's attributes of justice, honesty, duty, courage and selflessness. He was a victim of other men's incompetence. His courageous sacrifice at Isandhlwana was tarnished by blame for the fall of the camp unjustly laid by the military establishment. Edward Durnford declared that his brother was well aware of the dangers to the camp and died trying to save it. But Edward had considerable difficulty in proving that his brother had not assumed command of the camp.

Unfortunately the evidence that Edward Durnford selected from survivors to reconstruct the course of the battle was inconclusive. Only a limited number of accounts were available at that time. Many vital pieces of evidence only came to light after the book was published – the orders given by Chelmsford on 19 January 1879, for example, would have been useful to his cause. In its efforts to present Anthony Durnford in a squeaky clean image, the book lost much of its veracity. Couple that with the waning interest in the Zulu War at the time of its publication, and an explanation can be found for the poor sales of the book.

This did not discourage Nell Colenso from pursuing the matter of the 'missing papers' with an energy quite considerable for one so frail. She ferreted out witnesses with vague memories, and convinced successive commandants of the Royal Engineers in Natal, Colonels R. Hawthorn and C. Luard, that the *honour* of the Engineers was at stake and therefore the case was worth investigating. Both men ended up by believing that there was some doubt whether Offy Shepstone had told the truth. Luard was prepared to prosecute. Shepstone was finally convinced by his friends that the whole question should be settled by a court of inquiry.

Lieutenant-General H. Torrens, acting High Commissioner and Officer Commanding Imperial Troops in South Africa, foresaw the danger of imputations against Chelmsford arising at the inquiry, and wrote to Luard before the court convened in late April 1886: 'I have taken measures to limit proceedings and to prevent, I trust, the possibility of other names, distinguished or otherwise – being dragged into it'.

The inquiry was to be limited to whether papers had or had not been removed from Durnford's body. Luard found that the court was not interested in *why* the papers were removed. His witnesses, when brought before the court, contradicted themselves and made a poor impression. Frances Colenso believed that the Shepstone family had put pressure on them, though there was nothing to prove that this was so. Other important witnesses could not get leave from the army or from the civil service to attend the inquiry. Under these difficulties Luard withdrew from the proceedings. The inquiry went on without him. Shepstone brought witnesses to confirm his story. The court believed him and he was cleared of the charges. Torrens ordered Luard to write an apology to Shepstone (which he did) and then penned a note to Chelmsford: 'In a note received by [_____] he tells me that you are gratified at the action I have taken in this wretched charge against Theophilus Shepstone, in which an attempt has been made to involve you.'

Frances Colenso wrote to the *Times of Natal* on 10 December 1886 insisting that 'Durnford's last orders were upon him when he fell'. Edward Durnford, in his letter to the *Times of Natal* on 5 January 1887, described the inquiry as 'eminently unsatisfactory' and reluctantly exonerated Offy Shepstone from the charge.

It is sad that Frances Colenso had wasted her energy on what turned out to be simply a paper chase. If she had directed her abilities toward exposing the ambiguity of that final order in terms of previous orders, she might well have succeeded in vindicating Anthony Durnford's reputation. On 29 April 1887 she died from tuberculosis.

In Natal colonial circles Durnford's reputation had gone through a metamorphosis. The manner of his death and the rallying of the Carbineers around him on the nek had become the talking point of the colony's newspapers. The *Natal Witness* asked: 'Could any man wish to die more happily than this? . . . receiving the affection of those who . . . were most prejudiced against him?' Both the *Natal Witness* and the *Natal Daily News* suggested that Durnford and Scott should be given the VC. Whatever differences between Durnford and the colonists existed before his death were now forgotten.

In October 1879 the Colensos decided to have Durnford's body brought from Isandhlwana and buried in the military cemetery at Fort Napier. The event roused as much interest among the colonists as the arrival of the body of Louis Napoleon, the Prince Imperial of France, had done a few months before. It was ironic that the return of Anthony Durnford to the town that had treated him as a villain was to welcome his flag-draped coffin as that of a hero. The *Natal Colonist* recorded the occasion:

The sky [on Sunday] afternoon [12 October] was dark and threatening, and there appeared every prospect of a heavy thunderstorm. Still, even this did not deter almost every inhabitant of Maritzburg from attending to show their last tribute of respect to the gallant leader . . .

At 4 p.m. the coffin, covered with the Union Jack and flowers and containing the remains, was placed on a Royal Artillery gun carriage and the procession slowly moved off to the cemetery . . . the band of the 99th playing the 'Dead March of Saul'.

Practically every regiment in Natal, both Imperial and Colonial, was represented. Soldiers numbering over 2,000 followed the cortege. 300 men of the 24th Foot composed the firing party. A short service was held in the garrison chapel of St George at Fort Napier and the route to the grave was flanked by the soldiers with their arms reversed.

The Reverend G. St. M. Ritchie, military chaplain, praised Durnford in the following manner at the graveside:

A brave and devoted soldier, a generous attached friend, he possessed almost every faculty which is calculated to make one

man the leader of his fellow men and this he emphatically was
... We shall never look upon his like again.

Memorials to Durnford were placed in St Peter's Cathedral,
Pietermaritzburg, where Bishop Colenso preached, and in St Vincent's Church built at Isandhlwana to commemorate the fact that
the battle had been fought on St Vincent's Day there is both a
tablet and a stained glass window dedicated to Durnford's
memory. Perhaps the most moving of these public memorials is
the Durnford Window in Rochester Cathedral in England. It is
located at the west end of the south aisle and was dedicated to
Anthony Durnford by the Corps of Royal Engineers who selected
him 'for special honour [for] bravely fighting to the last ...
endeavouring to cover the retreat on the fatal day of Isandhlwana'.
Three scenes are represented from the life of Judas Maccabeus
as a parallel to this gallant engineer. The upper scene is that in
which Judas defeats Apollonius and takes his sword 'and therewith
he fought all his life long' (1 Maccabees III, 12). The centre panel
represents Judas when opposed with his small force of 800 men
to the army of Alcimus and Bacchides (22,000 strong) saying:
'God forbid that I should do this thing and flee from them; if our
time be come let us die manfully for our brethren and let us not
stain our honour.' (1 Maccabees IX, 10). Durnford would have
been proud of the apt allusion. The lower scene represents the
death of Judas – as the narrative in the Apochrypha has it: 'Judas
also was killed and the remnant fled' (1 Maccabees, IX, 18).

The private messages of condolence to Durnford's parents
were equally moving. Hlubi, the young Sotho chief, expressed
his feeling openly:

I grieve deeply for the loss of the Inkos and things will be very
different now for me and my people. While he lived we were
happy and protected ... The Colonel always treated me as
kindly and well as though I had been a white man, and where
shall we find another Inkos who will do that? All the Basutos
lament him greatly, both for himself and for their own sakes.

The Bishop of Natal was equally generous in his letter:

Our grief for the loss of one whom we knew so well and so

In the Estate of the late Lieutenant-Colonel
DURNFORD, R.E.

_____

T. J. E. SCOONES,
Having been duly instructed, will Sell,

ON FRIDAY NEXT, THE 7TH INSTANT,
AT 11 A.M.,
AT THE
ENGINEERS' DEPARTMENT,
Two Minutes' walk from Government House, the whole of the
HOUSEHOLD AND PERSONAL EFFECTS
Of the Late Lieut.-Col. DURNFORD, R.E., amongst which may be Specially Mentioned,

Military Chest of Drawers, Four-Post Iron Bedstead and Mosquito Curtains, Feather Pillows, Towel Horse, Tables, Washstand, Toilet Sets, Leather Arm Chair (new), Looking Glasses,

ANTELOPE KAROSSE, TWO LION SKINS,
Bronze Candlesticks, Liquor Case, Madeira Chairs, Folding Arm Chairs, Vases, China Dish,

ZULU BONE CURIOS,

Walnut Whatnot, Marble Inkstand, Opera Glasses, Uniforms (new), Brushes, Dressing Gown, Saddles (new), Snaffle Bits, Belts, Gloves, Buckles, Box of Bits, Spurs, Headstalls, Saddle Cloths, Girths, Stirrups and Leathers, Canvass Clothes, Two Guns, One Westley-Richards Breech-loader, Five Pairs of Horns (mounted), a large quantity of Clothing (nearly new),

A SMALL AND SELECT LIBRARY,

Paintings, Electro-plated Ware, Knives and Forks (good). Also, at same time and place,

The Late Lieut -Colonel Durnford's Bay Horse,
and Lieut. Daly's Grey Horse.

961an   *T. J. E. SCOONES, Auctioneer.*

February 3rd, 1879.

The auction of a dead officer's effects was commonplace. This particular one revealed Durnford as a collector of unusual African curios.

much admired and honoured, is very deep ... You ... will
rejoice, amidst all your sorrow, in knowing that he died a
gallant soldier's death. But you may also have a special conso-
lation in the fact that his last great act as a civilian was to do
his part, amidst great difficulties, in securing the just rights of
the Zulus, by whose hand, alas! one of their truest friends has
fallen ...

After the eulogies, what of the truth? Were these accolades
deserved? Was Durnford a leader of men? Leadership derives
from a proper understanding of the needs and opinions of those
one hopes to lead, and the context in which the leadership occurs.
It also depends upon good timing. A man who is prepared to
take risks and achieves success makes a popular leader. This
presupposes an enormous self-confidence. In an analysis of the
psychology behind military incompetence, N. F. Dixon, Reader in
Psychology at University College, London, made these observations: 'Over the years military incompetence has resulted more
from a dearth of boldness than from a lack of caution, and more
from a pall of indecision than from an excess of impulsivity.'

If one accepts this observation as valid then Durnford would
appear to be the sort of commander that the English army needed
in the nineteenth century. What went wrong? He lacked neither
boldness, nor impulsiveness. He certainly was a popular leader.
Perhaps his timing was awry – he tended to delay withdrawal
from a conflict when it was too late. The retreat at the Bushman's
Pass might well have been less untidy if he had ordered a withdrawal earlier. His return to the camp at Isandhlwana after a
gallant flank defence against the Zulu left horn was too late. Whatever arrangements he might have made with Pulleine for tighten-
ing the perimeter of the defence were to no avail – the camp's
defences were already falling apart. One is tempted to speculate
what might have happened if the defence had held firm. Dixon
made a further interesting observation which could with little
difficulty be applied to Durnford's predicament upon arriving at
the camp at Isandhlwana:

Lack of direction from those at the apex of hierarchical authori-
tarian organisation provides a special dilemma for those at the

AFTERMATH   251

lower levels in the chain of command. Confronted with an
absence of clear-cut orders what are they to do? If they take
the law into their own hands they run the risk of being accused
of insubordination, particularly if their plans happen to miscarry, but if they do not show initiative then they are equally
likely to suffer for not having done so. At the Alma [in the
Crimean War] the field officers, for want of higher direction,
used their own initiative with considerable success. In so doing
they saved the day if not the campaign.

Durnford's plans did miscarry and he stood condemned. Ulti-
mately, success is the yardstick that measures military competence. However, his undoubted personal bravery and the
manner of his death detract from the controversial issue of his
leadership. The uncertainty of much of what had happened at
Isandhlwana leaves one doubtful whether he had succeeded in
proving to himself whether he was indeed a leader. Unfortunately,
in that respect, he had left behind him a catalogue of failure.

In order to obtain a more creditable portrait of him it is necessary to look more closely at this controversial character, not in
the role of the soldier but at his role as an humanitarian. His
obsession with honour and with proving to himself that he was
a military leader blinded him to his strong social gifts. His grace,
his manners, his humanitarianism, his sense of propriety and of
justice, his moral courage, were all admirable social attributes. As
a humanitarian he might well have soared to heights as pres-
tigious as those achieved by Bishop Colenso. Did he really fail to
see that his character blended better with social rather than military ethics? The answer is uncertain although there appears to be
a clue in Frances Colenso's claim that he had led 'a tortured life
... for more than 20 years' and that 'all the bright and noble
aspirations of his young life [were] crushed out and destroyed'.
There is the suggestion in this private recollection that he had
been forced into a career that did not suit his temperament.
His family association with the Royal Engineers predestined his
enrolment for that corps. The qualities of the disciplined Imperial
soldier could never fit comfortably with the free and independent
will of the humanitarian. Of course there was too the matter of
Frances' love for Anthony Durnford, and his love for her may

have been deeper than the evidence shows. He may well have felt trapped by Victorian social constraints; he could obtain no divorce without repercussions upon his family name. But he was also, it will be remembered, a very private person who kept his feelings suppressed.

Frances Colenso exposed much more of this enigmatic man when she wrote sadly: 'His life, when he died, was and had long been, one of such great and constant pain both mental and physical that the two women who loved him best – his mother being one – have always felt, through all their grief, that it is *well*, that it would be cruel and selfish to wish to have him back.'

Let this be his epitaph.

Appendix I

Roll of the Carbineers who took part in the Expedition to the Bushman's River Pass

1. PIETERMARITZBURG (TOWN) TROOP:

Lieutenant Woodroffe
Quartermaster I. Niekerk
+*Sergeant Major J. Taylor*
Sergeant G. James
Sergeant J. T. Button
Sergeant W. Whitelaw
Corporal A. Moodie
#Corporal G. Shepstone
Corporal C. Fletcher
Trumpeter H. Holliday
Trooper J. C. Boshoff
Trooper D. J. Boshoff
Trooper W. Berning
Trooper E. Bourke
Trooper T. Bower
*Trooper E. Bond
Trooper W. Chatterton
Trooper H. H. Church
Trooper A. Davis
Trooper D. Doig
+Trooper J. Egner
*Trooper R. H. Erskine

*Trooper J. Freeman
Trooper Gilligan
Trooper Goodburn
Trooper G. Jones
Trooper F. Kahts
Trooper P. Kevtel
#*Trooper W. London*
++*Trooper A. Macdonald*
Trooper P. R. Murphy
#*Trooper J. Pannewitz*
Trooper H. Pepworth
*Trooper C. D. Potterill
Trooper J. Player
++*Trooper C. Pistorius*
++*Trooper W. Royston*
Trooper C. Raw
#Trooper A. J. Shepstone
Trooper T. Spettigue
#Trooper J. Vanderplank
Trooper W. Wheelwright
Trooper L. Zeederberg
Trooper T. Ford

2. THE KARKLOOF TROOP:

Captain C. Barter

Trooper R. Speirs

#*Lieutenant E. Parkinson*   Trooper E. Otto
Sergeant A. R. Button   *Trooper J. J. Raw*
Sergeant J. O. Jackson   *Trooper C. Raw*
Sergeant T. B. Varty   *Trooper J. J. Hodson*
Corporal I. W. Dicks   Trooper J. Holmes
Corporal W. C. Shaw   Trooper W. Holmes
Trooper M. Fannin   Trooper G. Curry (Jnr)
Trooper G. Ross   ##Trooper R. King
Trooper W. M. Jaffray   *Trooper P. Preller*
Trooper H. Bucknall   Trooper G. Ford
Trooper E. Shaw   *Trooper A. Lindsay*
Trooper H. Kirby   Trooper T. Day
Trooper G. Wray   Trooper James Day
#Trooper E. T. Taynton   Trooper John Day
#Trooper D. T. Household   Trooper R. Otto
Trooper J. W. Household   Trooper A. Otto

Key to symbols:
* Known to have been at the Bushman's River Pass.
\# Known to have reached the Hlatimba Pass only.
\#\# Believed to have reached the Hlatimba Pass.
\+ Known to have returned to Meshlynn Farm during the ride.
\+\+ Believed to have returned to Meshlynn during the ride.
Names in italics indicate those who gave evidence at the court of inquiry.

APPENDIX II

An Engineer's Legacy: Fort Durnford, Estcourt

The panic that swept the Natal midlands after the defeat of the Carbineers at Bushman's Pass led to a decision by the government to erect a permanent fort at Estcourt. The foundations were started in November 1874 and completed the following year. Colonel Anthony Durnford, RE, the Colonial Engineer at this time, was responsible for what was at the time a good example of military architecture and construction. The main walls of the fort are over half a metre thick and 11.5 metres high. It is a two storey building with a basement which was designed to act as a storage tank for rainwater drained from the roof. As the diagram below indicates, the two towers, with loopholes shuttered on the inside, allowed all four walls to be covered by enfilade fire.

GROUND FLOOR

UPPER FLOOR

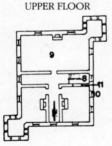

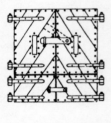

Double Shuttered Window

1. Moat
2. Vestibule with loopholes
3. Designed as a court room
4. Tower with loopholes
5. Guard room
6. Store room
7. Armoury

8. Hinged wooden stairway
9. Quarters
10. Shuttered windows
11. Loopholes

FLOOR PLAN OF FORT DURNFORD

The fort had an unusual feature in the double shutters which covered the barred windows which were preferred in the walls to loopholes. The outside of the shutters 'were covered in wood arranged so that the grain ran at various angles, the object being to retain assegais which lodged in the wood and so prevent them being used again'. The purpose of double shutters was so that the lower pair could be opened and cannon be depressed to fire at nearby targets. The upper pair could be kept closed, thereby affording some protection to the gunners.

The great front door was iron clad and double bolted from the inside. A vestibule, the walls of which were loopholed protected the inhabitants from an enemy who had managed to break through the door. An added feature was the hinged wooden stairway which could be raised by a block and tackle to isolate the upper storey. The block and tackle could also be used to lift the cannon upstairs.

The fort never had to withstand an assault. It became the barracks of the Natal Mounted Police and is today a museum. Durnford's instructor in fortification at Chatham would have been proud of his pupil.

Appendix III

THE DEFENCE OF NATAL COLONY

The four districts bordering Zululand showing magisterial divisions
and the number of men allocated for their defence.
[Minute by Sir Henry Bulwer, 20 November 1878]

District.	Division.	Magistrate, or Administrator of Native Law.	No. of men.
No. I.	Newcastle	Mr. Beaumont	300
	Umsinga	Mr. Fynn	1,500
	Ladysmith	Mr. Moodie	200
No. II.	Weenen	Mr. Patterson	1,000
	Upper Tugela	Mr. Allison	500
	Ulundi	Mr. Boast	500
No. VI.	Umlazi	Mr. Titren	500
	Inanda	Mr. Barter	500
	Lower Tugela	Mr. Jackson	1,500
		Mr. Fynney	1,500
No. VII.	Umvoti	Mr. Wheelwright	1,500
		Mr. Fannin	500
			10,000

The seven districts as determined for the defence of the colony, showing the posts of defence and arms in store:
[Minute by Sir Henry Bulwer, 7 December 1878]

	POSTS OF DEFENCE.	Rifles or Carbines.	Carbines For Europeans.	Rifles or Muskets for Natives.
I.	1. Newcastle ...	50	50	...
	2. Dundee	40	...	...
	3. Umsinga	10	...	100
	4. Ladysmith ...	50	50	100
II.	5. Upper Tugela ...	20	...	...
	6. Ulundi	...	...	...
	7. Estcourt	100	100	200
	8. Weston ...	...	...	...
III.	9. Howick	40	100	200
	10. Pietermaritzburg	500	...	...
IV.	11. Richmond ...	150	50	200
	12. Ixopo	...	...	...
V.	13. Harding	30	20	100
	14. Umzinto	50	30	100
VI.	15. Durban	500	100	100
	16. Pinetown ...	40	...	...
	17. Verulam	100	...	50
	18. Williamstown ...	10	...	...
	19. Stanger	50	20	80
	20. Lower Tugela ...	...	...	20
VII.	21. Greytown ...	100	50	200

APPENDIX IV

Corps and regiments of the Zulu army 1879

Corps or Regiment having a military kraal	Regiment composing Corps	Age of Men	Number in Regt	Number in Corps
Usixepi*		80		2,000
	Nokenke	30	2,000	
Mbelebele*		78		1,000
	Umhlanga	28	1,000	
Umlambongwenya*		75		2,000
	Umxapo	35	2,000	
Udukuza*		73		500
	Iqwa	35	500	
Bulawayo*		70		1,000
	Nsugamgeni	35	1,000	
Udhlambedhlu*		68		1,500
	Ngwekwe*	55	1,000	
	Ngulubi*	55	500	
Nodwengu	Mkulutyane*	64		
	Umsikabe*	54	500	
	Udududu	35	1,500	4,000
	Mbubi	35	500	
	Isanqu*	54	1,500	
Udabakaombi*		60	400	1,000
	Umkusi*	55	600	

Undi	Tulwana*	45	1,500	
	Nkonkone*	43	500	
	Ndhlondhlo*	43	900	9,900
	Indluyengwe	28	1,000	
	Nkobamakosi	24	6,000	
Udhloko*		40	2,500	4,000
	Amakwenkwe	29	1,500	
Umbonambi		32	1,500	2,000
	Amashutu	32	500	
Umcityu		28	2,500	
	Unqakamatye	30	5,000	9,000
	Umtulisazwi	29	1,500	
Uve		23	3,500	4,000
	Umzinyati*	43	500	

Note: All regiments marked * are married men wearing the head-ring (isiCoco)

The above list is taken from a detailed report on the Zulu Army, compiled by F. Bernard Fynney and published in Pietermaritzburg under the direction of Lord Chelmsford, the Lieutenant-General Commanding.

APPENDIX V

*List of Survivors whose Accounts have Contributed
to a Reconstruction of the Battle at Isandhlwana*

Imperial Forces:
1. Captain E. Essex, 75th Foot, Director of Transport, No 3 Column.
2. Captain A. C. Gardner, 14th Hussars, assigned to General Duties on the Staff of No. 3 Column.
3. Lieutenant W. F. D. Cochrane, 32nd Light Infantry, Transport Duties with No. 2 Column.
4. Lieutenant H. T. Curling, N Battery, 5th Brigade, Royal Artillery.
5. Lieutenant H. L. Smith-Dorrien, 95th Foot, Transport Duties with No 3 Column.
6. Private J. Bickley, 1/24th Foot, bandsman.
7. Private J. Williams, 1/24th Foot, Colonel Glyn's groom.
8. Private E. Wilson, 1/24th Foot, bandsman.
9. *Private S. Wassall, 80th Foot, attached to the Mounted Infantry.
10. Private H. Grant, 1/24th Foot, with the Rocket Battery.
11. Private D. Johnson, 1/24th Foot, with the Rocket Battery.
12. Private J. Trainer, 1/24th Foot, with the Rocket Battery.

Officers of the Natal Native Contingent:
13. Captain C. R. A. Nourse, 1st Battalion, 1st Regiment NNC.
14. Captain W. H. Stafford, 1st Battalion, 1st Regiment, NNC.
15. Lieutenant W. Erskine, 1st Battalion, 1st Regiment, NNC.
16. Lieutenant W. C. R. Higginson, 1st Battalion, 3rd Regiment, NNC.

Officers of the Natal Native Horse:
17. *Captain W. Barton, assigned to General Duties on the staff of No 2 Column.
18. Lieutenant H. D. Davis, Edendale Troop.
19. *Lieutenant A. F. Henderson, Hlubi Troop.
20. Lieutenant C. Raw, Sikali's Horse.
21. Lieutenant R. W. Vause, Sikali's Horse.

Mounted Volunteers:
22. *Trumpeter J. J. Horne, Newcastle Mounted Rifles.
23. Trooper W. W. Barker, Natal Carbineers.
24. Trooper W. Edwards, Natal Carbineers.
25. Quartermaster D. MacPhail, Buffalo Border Guard.
26. Trooper C. M. F. Sparks, Natal Mounted Police.
27. Trumpeter R. Stevens, Natal Mounted Police.

Black survivors: Natal Native Contingent:
28. Malindi, 2nd Battalion, 3rd Regiment.
29. Ntabeni, 1st Battalion, 3rd Regiment.
30. Uhloluvane 1st Battalion, 3rd Regiment.

Black survivors: Natal Native Horse:
31. Molife, Edendale Troop.
32. Nyanda, Sikali's Horse.

Non-combatants:
33. J. A. Brickhill, Interpreter.
34. M. Foley, conductor of wagons.
35. J. N. Hamer, commissariat and transport.
36. Abraham, wagon driver.
37. Hans Boer, mule driver.

Zulu: Centre:
38. Umhoti of the nKandampemvu (or Mcijo) regiment.
39. Gwabe of the nKandampemvu regiment.
40. Uguku of the nKandampemvu regiment.

Zulu: Left Horn:
41. Mehlokazulu of the Ngobamakosi regiment.
42. Ngune of the Ngobamakosi regiment.
43. Mandhla of the Uve regiment.
44. A warrior of the Uve regiment.
45. A warrior of the Mbonambi regiment.

Zulu: Right Horn:
46. A deserter from the Nokenke regiment.
47. A warrior of the Nokenke regiment.

Zulu: Reserve:
48. Umtegolalo of the Undi Corps.

* Fragments only.

SELECT BIBLIOGRAPHY

Ashe, W., and Wyatt-Edgell, E. V., *The Story of The Zulu Campaign*, London, 1880, South Africa, 1989

Atmore, A., and Marks, S., 'The Imperial Factor in South Africa in the 19th Century: Towards a Reassessment', from the *Journal of Imperial and Commonwealth History*, Volume 3, part 1, 1973

Bengough, H. M., *Memories of a Soldier's Life*, London, 1913

Bennett, Lt-Col I. H. W., *Eyewitness in Zululand*, London, 1989

Clammer, D., *The Zulu War*, London, 1973

Clements, W. H., *The Glamour and Tragedy of the Zulu War*, London, 1936

Colenso, F. E., *The Ruin of Zululand*, in two volumes, London, 1884

Colenso, F. E., and Durnford, E. C. L., *History of the Zulu War*, London, 1881

Colenso, J. W., *Langalibalele and the AmaHlubi Tribe*, London, 1874

Cope, R. L., 'Shepstone and Cetshwayo 1873–79', unpub. M.A., University of Natal, 1967

Coupland, R., *Zulu Battle Piece – Isandhlwana*, London, 1948; London, 1991

Cox, G. W., *The Life of John William Colenso, Bishop of Natal*, volume 2, London, 1888

De Kiewiet, C., *The Imperial Factor in South Africa*, London (Frank Cass edition), 1965

Dixon, N. F., *On the Psychology of Military Incompetence*, London, 1976

Droogleever, R. W. F., 'A Figure of Controversy: Colonel Anthony Durnford in Natal and Zululand 1873–79', unpub. D.Litt., University of South Africa, 1982

Durnford, E. C. L., *A Soldier's Life and Work in South Africa*, London, 1882

Durnford, E. C. L., *Isandhlwana: Lord Chelmsford's Statements compared with the Evidence*, London, 1880

Emery, F., ed., *The 24th Regiment at Isandhlwana – the Zulu War 1879*, London 1978

Emery, F., *The Red Soldier*, London, 1977

Etherington, N. A., *Preachers, Peasants and Politics in South-East Africa 1835–1880*, London, 1978

French, G., *Lord Chelmsford and the Zulu War*, London, 1939

Furneaux, R., *The Zulu War: Isandhlwana and Rorke's Drift*, London, 1963

Gordon, R. E., *Shepstone*, Cape Town, 1963

Guest, W. R., 'The Anglo-Zulu War; Natal and Confederation' – text of a lecture delivered to the University of Natal seminar on the Anglo-Zulu war, Durban, February 1979

Guest, W. R., *Langalibalele. The Crisis in Natal, 1873–75*, Durban, 1975

Guy, J. J., *The Destruction of the Zulu Kingdom*, London, 1979

Hamilton Browne, G., *A Lost Legionary in South Africa*, London, 1912

Hathorn, P. L. H., *Henderson Heritage*, Pietermaritzburg, 1972

Herd, N., *The Bent Pine*, Johannesburg, 1976

Holt, H. P., *The Mounted Police of Natal*, London, 1913

Jackson, F. W. D., 'The First Battalion, Twenty Fourth Regiment, marches to Isandhlwana', in the Zulu War Centenary publication of the Victorian Military Society, February 1979

Jackson, F. W. D., 'Isandhlwana, 1879 – The Sources re-examined', in three parts in the *Journal of the Society for Army Historical Research*: March–December 1965

Kennedy, P. A., 'The Fatal Diplomacy: Sir Theophilus Shepstone and the Zulu Kings 1839–1879', Unpub. PhD, University of California, 1976

Knight, I., *Brave Men's Blood*, London, 1990

Mackinnon, J. P., and Shadbolt, S., *The South African Campaign 1879*, London, 1880; London, 1973

Manson, A., 'A People in Transition: The Hlubi in Natal 1848–1877', in the *Journal of Natal and Zulu History*, volume 2, 1979

Martineau, J., *The Life and Correspondence of Sir Bartle Frere*, London, 1895

Maylam, P., 'The Official Mind and the War: The View from the Colonial Office' – text of a lecture delivered to the University of Natal seminar on the Anglo-Zulu War, Durban, February 1979

Mitford, Bertram, *Through the Zulu Country*, London, 1883; London 1992

Morris, D., *The Washing of The Spears*, London, 1966

Nicholls, B. M., 'Frances Ellen Colenso and the Zulu war' – text of a lecture delivered to the University of Natal seminar on the Anglo-Zulu War, Durban, February 1979

Norris-Newman, C., *In Zululand with the British throughout the War of 1879*, London, 1880; London, 1988

Pearse, R. O., *Barrier of Spears*, Cape Town, 1973

Pearse, R. O., and Clark, J. eds. *Langalibalele and the Natal Carbineers, being first-hand accounts by AmaHlubi and the Carbineers of the Bushman's River Pass affair*, Ladysmith Historical Society Publication, Ladysmith, 1973

Preston, A., ed., *The South African Journal of Sir Garnet Wolseley, 1879–1880*, Cape Town, 1973

Preston, A., ed., *Sir Garnet Wolseley's South African Diaries (Natal) 1875*, Cape Town, 1971

Rees, W., ed., *Colenso Letters from Natal*, Pietermaritzburg, 1958

Roberts, J., 'Victoria, Victorians and Victorianism', in Purnell's *History of the English Speaking Peoples*, Volume 7, No. 112, 1958

Smith-Dorrien, H., *Memories of 48 Years Service*, London, 1925

Stalker, J., *The Natal Carbineers*, Pietermaritzburg, 1912

Swinney, G. W., *A Zulu Boy's Recollections of the Zulu War and of Cetshwayo's Return*, London, 1884

Thompson, W. A., 'Wolseley and South Africa: A Study of Sir Garnet Wolseley's Role in South African Affairs, 1875–77', Unpub. PhD, Vanderbilt University, 1973

Verbeek, J. A., and Bresler, V., 'The Role of the Ammunition Boxes in the Disaster at Isandhlwana, 22 January 1879', in the *Journal of the Historical Firearms Society of South Africa*, Volume 7, part 6, December 1977

Vijn, Cornelius: *Cetshwayo's Dutchman*, London, 1880; London, 1989

War Office: *Narrative of the Field Operations connected with the Zulu War of 1879*, London, 1881; London, 1989

Worsfold, W. B., *Sir Bartle Frere*, London, 1923

Wylde, Atherton, *My Chief and I*, London, 1880

Young, John: *They Fell Like Stones*, London, 1991

INDEX